Omi

Mother Courage

Omi

Mother Courage

❧

by

Laurence W. Mazzeno

Omi ᕯ *Mother Courage*

Copyright © 2008
by
Omi Partners, LLC

Library of Congress Number: 2008902837
International Standard Book Number: 978-1-60126-105-2

Masthof Press
219 Mill Road
Morgantown, PA 19543-9516

Table of Contents

Acknowledgement From the Family

～

Omi: *Mother Courage* tells the story of our mother's efforts during and after World War II to provide for her family in harrowing times. It is the portrait of a woman of great courage who struggled against nearly insurmountable odds. At times, it appeared to her, and to her children, that the entire world was against them.

Looking back, we realize that there were many people in both East and West Germany who did their best to help us, even when they had little to give and were struggling themselves to survive. Some were family and friends, some were strangers. Some were government officials—both Americans and British in Berlin, and Germans and Americans in the West. If they did not seem to respond to our needs as promptly as we had wished, it may have been because they were overwhelmed by having to handle the problems of thousands of families like ours. We were fortunate to find similar people in the United States who went out of their way to ease the transition to our new homeland. We want to express our deepest appreciation to all of them for the assistance and support they provided.

- *The Schmidt Family*

Preface

On November 4, 1985, the Lancaster *New Era* daily newspaper carried the following notice:

Mrs. August Schmidt
Of Ephrata Is Dead

Hertha A. Schmidt, 75, a retired employee of former Nightwear Co., Ephrata, died Sunday morning at Ephrata Community Hospital after a long illness.

A resident of 825 Dawn Ave., Ephrata, she was the wife of the late August Wilhelm Schmidt, who died in 1952.

She was born in East Germany.

Surviving are two daughters, Barbara Frankford, Augusta, Ga.; and Annelore, wife of Richard Stoltzfus, Schoeneck; six sons: Rolf, Mohnton; F.W., Pennsburg; Einhard, West Germany; Friedrich W., Ephrata; Michael W., Winston-Salem, N.C.; and Joachim, Rothsville; 20 grandchildren; five great-grandchildren; and two sisters in Germany.

You can find notices like this one every day. If we are to believe the American writer Henry David Thoreau, most men—and women—lead lives of quiet desperation, seldom achieving distinction while they are alive, soon to be forgotten after their death. But inside this brief obituary lie clues to the tumultuous life of a truly remarkable woman who came to be known to her family and friends as "Omi."

As I began writing the story of Omi Schmidt and her children, I could not help recalling one of the most famous figures of the modern European stage: Bertholt Brecht's Mother Courage, the title character in the German dramatist's *Mother Courage and Her Children*. Brecht's play is set in the seventeenth century during the period known as the Thirty Years' War, but it is clearly intended as a protest against both the First World War and the conflict that was devastating Europe when *Mother Courage* was first produced in 1941. In the play Anna Fierling, known to the soldiers of both the Swedish and Polish armies as Mother Courage, struggles to keep her children safe from the ravages of war. At times, her methods may be questionable; never, however, is her determination in doubt.

That is how I came to see the central figure in the story of Hertha Anna Marie Jürgens. Born in a rural village north of Berlin in 1910, for forty years her life was touched first by two world wars and then by the horrors of the brutal Communist regime in the Soviet Zone of occupied Germany. Her marriage to Willi Schmidt was both her greatest joy and the source, albeit indirectly, of some of her greatest sorrows. How she managed to raise a family—and keep it together—under circumstances that overwhelmed hundreds of thousands of her countrymen, is indeed an epic tale.

It would be unwise, however, to draw too close a parallel between Hertha Schmidt and the heroine of Brecht's play. There are many aspects of Brecht's character that are, to put it mildly, "objectionable." But it is not straining comparison to say that, like her fictional counterpart, Hertha Schmidt was a survivor, bent on saving her children at any cost. Neither a sinister political machine nor an intransigent bureaucracy was able to defeat her. She was tenacious. She was determined. And most of all, she was courageous.

Hertha Jürgens Schmidt was born in a house that had no indoor plumbing. In the rural community where she lived, horses still provided the main source of power for farming. She lived long enough to see a man walk on the moon. And she was comfortable with the rapid pace of change that characterized the century in which she grew up, married, and raised her eight children. She would be the first to admit that her story is not unique. In some ways it is representative, though, repeated in the tales of thousands of women and men in Germany whose grand hopes for their families and their country were dashed first by two wars and then, for millions of those unfortunate enough to be trapped in the Soviet Zone of Occupation at the end of World War II, by the horrific conditions placed on their lives by the Soviets and then by the communist-led government of the ironically named Deutsche Demokratische Republik (DDR)—the German Democratic Republic (GDR).

It is hard now for many of us to comprehend how these oppressive authorities actually affected the lives of people who lived under these regimes. Only those who experienced the ordeal of life in a totalitarian state can fully appreciate its devastating and demoralizing effect on individual hopes and dreams. However, when one reads about what happened to people like Hertha and her children, one begins to get an idea of the grinding crush of the regime that took away their freedom, and in many cases, their lives.

Hertha Schmidt's response to the circumstances in which she found herself may not have been unique, but they are certainly extraordinary. This book is a chronicle of her determination, tenacity, and courage in rescuing herself and her children from a life which she was certain offered them no real future. It is a story compiled from family reminiscences and from "secondary sources"—books and articles that provide some insight into what life was like for the German people during the twentieth century. It is a reminder, too, of the overpowering allure of the American Dream, a vision shared by Hertha and her children—a dream they realized, in varying degrees, once they came to the United States to rebuild their lives, raise their families, make their fortunes, and support their communities and neighbors.

A Farm Girl in Germany
(1910-1932)

The story of the woman who would come to be known to three generations of her family simply as "Omi" begins in Alt Lutterow, a village about a hundred miles north of Berlin. There on February 23, 1910, Hertha Anna Marie Jürgens was born.

Hertha's mother, Marie Sadler, had married a local farmer, Richard Otto Paul Jürgens, a year or so earlier. The "pretty Marie," as she was known in the village, had been born in Alt Lutterow on November 30, 1888, two decades after the creation of the modern nation of Germany. She attended school in the nearby village of Flecken Zechlin, and after finishing her studies, probably through eighth grade, worked briefly as a sales clerk in a local store.

These were times of great social upheaval in this new state, as ideas from more progressive western countries began to circulate among people Marie's age. It is tempting to think she may have been affected by the "Young German Movement." This phenomenon occurred in the late nineteenth century when a number of organizations began encouraging young men and women to challenge the customs of their elders and make their own choices in life. What is certain is that before she was twenty Marie was engaged in a relationship with a young man who probably had no intention of marrying her. As a result of this liaison, she became pregnant.

Either Marie's parents talked some sense into her at this point, or she figured out for herself that her daughter Hedwig, born in 1907, would need a stable home life. Fortunately for her, Richard Jürgens, a man two years her senior, was looking for a wife. Like most small farmers in Germany, Jürgens worked outside the town limits on fields he leased. He owned a home at #11 or 12 Dorfstrasse—literally the "Village Street"—the single lane running for less than a quarter mile, along which all the residents of Alt Lutterow lived. Situated midway down this lane, the modest house was surrounded by garden patches where the family grew vegetables and flowers. Jürgens kept livestock and farm equipment in several outbuildings behind his home.

Apparently Jürgens was a good citizen, and was well liked in the village. Somehow, despite his busy schedule on the farm, he found time to be involved in the local cycling club. He offered Marie both stability and respectability—a combination that was hard to turn down. Marie and Richard married some-time in 1908. Theirs turned out to be a fruitful union. Together they had three daughters: Hertha was born in 1910, Elli in 1912 and Anni in 1913.

Hertha Schmidt's birthplace, Dorfstrasse 11-12, Alt Lutterow.
(photographed 2006)

Richard Jürgens, circa 1915.

In all likelihood, Richard and Marie Jürgens expected to spend their entire adult lives in this tiny hamlet, as their parents and grandparents had probably done before them. The village of Alt Lutterow is located in what is known to Germans as the Lake District. Stretching from a point north of Berlin to the Baltic Sea, the undulating countryside is dotted with lakes, which are in turn connected by a series of canals. A succession of wooden locks in many of the canals, including ones near Alt Lutterow and the neighboring villages, facilitate water transport so that an enterprising young German might, if he wished, travel by rowboat from Berlin to the Baltic.

Maria Sadler Jürgens and her children, circa 1914. Counterclockwise from left: Hedwig, Hertha, Elli, and Anni.

The landscape is covered alternatively by meadows and forests, and its rich soil had made the area suitable for farming for centuries. Wildflowers sprout profusely on the rolling hillsides and meadows.

Over time, small villages had grown up throughout the region to support the noble families who had built large mansions to take advantage of the beautiful lakes and woods. In the early twentieth century, country lanes led from these villages out to fields and pastures, through stately forests that provided a home for wildlife, as well as firewood and fertile ground for wild mushrooms and berries.

The branches of trees planted alongside the lanes years or even centuries earlier made a canopy that provided shade to travelers making the leisurely journey back and forth from village to village or out to the fields beyond the towns. The lakes and canals provided locals a ready method of transporting logs from their region to ports on the Baltic Sea, from which they could be shipped to other parts of Germany or other European nations. The region was virtually free of heavy industry—and stayed that way for the next fifty years, much to the good luck of the residents, who were to be spared the heavy Allied bombing that devastated major industrial areas and metropolitan centers in the country during the Second World War.

The tiny village had been part of the Province of Brandenburg, the ancestral domain of the Hohenzollerns, the ruling family in the Kingdom of Prussia. It had long been part of a loose confederation of semi-independent petty kingdoms and duchies known as "Germany." In 1866, however, the visionary Prussian Chancellor Otto von Bismarck welded these disparate entities into a single nation that could stand toe-to-toe with the major European powers—France, England, Spain, and Russia.

By 1910, the modern German nation was beginning to flex its muscles in the international arena. Whether in 1910 the villagers of Alt Lutterow cared that their region was now part of a more powerful nation is open to debate. What cannot be questioned, however, is that this saber-rattling by officials in Berlin was to have major consequences in years to come for Marie Sadler Jürgens and her family.

Change did not come overnight, of course. Despite efforts by national governments to create a new, unified country and improve the quality of life for its citizens, old habits were to die hard. Before World War I, and in fact until the rise of Hitler's Nazi party, the class system that had developed during feudal times was still alive in Germany. Kaiser Wilhelm II presided over a nation that was governed by an elite consisting of landed gentry and military professionals, a country whose business was handled by one of the most complicated professional bureaucracies in the world. Additionally, while there may have been no legal prohibitions to prevent members of the lower classes from advancing in society, the old system was still respected with a rigidity that made it difficult for farmers to think that their children, especially their daughters, could aspire to any life outside the agricultural community. A few might become merchants or shopkeepers in the local villages, but the idea of pursuing a profession was simply not fathomable.

Hertha and her sisters would be raised as farm girls, adored by their father and loved by their mother, given what would have been considered considerable freedoms in the backward farming communities of northern Germany, but certainly not prepared to follow their dreams into any career they might choose.

The Jürgens home in Alt Lutterow was typical of German farmsteads throughout the region. Inside the house a woodfire stove took up an entire corner of the ground floor. The stove served as the principal heat source in the house and was used for cooking and boiling water for a number of purposes. A special warming oven constructed inside the stove was used to keep food heated. Small children like Hedwig and Hertha had to use a footstool to reach the pots atop this stove—a circumstance that frequently led to accidents in other homes, but one the Jürgens family fortuitously avoided. There was no running water in the house, and no washing or toilet facilities. Marie Jürgens made soap patties, which dissolved in very hot water, for washing clothes and utensils. When they were old enough, the girls assisted their mother with those tasks. The children worked in the fields, too, helping to cut and bale the crops of rye, barley, wheat, and oats, rolling large bundles and tying them with string. Hertha recalled fondly the fields covered with seradella, a special gray-green seed plant used to feed the cows. It was said to be the secret to the sweet flavor milk and butter acquired from the cows that had eaten it.

At age six, Hertha began her formal education. Throughout the nineteenth century, the German elementary and secondary school system had been considered the finest in Europe, so much so that in the 1860s the British Secretary of Education sent an emissary to study the German system to see how it might be adapted in England. German educators stressed the importance of mastering bodies of knowledge, and although independent thinking was not encouraged, by the late nineteenth century the schools had become places where right conduct and civic pride were fostered.

Under the influence of the industrialists who began to wield considerable influence in Germany during the early decades of the twentieth century, the curriculum was changed to emphasize technical proficiency as well, preparing young Germans to enter a growing industrial work force. In addition to studying arithmetic, reading and writing, Hertha and her classmates spent their first years learning to love the Kaiser and the country his grandfather Kaiser Wilhelm I and Bismarck had created. She enjoyed school, even though she was so small the teacher would on occasion pick her up and place her on the teacher's desk so she could see the blackboard or recite before her classmates more easily. Her natural shyness kept her from saying too much in class, but she developed a love of learning that would stay with her for the remainder of her life.

Even before Hertha began attending school, though, the idyllic life on the Jürgens farm was shattered in August 1914. Since the turn of the new century, the country had been conducting a military buildup, waiting for a chance to lash out against its European neighbors for perceived slights and economic injustices. What many in Germany (and elsewhere) thought would be

Richard Jürgens (right) with members of his Army unit, circa 1915.

a swift and glorious war for national honor quickly turned into a bloody struggle of attrition and survival. As the months dragged on with no end in sight, nearly every able-bodied man was called to military service for a term of at least three years; even farmers were not exempted.

Richard Jürgens left his family sometime after 1914 for military training. He was eventually posted to a combat unit. He cut a handsome figure in his uniform; family photographs show him and his friends posing proudly in their form-fitting military tunics, snug breeches, high boots, and spiked helmets. But like so many young German men—more than 1.8 million, in fact—Richard Jürgens did not make it home from the war. He was serving on the front lines in France on July 15, 1918, when his unit engaged the enemy. What happened exactly is not clear, but Jürgens was killed on the battlefield. Ironically, he fell in the same month senior German military commanders determined it would be prudent to seek an armistice.

Marie Jürgens received the notice of her husband's death during harvest time. Several women and older men had gathered at the Jürgens farm to help bring in the crops, a common practice with so many able-bodied young men off fighting. More than sixty years later, Hertha could still remember seeing her mother sitting on the steps of the house, crying uncontrollably.

The note said Richard Jürgens had been killed instantly. Though this could not be verified, information received later suggests he may have died from poison gas. But word of a death without suffering certainly provided some comfort to Marie as she mourned for the man with whom she had intended to spend the rest of her life. Hertha remembered that, even though meals during harvest time were like holiday feasts, no one ate much that day.

Although she inherited Richard Jürgens' farm, Marie was now left alone to raise four small girls, with no one around to help her manage the property. There was no public welfare system to provide a safety net for Marie and her family. She was certainly not afraid of hard work, but she knew she was not up to the task of raising four girls on a farm that required considerable manual labor and constant attention, so she put the farm up for sale. Ewald Mahnke, a neighbor who owned the farmstead across the road at Dorfstrasse #4, made her an acceptable offer. Mahnke would later remodel and expand the property, creating a two-family dwelling out of the original Jürgens house and making it impossible to identify the exact dwelling in which Hertha and her younger sisters were born.

Executing the deeds of sale, Marie placed the proceeds in her savings account at the local post office. That decision seemed wise at the time, but it would have disastrous consequences in the coming years. At the same time, she began considering how she might care for her girls. Prospects for a widow in 1919 were grim, as there were hundreds of thousands like her in war-ravaged Germany. She was convinced she would have to find work, and soon. Immediate re-marriage seemed unlikely, as so many men of marriageable age had died in the war. Nevertheless, she was certain that eventually she would have to find another husband who could provide for her family—no small task, considering that she had four daughters! Fortunately for her—and for them—a "white knight" rode into her life shortly after the hostilities ended.

After selling the Jürgens farm, Marie decided to look for a job three kilometers away in Flecken Zechlin, where her daughters attended school. Since the town was considerably larger than Alt Lutterow, Marie thought prospects for employment would be better there. She was right. In short order, she was hired as a maid at the Hotel Zur Alten Eiche on the village square. She moved her daughters into the workers' quarters on the top floor of the hotel.

Founded in the thirteenth century, Flecken Zechlin was one of thousands of towns in Germany that served as a "hub" for farming communities. In 1919 about a thousand people lived there. Located on the shore of the Schwarzer See, the homes and shops that made up the town were constructed on the slope of a hillside on the southwest corner of the lake. Flecken Zechlin was home to fishermen who plied the quiet waters of the lake for sturgeon and other delicacies. Dozens of farmers made their homes in town, keeping livestock in outbuildings behind residences built right up against the sidewalks of streets that wandered along the hillside. On the plateau above the town, the terrain stretched out flat for miles, providing ample room for fields and forests where a number of Flecken Zechlin's residents worked daily.

The town's streets and central marketplace were paved with cobblestones, and there was an outdoor garden beautifying the square. Two large oak trees stood in a small green patch in the center of the marketplace beside which passed the main roads out of town to villages within a day's distance on foot. A monument to the local men who had fallen in the Franco-Prussian war of 1870-71 had been erected at the northeast corner of the square.

As in many German cities, a small but impressive Lutheran church rose in the center of the marketplace. This building served not only as the spiritual center of the community, but also until the late nineteenth century as the official repository of records. Birth and death certificates of everyone in the community were housed in the church's archives. Plaques on the walls commemorated not only the saints of the church but also the prominent citizens of Flecken Zechlin and its suburbs, including Alt Lutterow. That is why, on the memorial placard for those who had fallen in The Great War, the name of Richard Jürgens was inscribed, second-to-last from the bottom.

Flecken Zechlin was also the site of the school that served boys and girls who resided in town and in neighboring villages. Marie had gone to school there two decades earlier. Her eldest daughter Hedwig had walked the three kilometers from Alt Lutterow through the marketplace to the two-story building

The town of Flecken Zechlin at the turn of the twentieth century.

at the foot of Amtstrasse for a few years before the family moved into town, and certainly Hertha had joined her on the walk to and from classes for at least several years.

Shops dotted the streets of the town, offering goods and services to the farmers and tradesmen, and to the tourists who swelled the population during the summer months. Later, probably in the 1930s, a kino, or movie house, opened on Wittstockerstrasse, the main thoroughfare leading up from the marketplace and out of town toward the west.

Sometime during those same years, a railway station was constructed on the southern edge of town, making it easier for outsiders to reach Flecken Zechlin. Even before that time, however, many made the journey to the village from Berlin and other cities. Its' location in the Lake District had made Flecken Zechlin a popular tourist destination. For years the hotels and *Gasthäuser* (accommodations similar to bed and breakfast establishments) had been attracting visitors during the summer months. When Berliners wanted to get away from the heat of the city for a week or two, they often sought refuge in the Lake District.

In Flecken Zechlin, docks ringing the lake offered boats for rent, and a number of large tourist crafts sailed the *Schwarzer See* in good weather. In addition to finding accommodations in commercial establishments such as the *Hotel Zur Alten Eiche*, visitors rented rooms in private homes, frequently renting from the same families year after year.

On the north side of the hotel at which Marie worked, on the point at which Mirowerstrasse and Amtstrasse intersected, was the home of one of the more affluent farmers in the region. His outbuildings contained not only his farming implements, but also his livestock, including two horses—a sure sign that he was better off than most of his neighbors.

Across from this farmer's house on Mirowerstrasse facing the market square stood the home where the celebrated German cityscape painter Eduard Gärtner had spent the last seven years of his life. Known throughout the country for his exquisite, detailed canvases of Berlin's thoroughfares and alleyways, Gärtner had retired to Flecken Zechlin with his wife in 1870. His home would eventually become a museum and a destination for tourists that supplemented the town's other attractions.

Across the alley next door to the hotel at which Marie Sadler worked stood the home of the Dittmann family. Am Markt #2 was one of the oldest buildings in Flecken Zechlin, built sometime in the fifteenth century. The exterior walls had been constructed by covering thick wooden beams with a mixture of mud and gravel stiffened and held together with horsehair.

The main house consisted of two stories, with a parlor, large dining room and kitchen on the ground floor; smaller rooms were nestled next to them. The kitchen contained a large cooking stove that also provided heat for downstairs in winter. Upstairs there were bedrooms, including some that summer guests occupied regularly. Some of the bedrooms were outfitted with a *Kachelofen*, a tile stove that gave off heat and served as a great place for small children to prepare baked apples. In 1919

The Dittmanns' home on the Market Square in Flecken Zechlin. The Hotel Zur Alten Eiche (no longer standing) can be seen at the left of the photo. (photograph circa 1930)

the house had no indoor plumbing. Water was carried in from a well in the garden; the family used an outhouse in the farm yard behind the main house.

At the rear of the house, lay a cobblestone yard containing a number of outbuildings, including a large barn where the Dittmanns kept a few cows, two or three pigs, and a horse used for plowing and pulling wagons and sleds. Chickens and other fowl were kept in the yard. Inside other buildings were a wagon, a threshing machine, and other farm implements. A large wooden fence, attached to the house, surrounded the outbuildings and made an inner courtyard where a large woodpile was kept.

There was also a pile of manure, situated over a grate with a cement trench beneath it, so that rain water could run through the manure and liquefy it; this liquid was spread on the fields each spring. The Dittmanns had erected a blacksmith shop in the yard, and earnings from that enterprise provided additional (and much needed) income.

Set into the north side of the fence near the point where it was affixed to the house was a large wooden gate, an exit for farm equipment and livestock when they were taken to the family's fields and pastures. A smaller gate on the east side of the fence opened onto a garden at the rear of the property; a set of steps descended from the gate into the garden. Inside the garden the Dittmanns grew flowers and vegetables. An artesian well provided plenty of water for the family and its livestock. Beyond the garden a lawn sloped toward the edge of the lake where a beautiful willow tree stood, its branches hanging over the water. From beside the Dittmanns' willow tree one could look across the Schwarzer See, a freshwater lake whose shoreline was ringed with stately willow trees that shimmered in the afternoon sunshine and reflected in the mirror-like surface of the water.

The Dittmann home was one of three buildings that faced the open space of the marketplace. At Am Markt #3 was a bakery which had opened its doors in the nineteenth century and continued to operate long after the Schmidts had departed from Flecken Zechlin for good and the Dittmanns had died. Attached at Am Markt #4 was another residence, one that would house some of the Dittmanns' family briefly after World War II.

In 1919, Wilhelm Dittmann—Willi, as he was known to his friends and associates in Flecken Zechlin—had taken over management of the farm from his father, his sister having married and moved away.

Like Richard Jürgens, Willi Dittmann was one of the handsome young men in uniform who had left his home to serve his country during the war. When at home on leave from the special guards unit to which he was assigned, he paraded around the village in his plumed helmet and form-fitting tunic and trousers. Combat, however had proven to be no parade; he was wounded during the war. Fortunately the injury was not serious, and he was still capable of working his land. The kind of farming he engaged in, however, did not bring in a large income. Consequently, in addition to raising crops and running a blacksmith operation part-time, Dittmann supplemented his income

Summer scene at the Dittmanns' in Flecken Zechlin. Left to right: Hertha's sisters Hedwig and Elli, Hertha's grandfather Sadler, two summer guests, Hertha's mother Marie (Sadler) Dittmann. The cart is a Handwagen. (photograph circa 1930)

in the winter by hauling logs from the surrounding forests to the lake, where they were placed on barges for shipping outside the region. He, too, was well-liked in the village, and in the 1920s, he found time to sing in the local men's choir.

Marie Jürgens may have been acquainted with Willi Dittmann before the war. In later life Hertha suggested that the two may have been close friends, and that Dittmann may have "had his eye on" Marie even before he went off to fight. One thing is certain: Marie made it a point to get to know him after she moved to Flecken Zechlin. The details of their courtship are lost to memory, but after the harvest season in 1919, Marie Sadler Jürgens and Wilhelm Dittmann were married. Marie and her four children moved into the Dittmann farmstead shortly thereafter.

For Marie and her girls, making their living on the Dittmann farm was remarkably similar to their earlier experiences

in Alt Lutterow. Marie kept the Dittmann house spotless, spending Saturday evenings scrubbing floors that had long ago lost
the luster of new wood and tile. As the homemaker, she spent
a good bit of time in the kitchen. Among her specialties was
bread-making. Family members recall that she would knead her
dough carefully by hand, using large trays to bake loaves some
two- to three-feet long. Once a week she would bake cakes and
confectionaries so that visitors on Sunday would be treated to
sweet goodies along with her lively conversation.

Though it was possible to buy some products at one of
the local butcheries or vegetable markets, the Dittmanns raised
most of what they ate, and it was Marie's job to prepare meals.
That meant not only cutting up vegetables or peeling potatoes,
but killing and plucking chickens or ducks. When it was time to
slaughter a pig—a common occurrence before World War II, but
illegal under the Soviets—she would work tirelessly to help with
the butchering, collecting the blood and innards for sausages,
cutting and smoking and curing the meat so that the family
would have pork for months. Despite the backbreaking schedule, she was always upbeat. Her daughter Hertha would learn
well from her mother, both in terms of maintaining a household
and keeping a stiff upper lip when things got tough.

Willi Dittmann spent much of his time in the fields that
he leased. Most of these were located some distance south of
town, although he had permission to harvest one meadow deep
in the beech woods north of town. To reach the arable lands he
tended, he would have to hitch his horse to the wagon and navi-
gate up the cobblestone streets of the town out to the plateau
where he grew rye, barley, wheat, oats, beets, and potatoes.

In harvest season Marie worked in the fields alongside
her husband, helping to cut the hay and barley or pull up potatoes, and load the wagon for the journey back home. There
were heavy chores for children to perform as well—caring for the
animals, harvesting grains, and picking potatoes. This last task

was backbreaking, as it required the use of a three-pronged tool to pry loose individual potatoes from the soil. The work had to be done on one's knees. Hertha found the task interminable, especially in cold weather. Frequently one or another of the girls picked up infections from the soil, and invariably their hands dried and cracked at the fingertips from constant contact with the soil. Whether planting or tilling or harvesting or storing the crops, the work was backbreaking. There were days when Hertha and her sisters thought it would be impossible to get up and go out again to work in the fields or in the barns. But they did, because it was the only life they knew.

Bringing in the harvest was a particularly challenging and even a dangerous chore. Dittmann's wagon was of typical German construction. The wheel base sat high, between three and four feet off the ground. The wagon bed was approximately six feet wide, but the staves that rose upward to form the sides leaned outward so that more harvested crops could be tossed up into the wagon, allowing the farmers to make fewer trips back from the fields to the village.

Since all the roads leading from the fields to Flecken Zechlin were at a higher elevation than the marketplace, coming home the wagon had to travel downhill on the town's cobblestone streets. Farmers like Dittmann had to negotiate the streets with a load of hay or grain crops swaying precariously some ten to fifteen feet above the wagon bed. Anyone riding atop the harvested crops would have to hang on tight, constantly fearing that the load might spill over!

If that were not bad enough, when the wagon reached home the wide double gates would be swung open and Dittmann would gently coax the horse inside, wagon in tow. Then a set of brakes would be affixed under the wheels and lines run off the sides; Marie and her children (and later grandson Rolf) would hold the lines, and the brakes would be set and released carefully as Dittmann maneuvered the wagon down the slope in the yard to the grain bins located half-way down the barnyard. One slip and the wagon would go sliding into the horse and the buildings below!

At that time in Germany, it was customary for several generations to occupy the same home, and Hertha remembered her grandfathers living with the family. Although "Opa" Dittmann was no longer farming actively, he did maintain a few crops of his own in small gardens, among them a patch of tobacco. One brand, Hertha recalls, was named "Maryland." Opa Dittmann would pick leaves carefully and then hang them on wires to dry; when they had lost enough natural moisture, he would soak the leaves in some foul-smelling liquid as part of the curing process. The children helped their grandfather roll cigars, which were shaped in a press Opa Dittmann had made himself.

Every man who came to visit the farm received a home-made cigar—but, Hertha recalled, most tried to avoid accepting them, because they did not smell or taste very good! Certainly, they were no match to those which her stepfather smoked on Sundays. It was certainly Willi Dittmann's cigars, and not those smoked by his father, that Hertha remembered fondly when she observed later in life that she enjoyed seeing a man smoke a good cigar.

Opa Sadler, Hertha's maternal grandfather, on the Dittmann farm, with Rolf. (photograph circa 1935).

Willi Dittmann's father. (photographed in the early decades of the 20th century)

  Willi Dittmann's father also made *Harzer Käse*—a kind of cottage cheese with a sweet taste but a strong smell that makes Limburger seem mild! Apparently he found it necessary to age this cheese for some time, keeping it under loose-fitting covers. He told the children he had to keep it in this fashion so that flies and maggots could get to it. When the maggots were on the cheese, he said, it was ready! They had only to scrape off the maggots then eat the cheese. The young Marie Dittmann would get exasperated with her father-in-law because he would use Marie's dough tray to make this cheese, fouling the tray and causing her to spend hours scrubbing it to clean out the odor.

  Opa Dittmann slept in a tiny room off the dining room on the ground floor, settling himself into bed each night with a small glass of brandy. He lived to his hundredth birthday, serving as a bridge between the old generations of Brandenburgers and the younger generation of modern women that Marie Dittmann brought into the house when she married Willi.

  By 1920 the new family had settled into a life that promised some stability and offered some prospects for happiness.

But events far beyond their control would soon intervene to make sacrifice necessary once again. One might think that national and international events would have had little impact on the life of farmers, especially in a country where transportation was limited and agricultural practices still favored subsistence farming. That was not the case, however; one still needed money to purchase equipment, clothing supplies, sundries and the like. Consequently, in 1922, the Dittmanns found themselves suffering along with millions of other Germans the effects of what became known as "the Great Inflation." In a span of two years from 1922 to 1924, the value of their hard-earned currency plummeted.

The causes were tied directly to Germany's defeat in World War I. When the hostilities began, a U.S. dollar was worth 4.2 German marks. By the end of the war, its' value had diminished so that it took 14 *marks* to purchase a single U.S. dollar.

The rear yard at the Dittmanns in Flecken Zechlin. The large wagon used to haul crops from the fields outside the town can be seen at left. (photographed circa 1940).

Worse things were to come, however. At the Treaty of Versailles, the Allies demanded that Germany pay burdensome reparations to the victors. Additionally, much of Germany's manufacturing capability was either taken away (equipment was actually carted off to France and Russia) or used to make goods for other countries as part of the payment of reparations.

Leaders of the new Weimar Republic, a government named after the city where leaders had met to draft a new constitution after the fall of the Kaiser's regime, seemed almost powerless to control their economy. The ruling political party began printing more and more currency to meet the nation's obligations. As a result, rampant inflation set in. By January 1923 it took nearly 18,000 *marks* to purchase one dollar, and within two months the ratio was 4.6 *million* marks to $1.00 U.S. The spiral increased precipitously, so that by late 1923 the value of German currency had dwindled to an almost meaningless level: $1.00 was now worth 4.2 *trillion* marks. Stories circulated of workers in the cities being paid twice daily so they could purchase needed foodstuffs and supplies on their lunch breaks, before prices went up in the afternoon. As difficult as it may be to believe, salaried and hourly-wage employees needed baskets and wheelbarrows to cart home a day's pay.

Eventually the government got inflation under control, and the country's economy was stabilized once more. But on the personal level, this four-year period hit people exceptionally hard, even subsistence farmers who, like the Dittmanns, may not have been as dependent on cash income as their counterparts in the city. In fact, Marie was not spared, from the catastrophe. Sometime during the period of soaring inflation, she found it necessary to purchase some simple supplies. Having no ready cash, she withdrew from the local bank the funds she had set aside from the sale of the Jürgens farm in 1918. This money, which represented generations of hard work by more than one owner of the small farmstead, allowed her to purchase only a few rolls of sewing yarn. No wonder every member of the family had to work hard to make sure the family could survive.

But life on the farm was not all work. There were days in the summer and fall when Hertha and her sisters went out into the forest to pick berries and mushrooms. In the winter, the girls could go ice skating on the frozen lake. There was time to play in the summers, too, when the girls would amuse themselves out in the barn, in the yard, and in the large family garden. There was fruit for the taking in the family orchard.

Of course, like most children, the Dittmann girls were not always satisfied with what they could obtain easily, and temptation lay just outside their fence. The Dittmanns had apple trees in their yard, but there was a larger one next door. One day Hertha and Elli snuck out of the fence, crawled under a hedge and entered their neighbor's yard. They proceeded to pick the ripening apples, gathering them up in their smocks. When they had all they could carry, they dashed back to their own yard by the way they had come, proud that they'd not been caught. Much to their dismay, however, their neighbor came to the door a half hour later, carrying a large basket of apples. When Marie Dittmann opened the door for him, he handed her the basket and said, "There's no need for the girls to crawl through the hedge; if you need apples that badly, here's a basket for you!" Hertha did not report on the aftermath of this adventure, but one might imagine that the embarrassed parents had something to say to the two girls about their escapade!

After the war, Hertha and her sisters continued their education in Flecken Zechlin. The Dittmann girls were all good students. Their mother recalled that all four were consistently assigned to sit in the front row in their classroom—the place reserved for the best scholars. In the years following Germany's defeat, however, the curriculum changed markedly. Kaiser-worship was replaced by instruction that stressed the wrongs done to Germany by the victorious Allies. New textbooks continued to glorify the German nation and stressed the natural superiority of the Germans over people from other countries.

In some ways this was a not-so-subtle type of propaganda that promoted not only aggressive nationalism but also ideas of racial superiority. The system promoted the need for acquiescence to authority, along with a strong sense of community; children were taught that it was noble to sacrifice one's personal ambitions for the good of the Fatherland. The government's aim was to build in the next generation a strong sense of national pride—something that would unfortunately play into the hands of Adolf Hitler and his henchmen when they began their meteoric rise to power in the early 1930s.

When she was not in school or out with her sisters and friends, Hertha enjoyed reading. Her favorite books were science fiction. She devoured the works of Kurt Lasswitz, the father of German science fiction, as well as those of Hans Dominick and Rudolf Daumann. She would escape from her present woes into a future world depicted in novels such as Lasswitz's *On Two Planets*, a stirring tale of Martian invaders, or Dominick's *The Legacy of the Uranids*, which featured amazing inventions that all the nations of the earth could use against evil forces in the galaxy.

Among other books she read as a child were ones that described that far-away land known as "America." Places like Delaware and Philadelphia and New York captured Hertha's imagination as much, perhaps, as those science-fiction novels had done. "Who would have thought then," she remarked much later in life, "of living in America at all?" She probably figured she had as much chance of going to the United States as she had of visiting the worlds created by Dominick and Daumann! In the days before convenient auto and train travel, people from farming communities in northern Germany traveled only infrequently to the capital towns of their region, and only a few ever made it as far as the nation's capital, Berlin.

At the Dittmanns sometime in the late 1920s. Left to right: Willi Dit-tmann's father and sister; Hertha's grandfather Sadler; Hertha's sister Hedwig; Hertha; Marie and Willi Dittmann.

When Hertha completed her secondary education, she was forced to confront an issue that most German women of previous generations did not face: What would she do next? Prior to World War I, upon finishing school most young farm girls, and even many in the cities and towns, would have begun thinking about their future as wives and mothers. Most would have stayed at home perfecting their domestic skills in anticipation of meeting the man who would be a good husband, father, and provider for them and their children.

There were some rebels among these pre-war women—Marie Sadler had been one, opting to get a job as a hotel maid rather than waiting patiently at home until she met "Mr. Right." After the war, however, it became more acceptable for girls finishing school to consider some form of trade or profession. In fact, the schools had been restructured (at the insistence of the new breed of industry leaders that had emerged in the late nineteenth century) so that young women would be encouraged to develop skills other than those needed to run a household. As a consequence, when her formal schooling came to an end, Hertha began to consider seriously what career she might want to pursue. Besides, getting a real job would give her some independence.

She may not have been aware of it at the time, but Hertha was joining a growing number of young German women who were opting for careers over marriage, at least right out of school. This trend would continue for only a few more years, until the Nazis took steps to return women to the home and increase the country's birth rate. For a time, though, it was both acceptable and fashionable for a young woman to see herself as a career woman, and Hertha found this prospect most tempting.

Initially, Hertha settled on the banking field, because as a student she had liked working with numbers. She had even managed to get a job in the local bank during her last year of school. For three and a half years, she devoted herself to becoming proficient in the skills required of an entry-level bank clerk, and she became good at what she was doing. Unfortunately, she was the victim of bad timing. Just when she completed her apprenticeship, Germany had begun to suffer from recession and she lost her job. Hertha was qualified for a position at the post office, but none were open. So she took a job at a retail establishment, a kind of general store where she worked in *haberdashery*. It was not what she wanted, but she realized she was lucky to be earning any money at all.

At age twenty, Hertha Jürgens Dittmann was a dark-haired beauty. She dressed as smartly as the family budget permitted. Standing barely five feet tall (her daughter Annelore reports she was 4' 9¾") she was probably considered "forward" in Flecken Zechlin, a village that still maintained many of the traditions that dated back to the nineteenth century or even earlier.

In this region it was common for women to dress in ankle-length frocks, to adorn their clothes with lace and frills that looked like something out of a Victorian sepia photograph, and to keep their hair long and braided. Some were even expected to marry the men their parents selected for them—often men as old as their father. Marie Dittmann did not want to limit her

The Jürgen girls circa 1930, clockwise beginning at top left: Hertha, Elli, Anni, and Hedwig.

daughters' future in this way. An excellent seamstress, she made all her daughters' clothes, and taught them to sew as well. She always dressed them as elegantly as her limited means permitted, and she had little use for antiquated customs.

Hertha and her sisters had their hair bobbed—the first girls in the village to do so. They were encouraged to seek careers that would interest them, as Marie had done when she was younger. But they were no doubt encouraged to also find a man they could love and marry.

Hertha certainly knew what she wanted—and what she did not. One thing was certain: she did not want to become a farmer's wife and live the rest of her life in the same circumstances in which she had grown up. That might be fine for her mother, who seemed to accept gladly the burdens attendant to farm and household management. Her sister Elli showed no signs of wanting to leave home or the farming life; even Anni was adjusting to the routine. But Hertha had no love for farming. In later life, she told her children, "I didn't want to farm. It smelled—and I did not like taking care of farm animals!"

She did enjoy working and having spending money to use for outings with her friends. When she found she did not like her position at the small store in Flecken Zechlin, she made her displeasure known to the store owner. Whether he felt sorry for the young woman or just wanted to get rid of a disgruntled employee, the owner suggested that Hertha may want to work in a larger store—away from her home town. He had been a manager at just such a store in Kolberg, south of Berlin, and he used his connections to secure a position there for Hertha. Moving so far away from home—nearly 160 kilometers in an age when travel by car was nonexistent and train travel slow at best—was both exciting and a bit traumatic for the twenty-year-old, as she had never been out of the area around Alt Lutterow and Flecken Zechlin. Her fears did not stop her, though. Bravely she made her way to Kolberg—alone—where she rented a room in town.

Her pay at the store was minimal, however. What little money she earned went to pay for room and board, so she had precious little to set aside for herself.

Further bad luck would strike again, and quickly. In 1930, Germany entered another period of significant economic hardship. The Great Depression in Germany was a direct result of the United States stock market crash of 1929. American financiers and investors who had loaned money to the Weimar government after 1919 began calling in their loans to make up for losses suffered at home. The Germans began to feel the pinch as businesses closed or began reducing their payrolls by letting people go. By the end of 1930, more than five million Germans out of a workforce of 29 million were unemployed. Among them was the young Hertha Jürgens, who was laid off and forced to return to Flecken Zechlin where no work was to be found.

A ray of hope shone upon her soon after her return, though. Her older sister Hedwig, who had never learned a trade, had taken a position as a maid in the home of a doctor in Flecken Zechlin. When the doctor was offered a better position in Wuppertal, a city in western Germany near Düsseldorf and Cologne, he took Hedwig with the family. Sometime after Hertha returned to Flecken Zechlin, she received a letter from Hedwig suggesting that if Hertha could not find work at home, she might want to come west to try her prospects in a larger city.

Hertha thought the idea had merit. After all, she reasoned, a city like Wuppertal would have plenty of stores, banks, and other places where a young woman with her skills might find employment. So she set off to join her sister. Of course, she could not stay with the doctor's family; she had to find a place for herself. Wuppertal was indeed a larger city, but because of the Depression there were even more laid-off industrial workers seeking the few jobs that came available. Lacking the professional experience she needed to compete for positions against these men and women, she decided to seek employment as a housemaid.

Hertha found a position with the *Landgericht Direktor—*the District Administrator—a local political official, as a combination house maid and part-time nanny for his children. He had two boys and two girls, each two years apart. The family lived in a large apartment in the city. Hertha had a little room to herself in their quarters. Among the tasks she had to perform to earn her keep was cleaning the apartment's ten rooms. The heavy carved oak furniture had to be dusted, wiped, cleaned, waxed, and shined each week. So did the floors. The house was filled with large carpets and runners covering the hallways, and periodically Hertha was required to clean these as well—which meant dragging them outdoors, beating them to remove dust, and then hauling them back inside. The work seemed endless, since the *Direktor* and his wife expected the house to be spotless when their many guests came calling.

Hertha ended up doing everything by herself, even though she had been promised that the children would help. Only the youngest boy, age 8, volunteered assistance. He had a special motive: He wanted to marry Hertha! He fawned around her, and was really more hindrance than help. What's more, when the *Direktor's* wife learned Hertha was adept at darning and mending, she asked Hertha to take on this task as well. The work was tedious, but Hertha did it, mustering up as much good cheer as she could. Then the mistress of the house discovered Hertha could cook, so the housemaid had another task dumped on her.

With Hertha handling more of the housekeeping chores, the Direktor's wife found she was free to expand her activity in the National Socialist Women's League. This group was the female auxiliary of the NSDAP—the *Nationalsozialistische Deutsche Arbeiterpartei*, or National Socialist German Workers' Party. Many people referred to this relatively new political group as Nazis. The women's group was growing in membership as the Party rapidly gained influence on the national scene.

In retrospect, considering the Nazis' record of atrocities, it may seem hard to believe Hitler's organization was able to achieve a growing following so quickly. In 1930, however, the Nazis were seen as capable of ending both the chaos that existed in national politics, where nearly thirty parties struggled to gain some political power for their special interests, and checking the influence of the Communists, who were also growing more powerful. Whether the District Administrator and his wife were members of the party is not clear—most likely they were—but certainly both believed the future for Germany lay in its embracing Hitler and his agenda for change.

That Hertha's employers felt this way may give some insight into the kind of appeal the Nazis had at the time. The District Administrator had a background as an academic, and had been educated in German universities. His wife was the daughter of upper-class parents. In 1930 the choice for them was clear cut. No matter how odious some of their practices were—and few believed the rumors of the most brutal activities being attributed to them—the National Socialists were surely preferable to the Communists, whose promise of an egalitarian state sent shudders down the spines of those from the traditionally privileged classes. The Nazis had done a good job, too, in convincing the country's farmers that they would be better off under Hitler than under Walter Ebert, the Communist leader. In fact, the increase in the number of National Socialists elected to the German Parliament from 1929 onward was due in large part to the support Hitler received from the countryside.

On occasion, the *Direktor's* wife would take Hertha and the children to events sponsored by the Women's League. Hertha remembered some years later that despite the political overtones that colored the group's activities, she enjoyed such gatherings. She found the *Rheinländer* she met in and around Wuppertal significantly more open and friendly than the natives of her home town and region. "They opened their mouth and their heart more immediately," she recalled. Then, too, there may have been a very special, personal reason Hertha remembered these meetings so fondly. It was at one of the organization's social functions that she met a young tradesman from the Wuppertal suburb of Elberfeld: August Wilhelm Schmidt.

Willi Schmidt had been born August 29, 1909, in Elberfeld. The son of Wilhelm and Paula Schmidt, he had grown up with sisters Änne, Hertha, and Käthe. He had an interest in art and in cooking, a skill he would later demonstrate as the father of a growing family that relished his confectionary delicacies. Though his father was employed as a painter and paperhanger, the family considered themselves a cut above the common tradespeople with whom they associated—and another cut or two above the farming classes, a fact that would lead to heartache for Willi and especially for Hertha and her children in later years.

But if someone had told Hertha this in 1930, she probably would have paid little attention to the warning. She was immediately smitten by the lithely built youth with his wavy hair and ready smile. Although of medium height (probably around 5'8" to 5'10") Willi Schmidt no doubt seemed to tower over the diminutive farm girl from Flecken Zechlin. Like his father, he was a painter and paperhanger by trade, having completed his schooling several years earlier. By his own admission, he had been a lackluster student at best, preferring to concentrate on riding his motorbike,

August Wilhelm (Willi) Schmidt, circa 1940. The photograph captures the winsome smile and debonair attitude that attracted Hertha to the carefree young man whom she married in 1932.

visiting fancy restaurants along the Rhine River, and enjoying the good life with his friends—acting, as he described himself in later years, "like a big shot." What impressed Hertha most of all, however, was his exceptional musical talent: he could play a tiny harmonica with his nose!

Although she was not often free from her chores, Hertha began seeing Willi Schmidt whenever she could. Frequently they would spend Sunday afternoons walking through the beautifully landscaped cemetery in Wuppertal—a practice that continues in Germany today. The courtship was going strong in the summer of 1931 when Hertha received a letter from home informing her that her mother was ill. Hertha was needed at home. With great reluctance, she quit her position at the District Administrator's home and headed back east to Flecken Zechlin.

There is some irony in her being called home at this time. For several months after arriving in Wuppertal, Hertha had complained in letters to her parents of the harsh conditions under which she was working. She had spoken of the misery she felt when, all alone, she would be on her hands and knees scrubbing floors in the apartment's ten rooms, or out in the snow beating carpets. Although she had been allowed to eat with the family, she received little monetary compensation. No doubt her letters touched a sympathetic chord in Marie and Willi Dittmann.

Always concerned for the welfare of their daughters, the Dittmanns finally acted to rescue Hertha from her travails in a way that would allow her to save face. They concocted a story of Marie's illness so their daughter could depart with dignity (and not receive a bad reference in the future, no doubt). But by the time Hertha received the Dittmann's plea for her to return, she was anything but eager to leave Wuppertal. Moving back to Flecken Zechlin would mean leaving behind the man with whom she had fallen in love.

By the fall of 1931, however, Hertha was home again. Willi wrote to her, of course, but since the family had no telephone, there was no way for her to hear his voice. She resigned herself to finding some kind of work in or near Flecken Zech-lin and spending time with her girlfriends. Although she was nearing her twenty-second birthday, she was in no rush to find someone else to marry. She might be considered an old maid by some, but she knew someday she would become *Frau* Schmidt; she was willing to wait awhile for Willi to make his move.

It did not take long for that to happen. After Christmas of 1931, Willi wrote to Hertha telling her of his intention to visit her in Flecken Zechlin; when there, he said, he would look for work. Even though jobs for painters and wallpaperers were scarce, he wanted to take his chances so he could be with Her-tha. Furthermore, Willi traveled east at considerable personal cost. Though there is no record of any conversation Willi may have had with his parents at this time, recollections by family members in later years indicate that the Schmidts were dead set against their son entering into a serious relationship with some-one "beneath his status."

Whatever may have transpired, nothing could talk Willi out of his plans. Sometime early in 1932, Willi Schmidt moved to Flecken Zechlin and the romance was rekindled. On Octo-ber 1, 1932, August Wilhelm Schmidt and Hertha Anna Maria Jürgens were married. A new chapter in Hertha's life was begin-ning.

Life Under the Third Reich
(1933-1939)

*I*mmediately after they were married, newlyweds Hertha and Willi Schmidt moved in with the Dittmanns while they began looking for a place to establish their own household. Once again, national events had a direct impact on their personal lives. At the same time they were searching for their own apartment, the National Socialists were coming into power and forming a new national government. While this would ultimately prove to be disastrous for Germany, the immediate impact of the Nazis' policies immensely benefited the young couple in Flecken Zechlin.

Under Chancellor Adolf Hitler, policies favoring family life were quickly adopted. Of course, only those who could prove they were Aryans with no Jewish blood could take advantage of these benefits, but at the time most Germans, including the Schmidts, did not think too hard about these discriminatory restrictions. After all, they had been educated in a school system that had drilled into their heads the notion that as German *Volk*, or native people, they had an obligation to raise the next generation of good Germans, and it seemed to them that the government was simply trying to help them fulfill this duty.

Hertha and Willi took immediate advantage of the program, qualifying for a special loan established to encourage young people to marry. Under the terms of the loan, a couple could get money to purchase furniture and other household items; the money would be repaid, at very reasonable interest rates, over several years—unless the couple had children, in which case part or all of the loan could be forgiven. The Schmidts applied and received their loan in the spring of 1933, and used the money to rent and outfit a tiny apartment on the upstairs floor of a home at Grävernitzstrasse #40, about three blocks west of the marketplace and just off Wittstockerstrasse, the main east-west thoroughfare in Flecken Zechlin. They purchased living room furniture, including a couch, and a dresser for storing linens.

Marie Dittmann provided her daughter—the first in the family to marry—with a bedroom suite. The accommodations were certainly not plush. The Schmidts' apartment had only two rooms, and like most of the houses in the town, there was no toilet inside. Like most of their neighbors, Hertha and Willi had to use an outhouse behind the building.

Undoubtedly, once she became responsible for her own household, Hertha carried on many of the traditions she had learned from her mother, diligently cooking hearty meals for her husband, cleaning their tiny living space and doing laundry for herself and Willi each week. Without the timesaving devices developed during the latter half of the century to help people complete housework with minimal exertion, Hertha probably devoted most of every day to keeping up with her chores. Additionally, since refrigeration was impractical for all but the wealthiest families, she had to shop daily for the goods needed to prepare meals. Although the Dittmanns no doubt provided some of the staples she needed, Hertha spent some time every day going to one or more of the various shops where foodstuffs were sold: the bakery, butcher, greengrocer, and spice-store. For the first years of their marriage, the Schmidts were able to eat reasonably well, as food was plentiful in Germany and government policies decreased its costs.

The Schmidts could certainly use all the help that the family or the government provided, because on February 10, 1933, in the apartment in Flecken Zechlin, Hertha gave birth to a baby boy. There is no surviving record of the circumstances surrounding the birth of Rolf Dieter Schmidt, but certainly Hertha received no professional medical assistance. A midwife would have attended her, and the women of the family may have also lent a hand. The baby, who would be called "Dieter" throughout his childhood, was healthy—and "early," if one calculates back to the date of Willi and Hertha's wedding—but the young couple were immensely proud of their young "love child" and were more than ever determined to make a good life for him and the brothers and sisters to come.

Making that good life proved something of a struggle, though. Since coming to Flecken Zechlin, Willi had worked at odd jobs as a painter and day laborer, but his lack of technical skills proved a real handicap. Although he was artistic like his father, Willi never did much in the way of portrait or landscape painting; the only ways he demonstrated that kind of artistic talent was in his work to decorate cakes for the family and in some occasional woodcarving. He would not have been held in high regard by the citizens of Flecken Zechlin, who were still ideologically bound to a class system that regarded unskilled workers as being "beneath" those engaged in skilled trades or business. The stigma of the class system would continue to haunt the Schmidts for the remainder of their time in Germany.

Things began to look brighter, however, as the summer of 1933 approached. Hitler's government had already begun a series of massive programs to give people employment and secretly rebuild Germany's military might. One of the first steps toward this goal proved to be most beneficial to Willi and Hertha. In 1933, the National Socialists embarked on a clandestine program to reinstitute military testing at the air base near Rechlin, a town just a few kilometers north of Mirow and only

25 kilometers from Flecken Zechlin. To do so the government needed a labor force, and Willi Schmidt was available and willing to accept a position there.

The Nazis were taking a real risk in beginning to build a major aviation testing station in blatant violation of international agreements. Although the terms of the 1919 Treaty of Versailles had prohibited Germany from having any military airpower, as early as 1920 the new Weimar government had acquiesced to demands from the German General Staff to begin rebuilding the country's air forces in secret. Operating for years under a secret agreement made with the Soviets at Rappallo, Italy, in 1922, the Germans had been training combat pilots and developing military aircraft at a base near Lipetzsk, Russia. When Hitler assumed power, one of his first acts was to direct his deputy, Hermann Göring, to build a strong air force. In 1933, however, Hitler and his henchmen in Berlin felt they had to continue operating in secret, because they feared the Allies were still in a position to impose strangling economic sanctions on Germany and hinder the Führer's plans to resurrect the country's economic and military might.

The area around Mirow was a perfect place for the Germans to hide their aviation experiments. The community was largely rural, its people trusting and somewhat naïve. Facilities already existed at Rechlin, an airfield constructed during World War I but opened in late August 1918, just months before the end of hostilities. Because the airfield had been converted for civilian use after the war, construction and improvements there were relatively easy, and could be done beyond the gaze of Allies bent on keeping the Germans from regaining any kind of air power. Further, the people in the region were happy to see the development, since growth provided jobs and increased the workforce in the region, thereby benefiting retail businesses and property owners who had houses to rent or sell. Civilian and military workers at the testing station were housed in the nearby villages and towns. A contingent lived in Rechlin itself, but many lived in the larger communities of Röbel to the northwest or Mirow to the southeast.

Willi was first hired on the labor force at Rechlin, digging foundations for buildings and handling other, similar construction tasks. Eventually he was able to move into the paint shop, and before too long he was assigned to painting planes at the airfield. The job must have been both interesting and challenging, as the Germany *Luftwaffe* was experimenting with aircraft finishes at the same time it was testing new engines and aircraft designs. In addition to painting on identification marks, Willi and his co-workers were helping to develop new patterns of camouflage that would make aircraft less easy to spot from the ground, and to apply different combinations of substances that would make the planes more aerodynamic.

Of course, getting and keeping a job in the Third Reich was not without cost. Labor was centrally controlled, and under the terms of the Trade Bill passed in 1933, virtually everyone working at any craft or trade was required to belong to the *Deutsche Arbeiterfront* (DAF), the German Labor Front. In exchange for stable wages and guaranteed employment, the Nazi government, through the DAF, controlled movement from job to job within the labor force.

It became clear to workers soon after Hitler came to power that those who aligned themselves with the Nazis could be assured job security—and those who did not might end up unemployed, or worse. Willi and Hertha discovered that anyone who wished to hold a government job had to be in good terms with the Nazi Party. Willi's father had wanted to join the Party when it was first forming, only his injured pride at not being awarded a low Party registration number—which would signify his importance to the organization—kept the elder Wilhelm Schmidt from becoming a member. Willi and Hertha did not share the elder Schmidt's enthusiasm for the Nazis. As the years passed and they witnessed first-hand what the reckless behavior of Hitler and those around him were doing to Germany, they became even more skeptical.

Neither was exceptionally political, however, and in the 1930s they saw the advantages of making no waves in exchange for guaranteed employment. Many Germans, including the Schmidts, had experienced the hardships and degradations of unemployment during the three years' prior to Hitler's assuming the chancellorship of his country. People needed to earn money to feed their families and pay household expenses; few among the middle or working classes were saving for the future or splurging on niceties. Those who got jobs worked long and hard in order to keep them.

Hardly anyone in Hertha and Willi's circle of friends and acquaintances gave much thought to vacations. For a brief time during the 1930s, a few families like the Schmidts benefited from an initiative called "Strength Through Joy," a government-sponsored program that provided paid vacations for families of workers at factories and in government positions. But Willi Schmidt's name was never picked in the lottery used to determine which lucky family might spend a week in Spain or on the Mediterranean coast. So the Schmidts stayed near home most of the time, and though he was never enamored with the Nazis, Willi kept his mouth shut, went to work, and collected his paycheck.

Initially that paycheck was minimal; Willi earned approximately 30 *Reichmarks* per week (less than $8 US). It was a steady job, however—something that must have seemed a godsend after the Depression years—and there were ways for the family to supplement this base pay. Willi worked overtime whenever he could. Additionally, because the Schmidts now had a child, the government began paying them *Kindergeld*, a supplemental grant that Hitler hoped would encourage Germans to have large families.

Looking back from the vantage point of history, it is easy to accuse Hitler of trying to bribe the German people into producing a fighting force to carry out his megalomaniacal scheme for world domination. In 1933, however, the idea certainly appealed to Willi and Hertha Schmidt, and to millions of other families, since the extra money made it possible for them to acquire a few more necessities, and occasionally some "extras" that would improve their standard of living. As the family grew, so did *Kindergeld* payments.

By making do with second-hand furniture and limiting expenditures to necessities, the Schmidts managed to provide for themselves. Willi also decided that, with one child at home and the prospect of others on the horizon, it was time for him to do something about a career. It was too late to go back and do an apprenticeship, but he learned the government was willing to pay for his schooling if he enrolled in courses offered at the air base. He might even learn to fly! So he enrolled in classes that would provide him skills in areas such as navigation, and though he did not become a pilot, he did improve his ability in mathematics and learned some management techniques as well.

One of the drawbacks to getting the job at Rechlin, however, was that Willi had to travel quite a distance to work each day. He had no automobile, nor did anyone living near the family in Flecken Zechlin. Public transportation from his home to the airbase was slow and made for an intolerably long commute, since he was required to travel first to Mirow, twenty kilometers north, and then get another bus to the airfield. Whether he took his motorbike or used a bicycle, travel time was extensive. He would have to leave before sunup and return long after darkness set in, and as the summer passed travel could be impeded by snowfall and would in the best of circumstances be uncomfortable in the bitter German winter. So he and Hertha decided to move to Mirow.

The wedding of Hedwig Jürgens to Paul Kobow (center) on April 2, 1938. Willi Schmidt is in the last row, behind Kobow. Hertha can barely be seen beside Kobow's father, who stands left of Hedwig. Marie Dittmann is third from right, Willi Dittmann at far right. Hertha and Willi's eldest son Rolf is standing beside Hedwig.

When the Schmidts resettled in the town on the south-eastern shore of the *Mirower See*, Mirow boasted approximately 3,000 inhabitants, a number of them recent arrivals due to the increase in the work force at Rechlin. Founded in the thirteenth century, Mirow had been part of the Duchy of Mecklenburg-Strelitz for centuries. The principality known as Mecklenburg, with its northern border along the Baltic Sea, extended southward for nearly a 100 miles into the larger region of Prussia. The Duke of Mecklenburg-Strelitz established a residence in Mirow in 1701.

After a fire destroyed almost every building in 1730, the city was rebuilt just in time to bid farewell to one of its most famous citizens. In 1761 Sophie Charlotte, sister of the region's ruler Adolf Friedrich IV, left her home for England, where she married the new King—George III, who would, twenty years later, lose his country's most prosperous colonies in North America.

Over the years Mirow had become a trading hub for merchants. The town was proud to claim it was home to one of Germany's first newspapers, the *Wendischer Bote*, which began publication in 1848. What the town did not have in 1933, or de-velop in the next decade, was any appreciable amount of heavy industry—a fact that was to be in its favor during World War II, when the Allies sought out locations that were contributing significantly to the war effort and bombed them heavily. The absence of industry was to spare Mirow that terrible fate.

Finding a place to live in Mirow proved easier than Her-tha and Willi had expected. At the time Elli, Hertha's sister, was working for a dentist in the city, living in the servant's quar-ters above the dentist's office and home on Bahnhofstrasse. She learned that an apartment had become vacant in the home of a veterinarian across the street from where she was living, so she sent word to her sister and brother-in-law, who quickly arranged to rent the place.

The second-story apartment on Bahnhofstrasse was cer-tainly an improvement. The family now had two rooms and a

Hertha and Willi Schmidts' first home in Mirow, on Bahnhof-strasse. (photographed 2006).

kitchen; additionally, a door from the apartment led to a small sun porch built over a veranda attached to the house. Hertha had more to clean, but she attacked her tasks cheerfully—even waxing the floor of the porch and hanging beautiful lace curtains to give the apartment a cheerful feeling no matter what the weather outside. While the vet stayed below taking care of large and small animals, Hertha stayed upstairs, caring for her towheaded youngster.

Late in 1934, Hertha became pregnant again, and on July 6, 1935, she gave birth to the couple's second child, whom they named Annelore Hertha Hedwig Käthe. Certainly quite a few of the young Annelore's aunts must have been pleased to have a namesake! Like all of the Schmidt children except Barbara, "Lörli" Schmidt was born at home. The midwife came to assist Hertha with the delivery. Over the years, this same mid-wife would come five more times.

Rolf remembered the midwife bicycling up to the house in her "sister" frock (the sign of someone in the nursing profession). She instilled fear in the small boy as she entered the house and commandeered equipment and supplies to begin her task.

Frequently, Willi was away when his children were born, and those attending Hertha would shoo away Rolf (and later, the other siblings) while their mother was actually delivering the new baby. There was a distinct smell that hung over the house during the birthing, and when the cries of the newborn emerged from the bedroom where Hertha lay, the older children were allowed to enter to see the newest addition to the family. It was a proud moment for them as they were allowed to hold the infant, still wet and still possessing the remnants of its umbilical cord, before the midwife took the child away to bathe it.

In the 1930s, German doctors prescribed a nine-day bed rest for women who had just delivered a baby. Of course, if a woman were to stay in bed for even a few days, someone had to look after her family and her household. There was no "paternity leave" for the husband, who was still required to report to his job while his wife was recuperating. That meant relying on family and friends for help.

Elli Jürgens would cook for the Schmidts and clean house—tasks she had performed at home in Flecken Zechlin. These jobs got harder as Hertha's clan grew in numbers, and even though Hertha seldom stayed in bed for the entire nine days, the work could be grueling for her unmarried sister. For years the children considered "Tante Elli" their favorite aunt, no doubt because she devoted so much time to them. But it is almost certain that Elli was delighted to return to her own home when Hertha was strong enough to resume her routine as matriarch of the household.

That routine now included watching two small children. Rolf was a toddler, and like most children his age, quite able to get into trouble around the house if he were not watched constantly. The sight of men dressed in their suits and bowler hats heading to the train station down the block held a special fascination for him. On more than one occasion, he found a way to escape from his crib. Once, dressed only in a u-necked undershirt and diaper, he made his way downstairs from the apartment, donned his father's hat, picked up an umbrella or a satchel, and toddled out the door, hat hanging over his eyes. Surprisingly, he made it all the way to the railway station before someone who knew the Schmidts spotted him and returned him to his mother—who must have been frantic with worry by this time!

Hertha discovered a safer way to keep her daughter entertained. Lori remembered years later how she would amuse herself on the sun porch. Because the veranda over which the porch had been built had a sloped roof, the floor was not perfectly level. Lori would sit atop a small pot (similar to a chamber pot) placed at the high corner of the porch. She could then push herself away from the wall, and the pot would slide across the waxed floors to the opposite corner, providing a "joy ride" that kept her busy for hours!

Before long, however, the apartment on Bahnhofstrasse began to feel cramped. Rolf was running underfoot all the time, and Lori was beginning to toddle about. Because they lived on a busy street, Hertha could not simply send her small children out to play. Their inclination to start looking for a larger place became a more urgent priority when, on December 20, 1936, Hertha gave birth to the couple's third child, Wolfgang Fritz Wilhelm Schmidt.

Once again, Hertha and Willi were in luck. The expansion of the air base at Rechlin meant that additional housing and other facilities were needed for the growing work force in

Granzowerstrasse #37, Mirow. The duplex was home to Hertha and Willi and their growing brood of children from 1936 until 1945. (photographed 2006)

the area. Mirow and surrounding villages saw a boom in construction. Sometime in the mid-1930s, the German government began building homes in and around the city to house workers at the testing station and airfield. Most of these government-sponsored developments consisted of tract housing that was simple, sturdy, and functional. Because the Nazis continued to favor men with large families, in late 1936 or early 1937 the Schmidts were able to secure a larger place, one side of an attractive duplex newly constructed on Granzowerstrasse, a main road leading north out of Mirow.

When the Schmidts moved into the duplex at Granzowerstrasse #37, they must have felt that, for the first time in their married life, they truly had a place of their own. The ground floor contained a living room, a small kitchen, a bathroom—with indoor plumbing!—and a bedroom that Willi and Hertha took for themselves. Upstairs were two large rooms, one used as an attic, the other as the children's bedroom. In a small space behind the living room, Willi placed an old desk, above which he hung a portrait of his father bedecked in the garb of a North Sea rescue squad boatman. The children were all fascinated because their grandfather's eyes seemed to follow them no matter where they stood in the room.

Outside was a yard, fenced in by rows of bushes, and a small garden. Behind the house was a storage shed where the Schmidts kept wood for heating and cooking. Beneath was a coal bin for storing coal briquettes. A beautiful wooden lattice fence, stained to preserve its natural beauty, ran along the property in front of the house. Just inside the fence stood a large metal trash can, which got blazingly hot in summer but whose lid provided a warm spot for sitting and sliding on the ice and snow on cold winter days. A deep ditch separated the hard-packed sidewalk from Granzowerstrasse, along which grew large chestnut trees. The Schmidt children earned money for themselves by gathering chestnuts into large bags and hauling them to the Forestry Service office in the next village. Though they were paid only one mark for a sack weighing one hundred pounds, they felt they were rich with their own money in their pockets.

Because they were near the edge of town, it was an easy walk for the Schmidt boys to reach the sports fields that the city maintained adjacent to Beethovenstrasse, the last street in Mirow. Additionally, a stroll of just a few blocks took them to the *Mirower See*, where there was a bath house beside the lake so the family could change for swimming. Occasionally Willi would go fishing or eeling in the nearby lake, bringing home his catch and hanging it on a nail just inside the rear doorway, where the children would look on in morbid fascination as their father skinned the eels that, though dead, still twitched as though alive.

The new home was located in a neighborhood of young families, many of whom loved to socialize. But Hertha had little time to spend with the other wives and mothers. Preferring to keep to herself, she spent most of her day doing her household chores. There was always a baby to tend, and that meant washing out dirty diapers, and there was other laundry to wash and iron—including the bed sheets and underwear! When her daily chores were done, and the children were in bed, Hertha would often eat her supper alone and then curl up for an hour with a favorite book.

In the summer, Hertha would go into the woods to pick berries, so that meant rising even earlier to clean house before departing for the forest. Hertha enjoyed this task, just as she had when she was a child, despite her fear of snakes. Although there were no poisonous snakes in the region, she still worried when she went into the woods or down by the lake; once she arrived and began picking, however, she quickly forgot her fears. Her treks into the forest became even more enjoyable, too, when Rolf was old enough to accompany her, and he seemed to have a knack for the work. Later the other children began to accompany her as well. Before 1945, the only drawback to these foraging adventures was the chance someone might be attacked by one of the wild boars that inhabited the woods. Sows protecting their litter of piglets could be especially dangerous!

Berry-picking was especially fun for the children because they could eat their fill of the berries as they picked them. When they returned home, hands and mouths stained and tummies stuffed, Hertha would go through their baskets, separating the leaves and twigs that they had failed to discard. She would often preserve the berries in one form or another, boiling them in their own juice and placing the mixture into bottles which she sealed with wax.

In addition to a cozy place in a pleasant neighborhood, the house on Granzowerstrasse proved convenient for the family breadwinner. Willi could make it to work in twenty minutes on his motorbike, or in less than an hour on a bicycle. Most of the Schmidts' neighbors worked at the air base—not necessarily a good thing, as it turned out. While it was nice to have something in common with the people around them, the Schmidts soon became painfully aware that the men all shared the occupational hazards of employment in what could at times be a dangerous place. Experimentation at Rechlin was not limited to new aircraft design. The Germans were also testing new technologies for paints as well, and the large paint facility that had been constructed for this purpose had little in the way of protection to keep the workers from inhaling paint fumes. During their time in the housing area, the Schmidts saw many of Willi's co-workers come down with various respiratory ailments. Their neighbor in the other half of their duplex died from a disease brought on by extended exposure to paint fumes.

On September 13, 1938, Hertha gave birth to her fourth child, Hans Einhard. Again, although her pregnancy and delivery were not exceptionally difficult, she called on her sister and mother for some help, and they responded immediately. Because of her duties on the farm, Marie was seldom able to spend more than a day or two with her daughter's family in Mirow, but as always Elli remained behind to serve as housekeeper, cook, and babysitter for her convalescing sister. With a mother, father, and three older siblings, little Eini, as the family called him, received more tender loving care than he might have wanted!

Although his family was growing, Willi did not have much time to enjoy his children. Even before the outbreak of World War II, he spent long hours away from Mirow at the air station. From Monday through Saturday of each week, he would leave home early each morning, before the small children were awake, to make the twelve kilometer trek to Rechlin. Frequently Hertha tried to have the children in bed in the evening before Willi arrived home, so her husband could have a peaceful supper and they could spend some quiet time together before retiring.

On the weekends, however, Willi became helpmate for his wife, playmate for the children, and cook for the entire family. He would treat Hertha like a queen, taking over all the household chores—quite strange for a man of the 1930s! He would often make elaborate meals that required hours of preparation. One of his favorite pastimes was to create scrumptious confectionaries that delighted his small sons and daughter. He had special tools for making intricate designs on these fancy cakes. Routinely he used whipped cream as a topping for these desserts, but from time to time he would use butter cream—which had to be whipped without benefit of an electric blender. Occasionally he would purchase a chocolate bar and shave off slices for each of the children.

When he was not in the kitchen, he would play in the yard with Dieter (Rolf), Lörli, and Wölfi. In good weather he would take them on walks along the streets of Mirow or in the woods outside the town, telling them stories all along the way. The children were all delighted when their father was home with them—and no doubt Hertha enjoyed the break from the drudgery of keeping house and babysitting all the time!

The holiday seasons were memorable in the Schmidt household. At Easter, there would be special candies for the children to share. Willi would take the young ones out for walks in the woods, dropping candy along the way. Between Easter and Pentecost, Hertha would make new outfits for all of them, new suits for the boys (with short pants until they grew older), and a new dress for Lori.

The Christmas season was the best of all times, though. The younger children looked forward with great anticipation to Christmas Eve. For hours they were kept out of the living room, where behind closed doors their parents, and later on the older children as well, would be decorating the Christmas tree. Then, dressed in their finest clothes, they would line up, the youngest at the front of the line, and march into the room. Before them was a beautiful tree, decorated with candies, cookies, and beautiful illuminated candles that gave the room a warm glow and cast shadows on the walls. Then, there was a *bang!* at the door, followed by loud footsteps, and in came Santa Claus! Santa would sit on a chair that had been placed there especially for him, and one by one the children would sit on his lap to recite a favorite poem or sing a Christmas tune. The little ones were amazed. How did Santa know so much about them? After they had all had a turn sitting on Santa's lap, and the singing was over, they would take turns blowing out the candles. What a wonderful time! Of course, the younger ones were a bit sad that their father was not around when Santa arrived. If only he had been able to be home with them—they were sure he would have enjoyed Santa's visit as much as they did.

Willi seemed to pay special attention to Lori, then his only daughter. When he was at home he seemed to single her out to be with him as he did his chores. When she had trouble learning to distinguish left from right, he taught her a simple "gimmick" that really worked. "Hold out your hands, palms down," he said to her. When she did, he pointed to the thumb on her right hand and said, "It's easy to tell right from left; *right* is where your thumb is *left!*" When she told her father about not liking her freckles, he explained to her gently that, "A girl without freckles is like a sky without stars!" Lori never worried about her freckles again.

Not all his gestures of affection worked so well, however. Willi once bought her a red-and-blue sweater that she admired immensely. Unfortunately, Germans often made fun of red-and-blue sweaters, because the German word for blue, *blau*, rhymes with the German word for pig, *Sau*, and people had created a rhyme: *Rot und blau putzt die Sau*—meaning that red-and-blue could dress up a sow! Lori hated to be the butt of this joke, but she adored the gift her father had given her, so she wore it anyway. She even put up with her brothers' teasing.

Willi teased his daughter as well. When she was learning to count, Lori proudly spread out her hand before her father and pointed out her ten digits, one by one. Willi said to her, "That's great, but I have eleven fingers!" Puzzled, Lori watched as her father spread his fingers and counted for her—counting *down* from "ten" to "nine, eight, seven, six"—finishing the first hand—and then, raising the other hand, declaring, "and five on this hand makes eleven!" It took Lori quite a while to learn how to refute him.

Perhaps because Willi was so seldom home, Hertha became the chief disciplinarian in the family. Every one of the siblings remembers getting a beating from her at one time or another. One of her favorite implements for such drubbings was a carpet beater. Over time she became expert at wielding it on the backsides of any child who dared break the rules of the household—something they did regularly, of course. Frequently the young children would be tempted by the long summer days to stay out well after 9:00 p.m., worrying their mother and making it harder for her to give her husband some quiet time when he came home. Often when this happened Rolf would end up as the target of his mother's displeasure since he was the oldest and considered the most responsible for the children's errant behavior.

Of course, when Willi was with the family, he did his part in enforcing discipline and building character. Rolf got his share of slaps from his father—and when he was older, the discipline became even harsher. Einhard recalls that sometime when he was about six or seven, he was out playing with a neighbor's child, and in the course of some heated dispute, he called her a "sow," a particularly vicious insult to German women. Unbeknownst to Einhard, his father was standing inside the doorway and overheard the conversation. Immediately, Willi stepped out of the door and called his son inside—where he promptly delivered a harsh blow and told him he should never again speak that way to anyone, especially a girl or woman.

At home in Flecken Zechlin. Seated: Hedwig, Hertha, Rolf, and Elli. Standing: Marie Sadler Dittmann, Willi Dittmann, and Paula Schmidt (Hertha Schmidt's mother-in-law). (photograph circa 1935)

Even Lori was once the target of Willi's anger—with some justification, as she admitted in later years. Willi had converted half of the shed behind the house into a playhouse for the children, a wonderful place to spend rainy days when one didn't want to be inside the house. On the other side of the shed Willi stored his motorcycle, as well as several cans of paint. One day Lori decided to take one of the cans so she could paint the carpet in the playhouse. When he got home, Willi was furious! Lori knew she was in trouble, so she raced out behind the playhouse and hid amid the gooseberry and red currant bushes while her father raced back and forth looking for her. Then suddenly he stopped—tired, perhaps, or perhaps embarrassed that he had become so upset over such a trifle—and then started laughing out loud. Lori knew it was now safe to come out of hiding.

While they lived in Mirow the family had only infrequent contact with Willi's parents. For some time, the elder Schmidts had continued to express dismay that their son had married "beneath" him. Perhaps this was one reason they did not visit frequently. However, sometime after Willi left home in 1932, his father and mother moved from Elberfeld to Horumersiel, a tiny fishing village on the North Sea, where Opa Schmidt continued his work as a painter and volunteered to help with the coastal rescue squad. When the Schmidt grandparents did visit Mirow shortly before war broke out, however, the children got a glimpse of what kind of woman their Oma Paula Schmidt really was.

Shortly after she and her husband arrived at their son's house, Willi took Hertha out for a special occasion (probably Hertha's birthday or their wedding anniversary), leaving the small children with their Schmidt grandparents. While they were out, Willi bought a box of chocolates to bring home to Rolf, Lörli, and Wölfi. When his mother saw him give the chocolate to the children, she became indignant. He had brought nothing for her! After she had agreed to watch these children for him! How ungrateful a son he was! These children could not appreciate chocolate—but she certainly could. The next day, the Schmidt grandparents left in a huff. It would not be the last time, however, that Oma Paula demonstrated to her grandchildren her incredible self-centeredness.

The family's relationship with their other grandparents was, by contrast, almost a source of unending joy. Occasionally, the Schmidts made trips back to the Dittmann household for visits or special events, traveling with Opa Dittmann in his wagon. When they were in Flecken Zechlin, Omi Dittmann made them feel special, and Opa Dittmann was a wonderful grandfather who entertained them no matter what the season. The older children got to spend time on the farm in the summers both before and during the war. As the eldest, Rolf accompanied Willi Dittmann to the fields, where his step-grandfather taught him to sharpen a scythe and cut down crops.

On rare occasions the others had their chance to experience farming life, too, including opportunities to operate the bellows in the blacksmith shop. This massive wind machine hung above the fire, with a long rope run through an eye on the roof beam. Pulling on the rope made the bellows contract, sending a stream of air across the coals and causing a sheet of flame to erupt inside the fire pit. Lori and her cousin Margarete would do their best to pull the heavy rope, but frequently Opa would have to lift them up so they could grab higher up to get leverage. As they hung onto the rope, they would be pulled off the ground by the force of the machine!

If the Schmidt children visited on a Sunday, they might take a walk with their grandmother to the local cemetery, where she and her neighbors spent pleasant afternoons wandering the pathways or decorating and maintaining the graves of loved ones. One Sunday in the fall was set aside to honor the dead, and Omi Dittmann would prepare for this special day weeks in advance. Accompanied by whichever grandchildren were with her at the time, she would take a small wagon into the forest to gather evergreens. Back at home, she would make wreaths and bouquets from the evergreens and flowers from her garden. On that special Sunday, Opa Dittmann would hitch up his horse and fill the wagon with all of Marie's wreaths and decorations. Marie would take these to the cemetery to place on the graves of family members or others who had no one to tend their resting places.

Hans, Willi Dittmann's faithful horse, with a visitor's child on its back. Hedwig Jürgens Kobow and her children are in the wagon bed. (photographed in the early 1940s)

When the Schmidt children were lucky enough to be in Flecken Zechlin in winter, they were in for an even greater adventure. As he had done for his own daughters, Willi Dittmann would hitch the horse, Hans, to the sleigh he kept in the barn. Meanwhile, their grandmother would put bricks in the warming oven until they became a bit too hot to touch, then remove them and wrap them in towels. The children would climb into the sleigh and off they would go! Opa Dittmann would drive them through the snow-covered woods, stopping somewhere on the route to pull out a thermos of hot cocoa. As they went along he would tell them stories that kept them entertained throughout the ride. When they returned home, Omi Dittmann would be waiting for them with a tray full of warm apples.

When Rolf and Lori were young, Opa Sadler, Marie's father, was still living with the Dittmanns. He would spend most of his time in the small room he occupied off the dining room in the main house. But each year, he would plant a few rows of corn to grow for his geese. Well before the holidays he would select one of the flock to be the "Christmas goose"—the main meal for the family's holiday dinner. As was the custom on farms throughout Germany, starting shortly after the annual harvest he would begin force-feeding the corn he had grown to the "lucky" goose. Fascinated, the Schmidt children could watch him as he went through the ritual. He would place the goose on his lap, take its beak in one hand and stretch it upward, extending the goose's neck, gently squeezing the beak to make it open. He would then scoop up corn in his other hand and pour it down the bird's gullet. Every day he would repeat the procedure, and every day the goose began to look just a little plumper. Watching the ritual the children could look forward with great anticipation to a hearty meal on Christmas day!

Once in awhile a wedding or similar celebration brought everyone back to Flecken Zechlin, and the extended Dittmann family would enjoy festivities that often included the four sisters' singing old songs they had learned in childhood. At these infrequent special occasions, the Schmidt children would see their cousins Gerhard and Margarete (Gretel) Kobow, children of their Aunt Hedwig, who had married a neighbor in Flecken Zechlin and moved into his house just down the street from the

Dittmanns. Later the Schmidts and the Kobows would see much more of each other, but under decidedly less pleasant circumstances.

The children may have been blissfully unaware of what was brewing on the national scene, but Hertha and Willi could sense their country was headed for another war. How long could Hitler continue to bully the world into submission and achieve all his objectives without ever firing a shot? For years he had defied other European countries and carried out his expansionist plans to gain more land and greater control of resources in central and eastern Europe. He had retaken the *Rheinland*, a region in western Germany that had been taken by France at the end of World War I. He had annexed Austria, claiming it should always have been part of Germany. He had gone after the Sudetenland, which had been given to Czechoslovakia in the Treaty of Versailles. Each time, the major powers that had defeated Germany just twenty years earlier capitulated to the Führer's demands, abandoning Germany's hapless neighbors.

As these events were unfolding on the world stage, Willi could see the stepped-up activity at Rechlin. In 1935 the government had informed the world that the *Luftwaffe* was being rebuilt. New airfields were constructed just a few kilometers away from Rechlin at Lärz and Roggenthin, and the site was officially designated an *Erprobungsstelle*, a testing station. By 1936 new planes such as the Messerschmitt 109 fighter, the Junker 87 dive bomber, the Dornier medium-range bomber, and dozens of other combat aircraft were being tested constantly—sometimes at great cost to the test pilots. Companies like Messerschmitt, Heinkel, Junker and Dornier were rushing prototypes to the isolated testing station where young men—and one young woman, Hannah Reitsch—risked their lives to check out new designs literally "on the fly." The German high command had begun to telegraph their advances to the world, and no less a celebrity than the American flyer Charles Lindbergh, the first person to fly solo across the Atlantic, was brought to Rechlin in October 1938, to try out one of the newest fighters, the Messerschmitt 109. Willi and his co-workers may not have known everything that was happening, but they certainly realized that the sheer magnitude of development suggested something big was going to occur—and soon. It is unfortunate that, in later years, Hertha did not recount in great detail the conversations she and her husband had with friends who came over in the evenings and on weekends to play cards and chat informally about the future.

On July 3, 1939, the top commanders of the Luftwaffe, Hermann Göring and Erhard Milch, arranged for Hitler to visit the airfield at Rechlin. They wanted him to see first-hand what progress had been made in developing a new generation of aircraft and other weapons of war. News of the Führer's visit spread among those working at the base, and Willi told Hertha on the evening before Hitler arrived that he would be at Rechlin the next day.

A dutiful mother and at this time still a loyal German, Hertha decided she would take her children to a place along the railway line so they could catch a glimpse of their leader. Stationed with Rolf, Lori, Wolf, and Einhard near a railroad trestle, she watched as the train carrying the Führer passed by. The large crowd kept Hertha's small children from seeing Hitler, but she managed to notice him standing at the window of the railroad car as the train passed the Schmidt family. "I can never forget," Hertha said years later, "the utter sadness of this man." Hitler was staring out the window at the people gathered there to greet him, a crowd made up largely of women and children. "It struck me then," she continued, "that perhaps he was so sad because he knew that war was inevitable."

Naively she felt then that Hitler hated the thought of his people suffering as they had only two decades earlier. She was not aware of the massive propaganda machine that had been hard at work to form her good opinion—and the good opinion of millions of Germans—toward their leader. Nor did she know how much the actor Hitler really was, how he was able to win over crowds by being alternatively maniacal and despondent—moods carefully adopted for political purposes. In 1939 she may have secretly been in awe of Hitler. Her attitude would change later, however, when she saw what his policies were doing to Germany, and especially to her own family.

If Hitler needed any convincing about his plans to conquer all of Europe, the trip to Rechlin went a long way to solidifying his decision to ratchet up the level of hostilities against Germany's neighbors. In the summer of 1939, he turned his formidable propaganda machine against Poland, "reminding" the Germans of the many crimes against their country committed over the centuries by the nation on its Eastern border. Never mind if there were truth to his accusations, he was preparing his own people and the world powers for yet another German takeover. Only this time it would not be a diplomatic victory.

Willi and Hertha must have wondered if Hitler would strike east through Poland toward Russia. After all, even before Hitler had come to power, the Nazi propaganda machine had fueled the German people's longstanding hatred for the Slavs of Eastern Europe. They must have been stunned when, on August 21, 1939, news of a German-Soviet Non-Aggression Pact was broadcast over the radio. What was Hitler up to?

They did not have to wait long for an answer. On September 1, 1939, Hitler sent elements of the Germany military across the Eastern border of Germany, launching the *Blitzkrieg* that would destroy the Polish armed forces and occupy the nation in less than a month.

Hertha and Willi were sitting at home on the evening of September 1 when they heard the news over the radio. The official German version was that the Poles had initiated the action, and Germany was retaliating against their hostile behav-

ior. Neither Hertha nor Willi was surprised. Certainly they had
realized war was inevitable when the government made an an-
nouncement on August 27, 1939, that a rationing program for
certain goods and staples would begin immediately. For six years
Hitler had been rebuilding the country's military might; Willi
and Hertha had been first-hand witnesses to the re-armament.

Like so many of the German people, however, they were
not excited about seeing their nation go to war again, so soon
after the devastating losses suffered in World War I. Both probably knew at that instant their lives were going to change rapidly.
They only hoped this new conflict would not be a repeat of
World War I, in which so many had lost fathers and brothers,
and so many families had been destroyed.

The Fatherland—
and a Father—at War
(1939-1945)

༒

$\mathcal{T}$he effects of Hitler's invasion of Poland were felt almost immediately throughout Germany. On the morning of September 2, store shelves began to empty. A second event of even greater impact followed swiftly thereafter. Although Hitler had built up the German army considerably in just six years, he did not have nearly enough men under arms to fight against Great Britain and France, who responded to the invasion of Poland by declaring war on Germany on September 3, 1939. Therefore, shortly after hostilities began, the German government instituted a draft of able-bodied men. Willi was in the pool of eligibles, although it is not clear when he was scheduled to be called up. It is also not clear if he was actually drafted, or if he volunteered. He may well have signed up on his own so he could be assigned to the *Luftwaffe*, Germany's air force, rather than be conscripted into the *Wehrmacht*, the German army.

Compared to millions of other recruits and conscriptees, Willi Schmidt was lucky in his military service. The *Luftwaffe* had its own logistics command, headed up by a Field Marshal and consisted of hundreds of units responsible for keeping troops in the field supplied with food, equipment, and ammunition. After completing a basic training course, Willi was assigned to this logistics command, and he traveled with his *Luftwaffe* supply unit to Albania, Greece, and Bulgaria, possibly to Romania and Hungary as well.

Unfortunately, his service records are not available, and because he did not share detailed stories of his wartime experiences with his children, it is possible only to speculate about the campaigns in which he participated. What is known for certain is that Hitler sent troops to "friendly" countries such as Bulgaria, Hungary and Romania, ostensibly to assist in training their forces to assist the Axis powers. In reality, Hitler wanted to be certain that he had "boots on the ground" to protect the Ploesti oil fields in Romania, a major source of Germany's raw material needed to meet the country's petroleum needs. Military forces, including *Luftwaffe* units, were in the area as early as the fall of 1940, and the buildup continued for the next six months. It would be plausible to assume that, since Willi entered military service shortly after Germany invaded Poland in 1939, he may have gone to the Balkans immediately after completing basic training.

While service in any war zone brings with it a certain amount of danger, being stationed with a ground unit of the *Luftwaffe* in the Balkan region during 1940-41 was, relatively speaking, a good assignment. Willi's unit was deployed in the area to support air operations for what is generally referred to in historical studies as Hitler's "Balkan Campaign." Hitler sent combat forces to this region to bail out the Italians who had been soundly defeated by a determined Greek army in Thessalonika and Albania. The combined forces of the *Wehrmacht* and *Luftwaffe* subdued Yugoslavia, Albania, and Greece, including Crete, even though the British had deployed troops to assist the Greeks in defending the invasion. The actual fighting began in late spring 1941 and lasted less than two months. Although the stinging defeat of the Allies' surrogates altered Winston Churchill's plans to defeat Germany by attacking from the south through the Balkans, Hitler's insistence on subjugating the region was actually more devastating for Germany in the long run; the campaign delayed the start of Operation Barbarossa, the Germans' invasion of Russia. Most of the German soldiers and airmen left the Balkans in late summer and headed immediately for the Russian border, finding themselves on the ground outside Moscow when the winter snows set in.

Apparently Willi Schmidt was most fortunate in being spared participation in the invasion of the Soviet Union. He may have stayed behind in the Balkans after full-scale hostilities ceased, because Germany left one *Luftwaffe* group in the area to conduct counterinsurgency operations against stubborn partisan groups hostile to the Axis powers and remain close to those valuable oil fields in Romania. At no time did Willi report to his wife or children that he had participated in any active combat operations while stationed in southeastern Europe.

While away from the family, Willi wrote to Hertha and the children almost daily. In the early years of the war, before casualties decimated the German fighting force, soldiers and airmen were able to obtain leave regularly, and Willi made several trips back home. When he came, he brought gifts for Hertha and the family: sweet-smelling tobacco, long cigarette holders intricately carved from exotic woods, brightly painted trinkets. Of course, it also seemed that every time he returned to the front, he left his young wife pregnant.

Though Hertha knew Willi probably could not avoid military service, she was not at all pleased that Willi was sent off to the Balkans. She was convinced he could have managed to stay at Rechlin if he had tried, since he already had a job there that the military required. What's more, he had a large family that needed him at home. Before Willi left for the Balkans, and during the times he was home on leave, Hertha never failed to express her displeasure at his decision to join the *Luftwaffe*. On one occasion, pregnant again and exasperated with having to manage the household by herself, she ranted that if something were to happen to him, she would be hard pressed to keep the growing family together. Willi smiled at her and said, "You'll do fine." He leaned toward her and said reassuringly, "I know you better than you know yourself." Ironically, he would be proven right not during the war, but in the years after.

While Willi was away, Hertha did her best to be both mother and father to the children. There were four of them when the war started, but on February 18, 1940, Friedrich Wilhelm Schmidt entered the world. There was much fanfare surrounding the birth of little "Willi," as the Schmidts' fifth child would be called at home. The National Socialist government

Hertha's children circa 1940. Left to right: Wolfgang, Rolf, Bill (on Rolf's lap), Einhard, Lori.

had always promoted large families, subsidizing couples with children and making a public fuss over those with four or more youngsters. As part of his propaganda campaign to encourage the German people to increase the birth rate, Hitler had proclaimed that every German woman who bore a child was worth as much as a general to him!

Hertha was still young enough and patriotic enough to believe she was doing a great service to her homeland by bringing more children into the world. Her newborn son's birth was announced over the radio, and Hertha was proud as a peacock! Naturally, as she had done with all her other children, she had remained at home to deliver "Willi"—who would become known in the family as Bill in later years. Her sister Elli again came to Mirow to help her with household chores while she recuperated from childbirth.

Despite the war, the family managed to keep some semblance of normalcy in their lives. Occasionally Opa Dittmann would come to Mirow with his wagon so the children could visit with their grandparents. Rolf got to bicycle down a bit more often, but the trip was a tough one. The roads were cobblestone near Mirow, but further south, past Schwarz, they turned to hard-packed dirt, and there was a shortcut through the woods that led directly south into Flecken Zechlin. Rolf recalls how sore he got riding his father's rickety bicycle along the cobblestones and making his way along deeply rutted roads.

As each grandchild grew old enough to have memories of the Dittmanns, he or she learned first-hand about the tough life of German farmers. Even in the best of times, both Willi and Marie Dittmann worked long hours, he in the fields and outbuildings, and she inside the house and stables. During the war, Willi Dittmann was required by the government to harvest trees in addition to managing the family farm. Additionally, Germany's armed forces required large quantities of food, so the government pressured farmers to increase agricultural production to meet that need. While most were willing to support the war effort, farmers like Willi Dittmann found themselves working long hours to grow crops to sell to the government or in the local marketplace and provide for their own families. There was little machinery to make a farmer's task easier; fields had to be plowed using horses, crops harvested with scythes, foodstuffs prepared from scratch, and clothing made at home.

It was no wonder Willi Dittmann seemed a bit stiff, relaxing only infrequently on weekends or for special occasions such as weddings and birthday celebrations. What the Dittmanns seemed to enjoy most was a quiet Sunday afternoon. When morning chores were finished, they would sit in their parlor. Marie would take up her darning, and Willi would light one of his aromatic cigars. They would carry on a muted conversation for awhile, and then, first one and then the other would fall asleep. What a luxury it was to take a nap! Farmers busy from sunup to sundown for six days a week relished those few hours of respite. And, no doubt, the war effort made such occasions doubly enjoyable.

Until the very last weeks of hostilities, the war did not interfere with the Schmidt children's education. Rolf went to school, and when she was old enough, Lori tagged along. At first, the teachers at the school would make Rolf walk his sister back home, but eventually they allowed her to stay. Hertha even began packing extra food in Rolf's bag, since Lori had no satchel in which to carry anything. As Rolf got down to the serious business of study at school, Lori would amuse herself with paper provided to her by the teachers. Eventually Lori began paying attention to the lessons, and before long she was also doing homework.

Hertha spoke to the authorities at the school and convinced them to allow Lori enroll as a student a year before she would technically have been eligible. To celebrate her new status, her Aunt Elli came to visit from Flecken Zechlin, bringing with her a special present: a *Schultüte*. These stiff paper or cardboard containers, a traditional present made to children on their first day of school, were almost as tall as those who received them. They were wide at the top and tapered to a point at the other end, brightly decorated with colorful pictures, ribbons and ruffles, and usually filled with candies, cookies, and other goodies.

Because rationing had been implemented, Hertha ended up finding creative ways to feed her growing children, all of whom ate, as she observed later, "like wolves." While conditions during the early years of the war were not as harsh as one might have imagined—they did become serious in the closing months of the conflict—Hertha often had little choice in preparing meals; she cooked what she managed to buy with her ration coupons. Of course, the family could still go out into the woods around Mirow to pick berries and mushrooms which grew in abundance there. Hertha spent a good bit of time preserving and canning fruits to tide the family over when other supplies might not be readily available. Like so many other women, she became adept at stretching the provisions she obtained, making things last as long as possible. Even in these tough times she managed to see to it that her children had as much as they wanted to eat.

Her ability to keep her family fed was no doubt aided by a thriving black market economy that had emerged throughout Germany shortly after hostilities broke out. There is no reason to believe the Schmidts did not make purchases through illegal channels; everyone seemed to be doing it. Perhaps, too, because the Dittmanns were able to supplement what Hertha and Willi were able to obtain until the late fall of 1944, they experienced few of the hardships some families faced in getting enough nutritious food. Then, too, there was the opportunity for the children to get rewards when they received their mandatory immunizations. Intended by the government to prevent the spread of disease through the population, these inoculations were often dreaded by the youngsters. But in the Schmidt family, little Eini was always happy to see that time roll around. Although he hated shots with a passion, he was always first in line to get his, because he knew the next thing he'd get was something good to eat!

Doing laundry for her growing children was a tiresome and backbreaking task. Like most German women, Hertha tried to limit washing to one day a week. Naturally, the work had to be done by hand. Clothes were placed in a large tub of water which had been boiled on the wood stove. While her children's garments did not always become as grimed as the shirts, pants, and smocks, Marie had had to clean on the farm, Hertha still ended up working her hands raw in the hot, hard water as she pounded out dirt from clothes, bedding, and towels, then scrubbed them on her washboard.

As was the custom in most German families, the Schmidts—children and adults—simply wore the same shirt, pants, or dress for quite awhile before the item went into the wash. Some of the children used to say that their clothes had to be able to stand up on their own before they went into the washtub! Unfortunately, some of Hertha's boys were bed-wetters, and she could not always wait until "wash day" to clean the soiled items. The work, therefore, seemed unending.

During the war it was impossible to procure soft diapers, so Hertha made diapers from worn-out pillowcases and bed sheets. It was not uncommon for Bill and the siblings that followed to suffer from sores on their bottoms and legs, especially when they developed diarrhea, as the rough cloth chafed the infants' tender skins.

At some point during the war—family records are scarce, so it is hard to pinpoint the exact date—the Dittmann family prepared to celebrate Marie's father's 100th birthday. The event was big news, and not just locally. The village of Flecken Zechlin planned a grand party, complete with a feast most unusual during wartime. The radio station in Berlin sent a correspondent to cover the festivities. In Mirow, Hertha spent considerable time making new outfits for her children. Lori got a new white blouse and a skirt made of peach-colored linen, and the boys new white shirts and short pants; their mother made each of them a sharp-looking bolero jacket. But on the morning of the celebration, great-grandfather Sadler did not wake up. The doctor was called. He examined Herr Sadler, then told Marie Dittmann not to try to wake her father. The old farmer never regained consciousness; he died shortly thereafter.

After Bill was born, Hertha began badgering the German authorities to have Willi returned home from the front. Hitler's penchant for promoting family life actually helped her in this instance. The government had established a policy whereby men with large families could request reassignment to a unit nearer their home where they could provide direct assistance to their spouse in managing the household and caring for the children. Apparently there was some resistance to this political mandate by the military hierarchy, who were reluctant to take able-bodied soldiers out of the front lines—especially when

Willi Schmidt in his Luftwaffe *uniform circa 1942.*

those men had already proven their worth in the first years of the war. But when the Schmidts' sixth child, Michael Walter Schmidt, was born on February 16, 1942, Hertha qualified for the award of the Silver Cross, an honor bestowed on women who were guaranteeing the future of the Fatherland by producing a new generation of Aryan warriors. Hertha was even more convinced that she deserved to have her husband stationed closer to the family—whether he wanted to or not. Under her relentless pressure, the authorities finally arranged for her husband to be assigned to the home front.

Hertha was thrilled that Willi was going to be relocated closer to the family, especially at this time. During the fall before Mike was born, a diphtheria epidemic swept through the country. In Mirow, houses where cases of the disease were discovered were placed under quarantine. This was nothing new, since it was common practice to quarantine an entire family whenever a child came down with even a routine disease (mumps or measles, for example). But Hertha was trying to raise five children already. This time her mother had decided to come from Flecken Zechlin to help. Marie Dittmann was not one to let a "quarantine" sign stop her. She pedaled her bicycle up to Mirow and marched into her daughter's house, ready to help out until Willi could return to his family.

Sometime after Mike was born, Willi Schmidt came home to a house full of children. Rolf, Lori, and Wolf were in school, but Einhard was still at home all day. Bill was there toddling about, and newborn Mike was whimpering away in his makeshift diapers. Having Willi home for some of the time—even if just for weekends—made a great deal of difference to Hertha. And to add to what they thought was their good fortune, Willi received orders to report to Rechlin, the aircraft testing station at which he had worked as a civilian before the war.

What seemed like a great stroke of good luck would come back to haunt the Schmidts, however. When Willi showed up for duty at Rechlin, he was given a choice of two assignments. The first was to be part of the guard force at the air base, pulling frequent night duty outside in the frigid weather. There was another option, though: he could use his talents as a logistician and work indoors—as an administrator coordinating the logistical support for activities of prisoners living at the forced labor camp located near the base.

The German government had established a labor camp close to Rechlin in 1939. Inmates came mainly from Russia and Eastern European countries; some were Jewish, of course, but many were not. The majority of the men at the Rechlin labor camp were Russian prisoners of war. Though not technically a concentration camp in the vein of Auschwitz or Dachau, the camp at Rechlin was run by the SS, and prisoners inside were often subjected to treatment similar to that received at more notorious sites. Most of the guards were not native Germans, but women and men recruited from Poland and other occupied countries who were considered suitable by SS higher-ups for the kind of brutal work expected of labor camp staff. Under the highly complicated system developed to oversee all of the camps, Rechlin became a sub-camp of Ravensbrück, the infamous women's concentration camp 46 kilometers southeast. Internees initially incarcerated at Ravensbrück were occasionally reassigned to Rechlin when the main camp was overcrowded.

From available evidence, it seems Willi Schmidt did not work inside the camp, and had little to do with the conditions under which prisoners lived. Instead, his job was to arrange to have laborers transported to the various worksites. Like every administrator, he was given an office and assigned a secretary. Young women who had been brought to the camp as prisoners but who demonstrated some skill at office work were usually chosen for these duties, and Willi was fortunate to have as his designated assistant a young Jewish woman from Czechoslovakia. Her parents owned a saw mill there, but like most Jews in any territory occupied by the Germans, their property had been confiscated and they had been arrested and transported to a camp for "further assignment." At some point the woman was separated from her parents, and did not know their fate. In all probability she was first sent to Ravensbrück, but because she had useful skills she was reassigned to the camp at Rechlin where she could be of service to the German military. She would become an important link between Willi and his family at war's end.

Hertha viewed Willi's new job most favorably. He was home—at least a good part of the time, in contrast to his infrequent visits when he was stationed in the Balkans. Both she and the children thought he had an important job in logistics at Rechlin. Only Hertha and Rolf had any real inkling of what he actually did, of course, as the others had no way to get to the base, which was heavily guarded and concealed by a series of camouflage nets to prevent aerial observation. Rolf made trips there on the family's bicycle so he could describe to the others what his father's office looked like—and it wasn't too special, actually. The family did participate in Christmas festivities sponsored by the testing station in the town of Rechlin, where soldiers from the base handed out toys to the children. Certainly no one in the family had any inkling that Willi's position at Rechlin would have serious ramifications later.

If the children thought at all about the place where their father now worked, they probably felt it wasn't such a bad assignment. After all, they had direct experience with the prisoner of war camp set up in the castle at Mirow, where French soldiers and officers were detained. What they did not realize, of course, was that this facility, unlike the forced labor camp at Rechlin, was run in accordance with the rules of the Geneva Convention. The soldiers performed tasks appropriate for POWs, often working at homes in Mirow to aid families with various household chores. Some even came to the Schmidt home on occasion, where

Hertha had them handle some outdoor chores and landscaping. She fed them hearty meals when they came—until she learned how well they were eating at the POW camp! Wolf remembers envying the French officers, who seemed to enjoy quite a nice life. They seldom did any manual labor, except to traipse along the ditches in the camp and around town—perhaps looking for frogs to supplement their diet. Every Saturday Wolf saw them carrying cakes to the bakery, where they would be baked for them. It certainly seemed to him that the lot of a prisoner was not such a bad one! That may have been true if you were not Jewish, or Polish, or Russian, and not out of sight in a camp such as the one that provided the labor force for Rechlin.

Although he adapted to his new position, Willi did not always seem happy to be back with his family. He had apparently enjoyed his service in the Balkans, and he may have been embarrassed at being taken out of a combat zone for family reasons. He may have thought it was not right for an able-bodied man to be living at home and working in a job that could have been done by someone not physically fit for active service. Hertha saw things otherwise, of course, and the two of them had arguments about this matter—usually late in the evening, when they thought all the children were asleep.

Once Willi was home and in his new job, the Schmidts settled down to a regular daily routine. For most of the time, it might have been hard to know that their country was at war. Although there was less choice in the stores than before the war, goods and services were still available. Women went about their daily chores just as they had before September 1939. Wash was hung out to dry. Windows were opened to air out stuffy houses. Continuing a custom that stretched back perhaps for centuries, each Saturday women could be seen outside their homes scrubbing the stoops in front of their doorways. And everywhere there were flowers: around the fountains, along the streets, in the parks, in boxes on window sills, and in the cemeteries. No one was going to let something as transitory as a war stop the Germans from planting their gardens and tending the flowers that added a touch of beauty to even the most dreary situation.

During the first three or four years of the war, the German government did all it could to help those not directly engaged in the fighting to lead a normal life. Unlike other countries such as Britain and the United States, where women were encouraged to take jobs in factories and offices to support the war effort, German mothers were encouraged to stay home to raise their children. The government established quite a number of wartime regulations—on top of those they had established before the war—designed to keep the population healthy and to educate the next generation for a time when the Germans would dominate all of Europe.

The curriculum at every level of schooling was revised to promote Nazi ideology. Youngsters who showed academic promise were sent to special schools to prepare them either for university or for specialized technical training. Of course, students at these institutions were subjected to intense Nazi propaganda. When he was ten, Rolf was selected for such a school. Unfortunately, he had to commute by train 90 minutes each way, making his day quite long. One small consolation, however, was that he got to do his homework on the train.

As might be expected, the boys especially began to follow the progress of the war with great interest. Rolf idolized General Erwin Rommel, the audacious tank commander whose actions in Poland, France, and later in Africa were to make him the most feared of all Axis field generals. Like their older brother, Wolf and Einhard would follow news of the war on the radio, and during the day they would peek out of their air-raid shelter as planes from both sides dotted the sky on their way east or south toward population and industrial centers. Tiny specks would dart back and forth as Allied aircraft swerved to avoid flak being shot at them from unseen antiaircraft guns. Then the German fighters would ascend to meet the enemy, and the Schmidt boys—even little Bill—would be mesmerized by the dog-fights taking place high above them. The war was, for some of them, just another game being played by adults for the entertainment of inquisitive children.

Like most boys Rolf had initially been enthusiastic about the war. By the time he was ten, though, he had begun to doubt the Nazis' rosy vision of the world under Hitler's leadership. He had begun to see for himself that the people who rose to power in the national and local government were often former "lowlifes" who immediately abused their authority once in office. Rumors had circulated that Germany's officer corps, most of whom were not Nazis but who were fighting for the Fatherland as good soldiers often do in wartime, had private reservations about Hitler's grandiose plans and about his social philosophy as well.

Rolf felt alone in his discontent, however, since there seemed to be no one to whom he could turn to discuss his reservations about Hitler's optimistic pronouncements regarding Germany's future. Not until much later did he learn that his mother and father felt the same way. Later, too, he started noticing that some of the best of the German officer corps—his hero Rommel among them—were disappearing under mysterious circumstances. There must be something wrong, he thought, with a government that did away with its best generals in the middle of a war.

To make matters worse for him, in 1943 he was required to join *Das Jungvolk*, the junior branch of *Die Hitler-Jugend*—the Hitler Youth. The organization was an outgrowth of *Jungsturm Adolf Hitler*, which had been founded in 1922 as a place to groom recruits for Hitler's Brown Shirts. Having adopted its new name in 1926, the group flourished when Hitler came to power in 1933, as its membership was greatly expanded and its mission changed under the leadership of Baldur von Schirach. By 1938 all boys were required to join *Das Jungvolk* upon reaching their tenth birthday; at fourteen they moved up the ranks into the Hitler Youth. The organization was dedicated to the formation of Aryan males, promoting physical fitness and preparing youth for military service. Organized along the lines of an armed force, the youth wore paramilitary uniforms and learned military tactics. They were taught to obey without question the orders of their superiors. Older boys were often given charge of younger members, and in some cases were actually encouraged to practice forms of cruelty as a means of toughening up the new recruits. Boys were also encouraged to know the heroes of the Reich, memorizing information about *Wehrmacht* generals and *Luftwaffe* aces. An elaborate initiation ceremony for new members was held on April 20th of each year, the anniversary of Hitler's birthday.

By the time Rolf became a member, the Hitler Youth had become a kind of military reserve force, the principal training ground for new soldiers. It was also a special source of recruits for the SS, who selected from the ranks of the Hitler Youth those young men who demonstrated exceptional zeal for Nazi ideology. Even at age ten, Rolf could sense that something was amiss.

While he did not experience outright cruelty and did rise to the rank of platoon leader, he could see quickly that favoritism rather than merit was the principal means to advance in the organization. Somewhere between 80-100 boys were enrolled in the *Hitler Jugend* in Mirow, already organized like an army outfit. The youth leader of his troop was a boy of twelve or thirteen who struck Rolf as "an absolute ass." He was not very smart, but he bullied the other boys unmercifully and with impunity—because his father was a Brown Shirt, a member of the group that had been doing Hitler's dirty work throughout Germany for over a decade. Rolf knew something was seriously wrong with a society that tolerated and even glorified such behavior.

Willi's presence at home in the evenings did not lessen the fear Hertha felt for her family and her neighbors. At night Allied bombers soared overhead on their way to targets in Berlin to the south and Hamburg to the west. Sometimes the explosions from miles away shook the windowpanes in their house. Hertha thought then how terrible it must have been to live in the city, with bombs falling and fires sweeping across block after block of urban neighborhoods. She felt fortunate her family lived in the rural district of Germany. There were few targets of interest to the Allies—few except for the place where her husband worked.

Although the inhabitants of Mirow may not have had to worry about being a target of Allied bombing, those who lived near the Schmidts had already begun to experience first-hand the tragedy of the war. As early as 1943, the Allies began to make passes over Rechlin, and disparate bombing took some toll on the site. Additionally, there was always the danger that a plane returning from the target area with bombs that had not been dropped, or ammunition not fired would simply release their unspent ordnance indiscriminately over the farms and cities they had passed over on their way back from places like Hamburg or Berlin.

However, the danger posed by the Allies was not as great as that posed by the hazards of the work there. As early as 1938 or 1939 test pilots had faced the unnerving possibility that the planes they were being asked to take up into the skies might not prove airworthy. As the military situation for Germany worsened, experiments with new high-performance aircraft became even more desperate. The Germans needed something to counter British and American air power, and they needed it quickly. The normal three-year cycle required to move a new aircraft design from the drawing board through testing and into production was reduced to one year. As a result, a number of ill-designed prototypes were rushed to Rechlin, and all too frequently they failed in their first real test.

As 1943 moved into 1944, the death toll of pilots at Rechlin exceeded one per week. The Mirow neighborhood became a somber place to live. Hertha and her neighbors must have thought every day, as they saw their husbands off to work, will they be home this evening? Hertha herself must have wondered if someday she would be forced to relive the scene she had witnessed in the summer of 1918, when her mother learned Richard Jürgens would not return from the war.

For the first five years of the war, conditions deteriorated slowly, almost imperceptibly, as the logistics system throughout the country broke down. Citizens were constantly encouraged to "tighten their belts" as a means to help the war effort, and most did so willingly. However, life began to change noticeably for the Schmidts and their neighbors in 1944. As the Allied bombing on cities such as Hamburg and those in the Ruhr valley took an increasingly greater toll on civilians of those regions, the German government began evacuating the population eastward into those regions of the country that were considered safer. While the evacuation was handled in an orderly fashion, the evacuees were not always welcome in their new "homes." Because Mirow was located in what was essentially a rural area, it became a destination site for these evacuees.

In the summer of 1944, the population of Mirow grew from 3,000 to 10,000 in a few short weeks. The city's infrastructure was severely taxed. Most families in Mirow were required to make room in their home for evacuees from the western part of the country. Though some attempt was made to provide additional food to the host families for their new "guests," in most cases Mirow natives ended up sharing their own rations with the people who had been assigned to live in their houses. Finally, the real tragedy of the war had come close to home. It was becoming impossible to hide the growing sense of desperation spreading throughout the populace. Was Germany going to lose *this* war too?

The last vestige of hope for the country's military success must have disappeared entirely by the summer of 1944
when a new wave of people began arriving. Earlier in the year
the Russians launched what would be the final offensive
against the Germans. Supported by Russian air cover, the Red
Army pushed across Russia's western border into Poland, driving toward Berlin. The formidable force consisting of nearly
two million soldiers destroyed virtually everything in its path.
As the Russians moved closer to the Oder River, Hitler's generals tried vainly to mount defensive operations. At every step
of the way, the Russians managed to beat back the German
defenders. When the Red Army entered a city or town, soldiers began killing the townspeople indiscriminately. Women
were raped. Animals were slaughtered. Buildings were burned
or torn down.

The inhabitants of the regions in what had been called
East Prussia and Silesia realized their only hope of survival was
to leave the region. Farmers who could stand the hardships of a
journey on foot that could last for weeks or months and stretch
for hundreds of miles packed their wagons with whatever they
could fit inside, tying their pets and livestock to the rear. People from the cities crammed valuables into suitcases and began
walking west by the thousands. Those who became seriously ill
were often left to fend for themselves. The ones who died on
the journey were buried in shallow graves or simply laid beside
the roadways.

As these refugees moved away from the advancing Russian armies, they were often strafed by Soviet aircraft who slaughtered them indiscriminately. Animals fared no better. Carcasses
of horses, cattle, sheep and dogs were strewn among the dead,
shot by owners who could no longer feed them or simply turned
loose when they were too weak to continue the journey. And of
course, not everyone chose to flee. Many old people simply gave
up all thought of being saved, remaining behind to face the fury

of the invading Russian forces. Eventually, tens of thousands met the fate they feared but expected.

The roads were clogged with groups of refugees heading to German cities and towns like Mirow. Often in tatters from the harsh winter and constant strafing, they struggled along, carrying little more than they could hoist on their backs or into small wagons. Broken and demoralized, thousands of them crawled into Mirow during the fall and winter of 1944-1945. These people would appear along the streets, often staring blankly ahead of them, too traumatized to go any farther.

Frequently, the townspeople received advance warning that another party was moving toward the city. This only heightened the collective level of anxiety. As one group after another stumbled into town, the citizens of Mirow watched in dismay and thought: How many more are coming?

It was immediately apparent that these people were very different from the ones who had come seeking shelter some months earlier. Refugees from the west had arrived in an orderly fashion. They expected to stay only for the duration of the conflict, and were looking forward to going home to rebuild their cities and their lives. By contrast, these new arrivals were a rabble. No organized effort had brought them to Mirow; they had simply wandered into town. Most came with little; some came with nothing at all. They camped wherever they could find an empty building or an open space, begging for food or shelter. Many were eventually driven on from the town which was already overcrowded with people facing the prospects of famine and displacement themselves. Some just simply gave up and died.

In the midst of this growing turmoil, on October 28, 1944, Hertha gave birth to her seventh child, whom she named Joachim. During these last chaotic months of the war, there was scarcely enough nutritious food available for the infant whom the family called "Hasi." Determined not to become demoralized, Hertha did the best she could with rationed supplies to keep him healthy; little did she know that conditions would become much worse for her and the children. Swaddled in clothing remade from the discarded garments of older siblings, diapered in old sheets that created serious rashes for him, Joe Schmidt was soon to partake in a family odyssey that would test the courage, fortitude, and ingenuity of all the Schmidts. Together they would have to face the challenges brought on by their country's defeat, and the subsequent occupation by the Soviets, who were bent on extracting serious retribution from the Germans who had invaded Mother Russia only three short years earlier. For what was speculation in the spring had hardened into sobering reality by the start of 1945: the war was lost, and there was nothing to stop the Russians from advancing through to Berlin.

The Schmidts and their neighbors felt an increasing sense of desperation as the war moved closer to them. For nearly five years, they had been misled by a Nazi propaganda machine that refused to report anything but the Fatherland's glorious victories. Even after the disasters at Stalingrad and Leningrad, Hitler's henchmen reported the *Wehrmacht*'s retreat as a "strategic withdrawal." Subsequent retrenchments were treated as calculated moves to strengthen the Germans' position against the Russian army, which was sure to collapse at any moment. As March moved into April, however, the people of Mirow felt the war coming ever nearer. Refugees fleeing from the Russian army brought with them tales of incredible horror: wanton raping, murder, pillaging, drunken soldiers impaling farmers on their own equipment and slaughtering livestock for sport.

During that spring rumors began to spread that Mirow would be a target, too, since the railroad station there was of some significance in moving troops and supplies. Bombs were hardly accurate, so any ordnance intended for the station could land anywhere in town. Warning sirens drove townspeople into air raid shelters regularly. The government had required certain families to make space available for the construction of air raid bunkers to supplement underground cellars in people's homes.

The Schmidt boys helped build an underground bunker, but although they were proud of their efforts, Hertha thought these air raid shelters were of little practical value. At first she had responded to air raid alarms by herding her brood into the basement, but eventually she stopped doing that. She realized that, if a bomb struck near enough to damage the house, she might not be able to get her family out, and their shelter would become their prison—or their coffin. Instead, she tried to get the children to sleep through the bombings. Hertha and her children could see the flares light the sky over the air base, signals for the bombers to drop their ordnance. The air defenses nearby filled the night sky with flak, but to little avail. By the spring of 1945, the airfield that had once served as Germany's principal test site for experimental aircraft was virtually useless as a location for any military operations.

The final air raid on Rechlin was carried out not by the Russians, as Hertha thought, but by two squadrons of the American 453rd Bomb Group on April 10, 1945. Despite cloudy skies that kept some planes from releasing their payloads, the results were devastating. Hertha saw the smoke billowing into the sky. Concerned for Willi's safety, she cycled up to the airfield. When she arrived, she saw countless bomb craters and unexploded bombs dotting the air strip and the farmers' fields surrounding it. Casualties had been heavy; the dead were everywhere. Frantically, she searched for Willi—only to learn that he had already gone home. When she returned to Mirow, she was greeted by her embarrassed husband who was sorry to see how frightened she had been for him.

Meanwhile, news of the Russians' final advance toward Berlin reached Mirow. There was word, too, that the Russian army was sending a force of some size—actually, more than a million men—north of Berlin, aimed at sweeping all the way to Denmark. Citizens of Mirow were in a panic; surely this force would overrun their city. The Hitler Youth group to which Rolf belonged had dug long trenches extending about 100 meters on both sides of the roads to serve as tank traps. The theory was that these trenches would keep the Russians from arranging their tanks in a wide line to sweep into the city. The main roads leading into Mirow were barricaded by constructing earthwork and timber palisades across a portion of the road surface, leaving openings wide enough for cars and trucks to pass but too narrow for tanks to squeeze by. Considerable effort was put into constructing these palisades, which ended up being a great place for young boys to play but which proved of little use in stopping Russian tanks.

When the Russians finally arrived, as everyone knew they would, the entrances to the city were to be defended by members of the local Hitler Youth group and the *Volkssturm*, a local defense force made up mostly of old men like Willi Dittmann. Even though some had seen service in World War I, many of them were exceedingly unfit for the kind of work they were being asked to do. Nevertheless, the Hitler Youth group and members of the *Volkssturm* conducted joint training exercises to prepare for their roles in defending the town.

Rolf and his fellow Hitler Youth were trained to use weapons, including bazookas, which would be employed against the Russians as they approached the city. The small boys could do little to counter the tremendous recoil of the larger weapons, but they were prepared anyway for what would certainly be a last-ditch effort against the Russians. Neither of these groups was issued arms or ammunition, but instead these old men and boys were to report when called, draw their weapons, and position themselves on palisades built astride the roadways. Rolf thought the plan sounded ill-conceived and desperate, and as he was to learn later, it met with devastating results.

Long before the Russians reached the city, Willi had told Hertha that she and the children should not stay in Mirow when the threat of Russian occupation became a reality. When the Red Army was close enough for them to hear the cannon and tank fire in the distance, they were to flee into the forest outside the city. The Dittmanns had a better idea: they would take in the Schmidt family at the farm in Flecken Zechlin. The idea certainly sounded sensible. Hertha may have assumed (wrongly, as it turned out) that Flecken Zechlin was less likely to be in the path of the Russian invasion force than the larger population center of Mirow. Additionally, six-month-old Joe was already showing the ill effects of undernourishment, caused by the poor diet Hertha was forced to feed him. She was constantly trying to get milk for him, so going to the farm might at least provide that staple. The thought of exposing her family to Russian soldiers who were rumored to be raping women and girls at random and killing even small children who got in their way made it easy for her to decide what to do.

Hertha knew, of course, that she could not take much with her if she fled. So when her stepfather arrived from Flecken Zechlin, she packed up her sewing machine with her needles, buttons, and thread, grabbed some clothes for herself and the children, then loaded the family into his wagon. Wondering what would become of all she was leaving behind, she bravely locked the door and climbed onto the seat beside Willi Dittmann. Little did she or any of her children know that it would be their last day ever in the house on Granzowerstrasse.

Going to the Dittmann farm proved to be only a stop along the way. Although Hertha's sister Anni had joined the Women's Auxiliary and was not at home at that time, Elli was still living with her parents. Their sister Hedwig had also moved in with the Dittmanns, bringing Gerhard and Margarete with her in the hope that being with her parents would provide her greater safety than staying at her own home down the street.

After the Schmidts arrived in Flecken Zechlin, Hertha learned the townspeople there were as concerned as those in Mirow about what might happen if the Russians showed up on their doorsteps. Everyone knew it would be dangerous to remain in the village if fighting broke out. But would the Russians come their way? That question was on everyone's mind—and no one had a good answer. So every day Hertha went out on the roads leading away from town to the east, inquiring of retreating German soldiers about the progress of the enemy. Sometimes, one or another of her sisters would join her. By mid-April they learned the Russians were less than ten miles away, advancing steadily. The *Wehrmacht* soldiers were fleeing from the advancing Red Army, retreating westward so they could surrender to the British and Americans rather than suffer at the hands of the Russians.

Sometime in April the Dittmanns found themselves with other guests as well. The family from Berlin who had been renting from them during the summers had shown up on their doorstep, panicked about the impending advance of Soviet forces on the capital city. Unlike most refugees, they had dragged many of their possessions with them. The father had the audacity to be annoyed when Willi Dittmann put most of their belongings, including the man's tools, in the basement. But Dittmann knew there were more serious things to worry about. He now had twenty people to care for.

Marie and Willi Dittmann realized they and their daughters' families were in grave danger if they remained in Flecken Zechlin. They would have to get out of town, at least until the Russian soldiers passed through. No one expected the invaders to stay in Flecken Zechlin for any time, but no one wanted to see first-hand what they might do once they arrived. Where could the family go, at least temporarily, to escape?

Willi Dittmann had an answer. For years he had been harvesting a meadow located in the woods north of Flecken Zech-

The woods northwest of Flecken Zechlin. The thicket ahead was the Schmidts' hiding place during the last weeks of World War II, April through May 1945. (photographed 2006)

lin. It was probably the same forest in which Dittmann worked occasionally, cutting down trees to earn extra money for the family. A series of logging roads crisscrossed the area, providing easy access to the deepest recesses of the woods. The meadow he was allowed to harvest lay at the bottom of one of these logging roads that meandered through the forest and sloped down into the hollow where natural grasses grew in abundance. Dittmann knew the area well; he had driven his hay wagon to and from the meadow for years, and he was familiar with the terrain all along the edges of these roads.

Dittmann thought that an area in the woods just up the hill from this meadow would be a perfect spot for the family to use as a hideout. The field was near the edge of a small lake that could provide fresh water. The forest surrounding the meadow was made up of tall European beeches. Many of these stately trees had been growing for a century. Spiking nearly a hundred feet toward the sky, their oval-shaped green leaves created a canopy that shielded the forest floor from sunlight. Beneath them layers of decaying leaves, fallen in years gone by, provided matting that in the springtime deadened sound and offered a comfortable place to lay a bedroll.

Dittmann revealed his plans to his wife and daughters, and to their "guests" from Berlin. There would be twenty of them hiding in the woods, and it would be necessary to construct a camp that would be undetectable by the Russians who would undoubtedly appear in the forest within days. There would be a lot to carry out of town, and a lot of work to set up camp. And time was pressing on them.

Fortunately, Willi Schmidt was able to get away from his unit at Rechlin, so he pedaled down from the air base on his bicycle, twenty-four kilometers along roads that could at any moment be strafed with rifle or tank fire. He arrived at the Dittmanns suffering from some form of virus, coughing and perspiring heavily. Nevertheless, he helped the family pack the wagon once again for their trek into the woods. But he knew he could not stay with them. Word from the high command had come down that deserters would be prosecuted to the fullest extent of German law, and their families punished as well—an empty threat, of course, but one that men like Willi had to take seriously at the time. Once he had seen his family safely encamped in the woods, he left Flecken Zechlin and headed back to Rechlin to figure out how he might escape capture by the dreaded Russian Army.

Meanwhile, the Dittmann party proceeded to set up camp. The size of the group made it necessary for them to split up. Approximately two-thirds of them settled on the east side of the logging trail nearest to the lake, and another third (including the family from Berlin) established a camp on the opposite side of the trail. The men and older boys cut smaller trees to create the walls of a shelter and built a canopy with tar paper Willi Dittmann normally used to repair his barn roof. This crude arrangement offered only modest protection from the rain that fell constantly.

Hertha had loaded an old carpet and some bedding onto the wagon; these items went into the shelter to offer some rudimentary accommodation for sleeping. The bedding would be rolled out at night and put away during the day, so children could be kept inside whenever the murmur of strange voices, the rumbling of trucks and tanks, or the crack of rifle fire through the forest indicated the Russians were getting too close for comfort. A primitive latrine constructed several yards from the tent served as their outhouse. The Schmidts and the family from Berlin were accustomed to indoor plumbing, so these conditions were no doubt demoralizing. These makeshift arrangements deep in the woods would be their home for two weeks.

Willi Dittmann brought his horse into the woods, but the family could not bring their other livestock. There was some debate about whether to simply leave them back in Flecken Zechlin or to try to care for the animals in some fashion. On this point, Marie Dittmann was adamant: she would go back and forth into town to tend for the family's livestock. She was not afraid of the Russians; she felt she could make herself look old and unappealing! Almost every day she would pedal her bicycle out of the forest back into Flecken Zechlin. When she could, she would sneak out additional provisions. She was able to witness the arrival of the Russian invaders as they moved into town and took up residence in homes and shops. It is almost certain the Russian soldiers accosted her and demanded to know what she was doing on the property—and where she was heading when she left. Marie never shared with the other members of her family how she managed to escape from situations such as these, and apparently no one probed too deeply for an answer.

Once they had set up camp, the Schmidt boys immediately began building a makeshift pen for the Dittmanns' horse. They were discovered by German soldiers who encouraged them to abandon the site initially selected, so they moved to a spot less visible to airplanes which dotted the sky. Hertha was not sure if these were British or Russian—but she knew they were not German. Every day the family could hear the incessant booming of the Russian artillery as the advancing forces lobbed shells onto nearby built-up areas and into the woods. In the evenings they would sit near the fire that had been built in a pit to keep its light from giving away their position to the Russians.

Occasionally a stray bullet would zing through their campsite. The youngsters thought this was exciting—but one can only imagine the consternation and fear this raised in their mother. Daily they saw German soldiers slinking through the heavy woods, often discarding their uniforms as they went, hoping that being dressed as civilians would save them from being shot on sight.

As the Russian forces drew ever more close, the boys could hear the huge tanks, as well as jeeps and supply vehicles. Listening carefully, they could catch the sounds of voices speaking a strange language out on the roads near their campsite. Every so often, trees nearby would explode into fragments, indicating that a tank commander had turned his turret toward the woods to fire at what he suspected to be a German soldier fleeing the Russian advance.

All of them lived in constant fear of discovery. The situation was made more difficult because there were two babies—Joe and an infant brought by the family from Berlin—that cried out constantly. The baby was always hungry. Malnourished herself, Hertha was unable to breastfeed him, and the poor diet she fed him forced him to soil his diapers constantly—leading, of course, to more crying. To make matters worse, the horse was neighing constantly, prompted perhaps by the sounds of horses the Russians were using to move their equipment in the area. Certainly all of the adults feared the Russians would soon try to find the source of this noise.

Back in Rechlin, reports of the Russians' drawing ever nearer to the air base circulated freely. Orders came down to the labor camp that all prisoners would either be killed or transported west to keep them from being "liberated" by the Russians. No doubt the German high command wanted to prevent the Soviets from gathering up these prisoners to use as witnesses against the Germans after the war. However, when word of this plan reached Willi Schmidt, rather than helping to carry out any executions he decided to help as many prisoners as he could and save himself in the process. In secret he drew a map for his Czechoslovakian secretary directing her to the Dittmann farm in Flecken Zechlin. At some point before the camp was finally evacuated, she managed to slip away and head south.

After arranging to send word to his family regarding his plans, Willi went about his duties arranging to transport camp officers, guards, and prisoners westward. Not knowing the fate of those he had left behind in Flecken Zechlin, Willi managed to place himself aboard a truck heading toward the Elbe River, where the Allies had halted their offensive. He was no doubt hoping to reach a British unit, since several of them had actually crossed the Elbe and were encamped in the western regions of Mecklenburg. It was, he thought, his only chance of escaping the Russian marauders. He was to be proven both right and wrong.

When the fighting was finally over, the Schmidts left their camp in the woods and returned to the Dittmann farmstead. By the time the family moved back into Flecken Zechlin, the Russians had already established themselves in various buildings within the village. The Dittmann house had been ransacked, foodstuffs taken away, furniture damaged or taken out of the house. Rolf remembers seeing the tools that the man from

Berlin had fretted over so much scattered all over the market-place. Worse, the Dittmann's home was being used by a group of prostitutes who had followed the Russian soldiers. The family was allowed to move back in, but they were forced to share the premises with some unsavory characters. The situation for Hertha's sister Hedwig was worse; the Kobow house had been taken over by the Russian commander, and she was not allowed to move back in. Instead, she ended up finding accommodations a few doors down from her mother and stepfather.

To make matters worse, the Dittmanns and Schmidts were suddenly out of food. Before they had set off for the woods, Marie and her daughters had packed a large metal tub with food-stuffs, including pounds of wurst, to tide them through what they feared might be a very long stay in hiding. When they were constructing their woodland hideout, the family buried the tub beneath a large tree just outside the camp, sealing it carefully to prevent decay or pilfering by animals that might have picked up the scent of the food. Rolf was given the task of marking the tree so the family could find the container when their initial supply of food ran out. But they had returned to Flecken Zechlin before needing the tub of food, and when they went back to retrieve it, no one could find Rolf's mark on any of the trees. Their frantic search ended in vain. The wurst remained buried, and the family had to tighten their belts even more and live off what they could scrounge.

The coming weeks would begin to show just how desperate the situation was in northeastern Germany. Shortly after the Soviet occupation force had moved into the village, Rolf and some neighbor boys hiked all the way up to Granzow, north of Mirow, where one of the boys' grandparents lived. Along the way they observed craters where Russian aircraft had dropped their bombs, or Russian artillery shells had torn up the terrain. The roads and woods were littered with uniforms of German soldiers, who had discarded them while fleeing from the Russians.

The boys saw animal cadavers strewn in fields and forests, along with burned-out Russian tanks and other debris where pockets of German resistance had achieved some limited success. Some of the abandoned tanks emitted a rank smell, probably the odor of rotting flesh.

On the road they came across a dead pig, half-eaten by maggots, stinking badly. The stench was so bad that it clung to the boys and stayed in their nostrils. After spending the night in Granzow, the boys came back through Mirow, where they surveyed the damage done by the invading army. Homes and shops had been damaged by artillery shelling. A house down the block from the Schmidts' home on Granzowerstrasse had a gaping hole in its side where a tank had pierced it.

While back in Mirow, Rolf learned the fate of his Hitler Youth troop. They had assembled when called, bravely climbed atop the barricades, and faced the Russian tank battalion approaching the city—and had been summarily slaughtered. The invaders had driven their tanks right into the earthwork and timber barricades, smashing first into one side then into the other until the structures caved in, leaving a harmless mound of debris for the Red Army tanks to climb over. The Russians blasted away at the outgunned defense forces, killing every member of the Hitler Youth in Mirow, as they did in virtually every other city and town where groups of boys and old men stood up against them.

Everywhere around him Rolf came face-to-face with the inevitable fact that Germany had been defeated. Now his countrymen were at the mercy of the victors—and everyone knew that the victors were not prone to show mercy.

Back in Flecken Zechlin, the Russians showed no signs of leaving soon. The occupation had begun.

Exchanging Fascism
for Communism
(1945-1946)

⌘

*I*n late April and early May of 1945, events were oc-
curring in other places in Germany that would have further
life-changing impact on Hertha Schmidt and her children. Even
before the Soviets took Berlin, they had prepared to install a
Communist government to follow Hitler's regime. During the
war, a cadre of German Communists had been training in Russia and in countries such as Sweden and Norway, just waiting
for the day when they could return to their homeland. The guns
had barely fallen silent when, on April 30, 1945—the day Hitler
committed suicide—a plane flew into Berlin carrying several men
who would play key roles in ruling the Soviet zone and eventually the country of East Germany. Their leader was Wilhelm
Pieck; his principal deputy, who would run the Berlin region
and eventually control the new German Democratic Republic,
was Walter Ulbricht.

By mid-May, the Soviets had installed regional leaders
in the territory they were allocated under the Allies' plan for
the "temporary" partitioning of the country. Eventually there
would be five regions, but initially there were three. Ulbricht
controlled the most important region in and around Berlin.
On May 6, 1945, Gustav Sobottka, a lifelong Communist who
had been living in exile in the Soviet Union since the 1930s to

escape Hitler's assassins, returned to lead the regional government in Mecklenburg. Sobottka established his headquarters in
Schwerin, a city whose population hovered somewhere around
75,000. From the fourteenth century until the end of World
War I, it had the distinction of being the former home of Dukes
and Archdukes of Mecklenburg-Schwerin, and had long been
considered a seat of power within the region. Now it became the
regional seat of power for the Soviet occupiers and the Germans
willing to cooperate with them in establishing a Communist
state. Some of the Schmidts would see all too much of Schwerin
in the coming years.

Although the Soviets moved quickly to install German-
led local and regional governmental structures, they were not
about to let these German Communists rule alone. Quickly the
Soviet Military Administration in Germany (SMAD) was set up
to serve not only as the military government but also as the final arbiter of policies their German puppets began to develop.
The Soviets were determined not to let the country slip back
into fascism—or develop into a democracy. Germany was going
to become a Socialist Republic, independent only as long as its
leaders followed Moscow's directives.

Meanwhile, an uneasy peace settled over Flecken Zechlin
and the surrounding territory in early May 1945. The Germans
had surrendered; fighting in the woods and towns had ceased.
But the Russians who had come to the region as invaders now
settled in as an occupying force, and in many ways things went
from bad to worse for the Schmidts and their neighbors.

Unfortunately, the most heinous rumors about the
atrocities committed by the Russians proved to be true. Women
and girls were raped routinely; age did not seem to matter much
to the occupiers from the East. People were shot for the most
trivial reasons. Farm animals were slaughtered, sometimes for
food to supplement the Russian soldiers' insufficient rations,
sometimes merely for sport. Russian soldiers took over houses

and office buildings. The ferocity with which they treated the German people was reminiscent of the barbaric actions of the Huns and Visigoths of old. Officially such activity was not condoned by the Stalinist hierarchy. Nevertheless, most soldiers had been stirred up by propaganda sanctioned by and emanating from Moscow during the war.

Prominent among the anti-German literature was the work of the anti-fascist writer Ilya Ehrenburg. In a leaflet titled simply *"Kill!"* Ehrenburg had encouraged Russian soldiers to treat Germans as subhumans, suggesting that a day without killing Germans was a day wasted. To rape a German woman, he exhorted, was the Russian soldier's right and duty.

The Russians who stormed into Flecken Zechlin carried out an unrelenting program of pillaging and desecration. They drove their tanks into the marketplace at breakneck speed, tearing up the cobblestones and sending sheets of small pebbles flying into the buildings surrounding the square. They commandeered many houses, ousting entire families. Disparate groups of Russian soldiers took up residence in the parlors and bedrooms of other homes, displacing residents or forcing them into servitude to accommodate the soldiers' needs.

The first band of marauders who invaded Flecken Zechlin were primitive men who thought nothing of ransacking valuables and destroying property. They seemed motivated by a deep hatred for anything German, and they wreaked havoc on people and property alike. Many of them had spent weeks inside tanks and other vehicles, so they reeked of diesel oil and grease. Others had trudged through the woods and were equally foul-smelling. Now that they were no longer fighting, many stripped off their uniforms and made the women of the town wash them; meanwhile, they donned clothes they found at hand, often ladies bloomers—a sight that might have provoked humor in other circumstances, but no one in the town was laughing. Once they were clean, they doused themselves with various strong perfumes.

Near the end of May, a second group of soldiers came in to replace the invasion forces. These were generally more restrained, and the Soviet authorities had issued strict orders that there was to be no interaction with the populace other than for official business. In early summer the Schmidts witnessed a formal change of command ceremony held in the center of the marketplace. Tanks and other equipment had been spruced up and polished for the occasion. The day-long event featured soldiers' marching and lining up to face one another. The Russians who were to remain kissed their brothers-in-arms to wish them farewell. The invasion forces clambered onto a column of horse-drawn wagons awaiting them and rumbled out of town.

The replacement troops would prove to be more civilized, but that did not lessen Hertha's anxiety for her husband, from whom she had still heard nothing. She wanted to make no plans until she knew if Willi were safe in the West, or if something bad had happened to him in those last, hectic days when soldiers of the Red Army were indiscriminately shooting those fleeing their advance. Under the circumstances, Marie and Willi Dittmann allowed the Schmidts to remain with them in Flecken Zechlin. But they never made them feel unwelcome; instead, she and Willi Dittmann handled this new hardship with grace, feeding her daughter and grandchildren from their own dwindling resources with open hearts. Perhaps Marie remembered how alone and helpless she had felt in 1918 when news of Richard Jürgens' death had reached her. She could not let her daughter and seven grandchildren fend for themselves.

Until they knew for certain what had happened to Willi Schmidt, the house at Am Markt #2 would be home to an extended family. To their dismay, however, a group of Russians had taken residence on the ground floor, forcing the family to squeeze into cramped accommodations upstairs. Some of the children were sent to sleep with their cousins, the Kobows,

The barnyard at the Dittmann's place in Flecken Zechlin, circa 1940. The woodpile in which Willi Dittmann created a hiding place for his daughters is shown at the rear.

whose mother had found accommodations at Am Markt #4, two doors down from the Dittmanns, when the Russians commandeered the Kobow residence.

Willi Dittmann did not trust the Russians, even the replacement troops, to leave his daughters and granddaughters alone. As soon as the Schmidts had returned to Flecken Zechlin, he constructed a special woodpile in the rear of the barnyard. From the ground it looked like any other stack of firewood, but it had a hollow center. There Hertha and Elli could hide from the Russians. The idea was that, if the young women needed to remain in their hiding place for a long time, the elder Dittmanns could lower food down in a bucket, and remove any waste the two might have by the same method. The family sought to protect the younger girls as well. Lori remembers her mother rolling her in a blanket at night and having her get under the bed in their room. Then Hertha would place bags or suitcases in front of the opening so the ten-year-old would not be discovered by any Russian soldiers who might burst in upon the Dittmanns unannounced.

About a month after hostilities ended, Hertha and her family received a visitor. The young Czech who had served as Willi's secretary at the labor camp in Rechlin finally made her way to Flecken Zechlin. She informed Hertha that not only was Willi alive in early May 1945, but that he had gone west to surrender to the British. He promised to be in touch as soon as he could.

The woman's message gave Hertha great hope. The Dittmanns invited the young Czech to remain with them for a few days until she was able to arrange to continue her journey home. She was only too glad to take them up on their offer. She slept with the Schmidt children, often sharing a bed with seven-year-old Einhard. However, what was originally intended as a stay of a few days stretched out for four weeks. At first the Dittmanns and their daughter were compassionate. Clearly the young woman needed some time to recuperate. Hertha probably understood better than her mother the plight of this young woman; after all, like her, Hertha and her children had been displaced and weren't sure what was going to happen to them.

While the young woman was living with them, she told the Dittmanns and the Schmidts about her own upbringing in the Czechoslovakian forests and about the horrific treatment her family had suffered at the hands of the Nazis—a tale that sounded a bit farfetched at the time, but which probably was true. As a prisoner at the Rechlin labor camp she would have suffered from malnutrition and poor care despite Willi's attempts to improve conditions for her. After awhile, though, the family began to wonder just how much longer they would have to share their food with this refugee.

To the townspeople of Flecken Zechlin, the soldiers of the Red Army seemed to be barbarians. The soldiers, in turn, seemed fascinated with the "elegance" of the homes there. Unfortunately, they were utterly devoid of any sense of propriety or decorum. Frequently they would simply take furniture with them as they moved from house to house, or dump the residents' belongings in the street or the yard if they needed more space inside.

Those living on the Dittmanns' first floor dumped all of Marie Dittmann's canned goods into the middle of the living room. They stole Willi Dittmann's work boots, making it difficult for him to carry out his farming duties. They did not always go to the outhouse to relieve themselves, either, and many homes began to smell badly. Sometime later, after the Schmidts had left Flecken Zechlin, residents of the town were amazed that these soldiers would sleep atop the large stoves in the kitchens. Of course, what seemed a silly and somewhat primitive custom was common winter practice in the peasant villages in Russia, where the floor-to-ceiling stove was often the only warm thing in the house on a cold winter night.

Worse, perhaps, were the Russians' treatment of the Germans' farm animals and equipment, and their wanton destruction of the environment. Apparently when a Russian felt he had need of a new horse, he would simply take one from a farmer, often the only one the farmer had to plow his fields. Sometimes the farmer would be "lucky," as Willi Dittmann was when a Russian who stole his horse Hans but left a decidedly inferior one in the same stall. At least Dittmann could still plow his fields! The Russians clear-cut many of the trees in forests that had been carefully cultivated, shipped the wood back to their homeland, or simply left it rot on the ground. They also poisoned many of the lakes, killing all the fish—in some cases simply for spite, as a kind of payback for what they felt the Germans had done to Russia three years earlier.

The Russians acted as if they were a law unto themselves. Small wonder, then, that the citizens of Flecken Zechlin took great pleasure in seeing bad things happen to their occupiers.

One afternoon, three officers took a canoe out on the lake. They did not return to their unit that evening, and in fact it was two days before their bodies were found floating in the lake. The Russian commander ordered his soldiers to drag the bloated corpses from the water. The bodies were laid out on the edge of the lake near the schoolhouse—not a pretty sight. If people in town were glad to see these Russians meet with disaster, however, they were soon to regret the whole incident. The Russian commander decided these men needed a fitting burial, so he had them buried in the center of the marketplace in an outdoor garden that belonged to the hotel on the square. He then had a small monument erected to their memory—a monument that remained long after the Russians had left town.

The Dittmanns felt the cruelty of their Russian occupiers directly. For years Marie Dittmann kept a dog. Everyone in the family loved the mutt, and in turn it was very protective of the family. One summer afternoon, when Lori was sitting in the barnyard with her grandmother, the back gate swung open and in came two Russian soldiers, obviously drunk. One of them swung his rifle off his shoulder and stumbled toward the house, pointing the barrel of his weapon at Marie and shouting, "Old woman! You have all these chickens and you still owe us a dozen and a half eggs from last month!"

Marie had had enough with the Russians. They had made a mess of her house; they were making a mess of her family's life. She wasn't going to stand by meekly and be insulted or threatened. "Look!" she shouted back at the drunken soldier. "I'm sick and tired of you trying to push us around! And besides," she added, pointing to the chickens, "I'm not the one laying the eggs! Tell them!"

The soldier cocked his rifle and aimed wildly in Marie's direction. Just then, the dog lunged at him, attempting to protect its owner. The gun exploded, emitting a flash of light and smoke. The dog slumped to the ground, dead.

Hertha Schmidt's niece, Margarete Kobow, with the Dittmanns' dog Senta, early 1940s.

As the soldiers retreated through the gate, Willi Dittmann came into the yard and picked up the dog. He realized there was no chance to save him. With a heavy heart he lay the beast down and began digging a grave in the corner of the yard. That was how the Schmidts' cousin Margarete, who had heard the shot from her own home down the street, found him when she burst into the yard to see what had happened. Sadly, she thought her grandfather had shot the dog himself, to avoid having to feed him. And even more sadly, no one told her the truth for a long time afterwards.

But there were occasional acts of kindness. Some Russians took seriously the official directive not to fraternize with the Germans or harass them. The officers seemed especially fond of children, and frequently would pick one of the Schmidts or their cousins and place the child on their laps, talking to them or singing unintelligible Russian songs. Apparently they missed their own children very much. On occasion a Russian officer or soldier would notice baby Joe Schmidt and give Hertha some milk for him. A Cossack from Georgia took a special liking to Joe, and made sure the family had oatmeal to feed him. It may have been the only thing that kept him from dying, he was so malnourished.

An even greater instance of Russian kindness occurred one afternoon during the summer of 1945 along the bank of the lake behind the Dittmann farm. Rolf and Einhard were down at the water's edge, climbing onto a small boat tied up beside the short dock that extended out into the water. The boat was old and unbalanced. Too engrossed in playing to be concerned about safety, Einhard made a hasty move and tipped the craft, spilling head-over-heels into the water. Rolf immediately tried to lift him up, but his younger brother was clinging desperately to Rolf's leg, making it impossible to rescue him. Fearing his younger brother might drag him under, Rolf began yelling for help. A Russian soldier loitering nearby rushed down to the lake, and risked his own life to bring both boys safely to shore.

Compounding the problem of the Russian occupation for the residents of Flecken Zechlin was the shortage of food. Like most people throughout Germany, they had been feeling the pinch of hunger and deprivation. The refugees from the east had experienced these feelings before the guns had gone silent, but after hostilities had ceased, everyone living in the Soviet zone learned what it meant to go hungry.

The war had devastated not only the industrial centers, but many farming communities as well, and what little the populace might be able to produce was often commandeered by the Russians. Rationing was quickly implemented, and many people had to find ways to stretch the foodstuffs they were able to acquire. Frequently, flour was mixed with sawdust before baking loaves of bread. Real coffee was impossible to find; barley and acorns and even horse chestnuts were ground up to use as substitutes. Acorn flour, ground up by the local millers, often ended up being used for bread as well; the loaf tasted bitter but at least it filled one up. People who were hungry enough grabbed anything to use for food, including bark stripped from trees.

As the months went on and the Communist system of commerce was more fully implemented, store shelves remained virtually empty. The stores themselves were taken over by the

State, and officials in charge of distributing merchandize seemed to have scant interest in keeping them stocked. What little there was to buy was not appealing. Further, sales clerks were discouraged from being customer-friendly, lest this behavior be interpreted as a form of subservience. In the "worker's paradise," no person should have to bow and scrape to another—unless that "other" was a Party boss, of course.

People had trouble getting clothing, since factories producing cloth did not have raw materials for weaving. Worse, it was impossible to get leather, so people had to fashion shoes from wood and old tires, cut up in strips to use as fastenings. Makeshift upper sections were nailed to wooden soles. People picked up bits and pieces of discarded rags to fashion into clothes. Pieces of combs found on the street were taken home and carefully preserved for future use. Real soap disappeared from store shelves, and in its place a liquid made from tar became the staple product for washing both people and clothing. The viscous substance produced no foaming action. It came in a jar, and resembled the grease that garage mechanics used. Some women used it to scrub floors.

Somehow, Hertha managed to survive these first months after the war, despite the constant threat of rape, pillage, and murder from the occupying Russian forces, and the daily demands to find food for herself and her seven children. Already in the advanced stages of pregnancy with her eighth child, she made a vow to herself to battle on every day, never giving up. After all, she knew she was not alone in her struggle: millions of her fellow Germans were suffering as much as she was, and she took comfort in knowing that she had a loving family to help her in this time of dire need.

Rolf, now age twelve, had mixed feelings about the war's end. He was certainly sad his country had lost. But his initial thought was "Good riddance!" to Hitler and the scores of inept politicians. They had dragged his country through six years of agony, the last two for no purpose at all, since it had become clear by 1943 that Germany and her allies could not win. Unfortunately, within a few weeks of the start of the Soviet occupation he began to think, "Here we go again." It appeared from his perspective, that Germany had swapped one bad dictatorship for another. At that point he did not know what was happening in the west, although there were rumors that in the Americans and British zones, the Allies were planning to help the Germans to rebuild their industries and their lives. Looking around him as 1945 turned into 1946, Rolf felt powerless to do anything to make his family's life any better.

Meanwhile, the family had not heard from Willi. They continued to hope he was safe, and that he would follow through on the plan he had described to his Czech secretary. Despite the hardships they were all suffering under their Russian occupiers, they refused to give up on their absent husband and father. Then sometime late in the summer, Willi Schmidt came to Flecken Zechlin. He stopped outside the town and sent word in to the Dittmann farm for Hertha to come out to meet him so he could discuss his plans for getting the family out of Flecken Zechlin. He did not want to enter the town for fear that he might be recognized and his past exposed. After all, not only had he escaped the Russian invaders, with a little bit of duplicity spurred on by his will to survive, he had already managed to find employment within the new governing body in the town of Hagenow.

The story of Willi's escape and survival in the months after the war ended is a combination thriller and fairy tale. In May 1945, the British were occupying the region around Hagenow, forty-five kilometers east of the Elbe River. Willi had made it that far with other German soldiers fleeing to the west, but he was not allowed to go any farther. The British–occupying force learned that he was a "home front soldier" with a family living not far away to the east. They did not want too many men like him separated from their families, as this would add to an already monumental problem of dealing with displaced persons. So Willi Schmidt had to stay in Hagenow.

Fortunately, Hagenow did not seem like such a bad place to end up. Founded in the twelfth century, the city accommodated a population of approximately ten thousand when Willi arrived. It boasted a number of farmsteads and small shops, and was the county seat in southwest Mecklenburg. An imposing thirty-foot-high water tower marked the entrance to the northeast, and a graceful neo-Gothic church rose above the surrounding homes and shops at one end of Lange Strasse, the city's major thoroughfare.

Initially, forced to remain in Hagenow proved to be advantageous for Willi. Perhaps he did not know the British had agreed to let the Russians occupy all lands east of the Elbe River. Almost immediately after the German POWs were detained and processed, the British began organizing relief efforts for the population in the region, trying to restore order so people could be provided food and protection from lawless elements that might try to take advantage of the chaos following the collapse of the Nazi government.

Administrators in the British occupation force put out a call for volunteers to assist in organizing local government operations, and Willi Schmidt stepped forward to help. He knew even before he left Rechlin that if the Allies found out he had worked at a labor camp, he might be considered suspect. So he dressed in the civilian suit he had taken with him when he left Rechlin to meet with British army officials. In the course of the interview, he was asked if he had been in a concentration camp. "Yes," he admitted—but he was careful not to disclose his precise role there. Additionally, before he had left Rechlin, he had prepared for this situation by having his Czech secretary sew into his suit a set of numbers similar to those which were placed on the prisoners' clothes at the camp. Apparently the interviewers assumed he had been incarcerated there, which meant to them that he was not a threat and could be put to work immediately. Willi managed to convince authorities he had experience as an administrator, so he was given the task of helping with the placement and care of refugees who had been trapped in Hagenow when hostilities ended.

Although he lacked much formal education, Willi had a natural talent for administration, and he stood out among the many workers who possessed even less schooling and considerably less ability. His skill in logistics quickly earned him a reputation as an adroit manager. When the Russians took over the region in July 1945 and made Hagenow the seat of the county government, Willi was offered a position as head of the local administrative police unit. Although this might seem strange in retrospect, given the Russians' suspicion of all Germans, Soviet authorities were in a bind. Because so few of them spoke German, they needed to depend on at least some Germans to help them establish law and order.

The Russians had a particular fear of SS troops and the Gestapo, so they were particularly eager to ferret out these individuals and punish them. On the other hand, the Russians gave special privileges to people they believed were former camp inmates. Like the British, the Russians thought freed concentration camp prisoners would be most trustworthy, because these people must have hated the Germans almost as much as the Russians did. Since they, like the British, assumed Willi had been interned at Rechlin, his assignment as part of the local administration made good sense to the occupiers.

Once he had a secure position and had convinced the Soviet authorities he was a man of talent and trustworthiness, Willi Schmidt went home to retrieve his family. He had already found housing for them in Hagenow, and arranged to have a truck pick them up and take them to their new home several weeks hence. He did not stay in the area long, but his brief appearance gave the entire family confidence that their luck was changing for the better. The Dittmanns were no doubt doubly pleased: not only had their son-in-law come through unharmed, but they would soon have eight fewer mouths to feed!

On the appointed day, the Schmidts scrambled onto Opa Dittmann's wagon to make a short trip to the road where the truck was to pick them up. Having brought few items from Mirow when they fled to Flecken Zechlin six months earlier, they had little to take with them to their new home in Hagenow: some clothing, a few scattered pieces of furniture, and of course, Hertha's sewing machine.

Tossing these few belongings into the truck bed, the younger children piled into the back beside their goods while the very pregnant Hertha and Rolf got into the cab with the driver to begin their 125-kilometer journey. The distance may not seem excessive, but to a family traveling in a farm truck in 1945 Germany, the trip was onerous. Roads heading west out of Flecken Zechlin—especially main thoroughfares—had been damaged during the war, causing people to travel by circuitous routes and inevitably forcing delays. Additionally, the vehicle had to pass through a number of roadblocks established by the Russians to control traffic. Many of the roadway surfaces were cobblestone, adding not only time but considerable discomfort to the journey. After a tortuous day's travel, the family arrived in Hagenow.

Since the Soviets did not respect individual property rights, every home in Hagenow was subject to confiscation by the State if there were "pressing needs." Among the reasons the State could commandeer someone's living quarters was to make the space available for government officials—of which Willi Schmidt was now one. Consequently, Willi Schmidt was assigned living space in Hagenow by the new governmental agency responsible for housing. Unfortunately, the housing allocated to the Schmidts was not yet ready for them when they arrived, so he found temporary quarters (no doubt also requisitioned by the government for him) in the village of Zarrentin twenty-five kilometers northwest. The trucker who brought the family west from Flecken Zechlin took them to their temporary home in a building that also housed a dentist. The apartment was sunny and very nicely apportioned—but much too small for the Schmidts' permanent residence!

It was good that they moved into the apartment in September, however, for on October 28, 1945—exactly a year after she had delivered Joe—Hertha gave birth to her eighth child and second daughter, Barbara Elli. This time she was able to deliver in a birthing center rather than at home—a circumstance that may have been particularly fortuitous, since she knew virtually no one in the community. Unfortunately, Hertha was not well enough to nurse her new daughter, and the quality of milk she managed to obtain was exceptionally poor. As a result "Nuni," as the baby was affectionately called, developed severe dysentery. The situation remained serious for several months, until the baby was able to get on a steady diet of solid food.

Rolf did not stay with the family in Zarrentin. After helping them unload the truck at their temporary quarters, he went with his father to Hagenow. Willi had arranged for Rolf to begin classes immediately in a special school located in the center of town. The facility, dating back to 1834, had been known throughout the region for its superb academic program, readying students to go on to the *Gymnasium* where they would prepare to enter a university, or give them technical skills needed for apprenticeships leading to a variety of careers. The brick three-story structure had an imposing oak staircase in the center, lending a sense of dignity to the academic enterprise—even if Rolf's teachers were a truly odd lot who were often only one day ahead of their students in mastering the subjects they taught. Behind the facility there was a large sand-covered playground (and restroom facilities), and across the street a dance studio where Rolf would learn to dance—as would his future wife, Renate Spingies, who attended the same school. Willi had even arranged for Rolf to live in a dormitory with other children attending the institution. Although Rolf would have to walk nearly half an hour across town to classes every morning, the opportunity for this kind of education was too good to pass up.

Rather than bring him directly to the dormitory, however, Willi took Rolf to his apartment, a modest flat on the upper floor of a building several blocks from the County Administrative Center where Willi had his office. Immediately upon walking inside, Rolf realized that his father did not live there alone. As he was to learn quickly, the other occupant was a young woman named Christine Herrlinger.

Like the young Czech woman who had come to stay with them in Flecken Zechlin, Christine Herrlinger was serving as Willi's secretary. Not more than nineteen or twenty, she came from the tiny village of Lutheran located near the town of Parchim seventy kilometers east of Hagenow. At first, Willi tried to offer his son excuses as to why Christine was sharing the apartment, but Rolf was not fooled. Unfortunately, at twelve years old, Rolf was in no position to challenge his father about his living arrangements. Nevertheless, he was enraged that his father could have been so cavalier about his commitment to his mother, who had not only borne Willi eight children but kept his family alive through the war and after.

At one point Rolf even confronted his father and the two actually exchanged blows. What surprised Rolf, as he discovered later, was that Hertha had already learned about Christine, and while she never openly condoned the relationship, she seemed to accept it as another one of those unfortunate circumstances brought on by the war. By the time Hertha and the other children moved to Hagenow in the fall of 1945, Christine was no longer living with Willi. But the relationship may not have ended amicably, as later events might suggest.

By the time his family joined him in Hagenow, Willi had become an important official within the county. As they had done in the countries under their rule, the Soviets had established two separate police forces. One was responsible for traditional law-enforcement duties such as ferreting out lawbreakers—but also for identifying those who were considered subversive. By contrast the administrative police, which Willi headed up, was responsible for ensuring that people followed new rules regarding such things as agricultural production. Modeling their policies on those established in the Soviet Union three decades earlier, the Communists abolished or strictly curtailed property rights and set up rigid systems for production of both manufactured and agricultural products.

Since the area around Hagenow had traditionally been farm country, the regional Party bosses drew up a set of rules for all farmers to follow in running their individual enterprises. The Party determined which crops would be grown and which species of livestock should be raised. The administrative police were responsible for seeing that farmers provided a certain amount of their crops and livestock to the State for redistribution—in practice, for Party bosses to reallocate as they saw fit.

As head of the administrative police, Willi was one of the few officials who had an automobile at his disposal. He traveled throughout the region to make sure complaints were handled expeditiously and that the new interim government was meeting the needs of the populace. His car was a DKW. The initials originally stood for *Dampf-Kraft Wagen*, or steam-powered car—a technology soon abandoned by the developers for the more reliable gas-powered engines. Among many Germans the initials came to signify *Das Kleine Wunder*, a kind of nickname applied to this unusual motor vehicle that featured bodies often made from prefabricated materials.

The cars still had mechanical turn signals that had to be raised and lowered manually. However, the two-stroke gasoline engine that had replaced the original steam motor, cross-mounted under the hood, was simple to maintain. Willi quickly located a mechanic in Hagenow who knew how to work on the car, and periodically he brought it in for servicing.

The model was well respected, and getting one for his personal use made Willi someone special indeed. Certainly it was still better transportation than most people were able to acquire. The version he owned was a Cabriolet, with leather interior and a top that could be taken down. The doors swung out toward the rear. Unfortunately, the cloth top leaked in winter and the interior had no reliable heating system. Even bundling up in warm clothing made minimal difference, since the cold seemed to seep up through the floorboards, making one's feet ice cold in a matter of minutes.

When Rolf was on vacation from school, Willi would let his son accompany him on trips through the countryside, where Willi would check to see that farmers were providing correct inventories of livestock and crops. Father and son would bump and rattle over cobblestone roads to remote sections of the county, traveling to out-of-the-way villages such as Friedrichshof, Kloddram, Jesow—and Vellahn. In the winter Rolf would help his father by wiping the windows with a cloth soaked in salt to keep down ice buildup. Later, Willi's possession of this car became the subject of contention when he found himself at odds with the new Communist regime.

One of Willi's additional tasks was to help former concentration camp prisoners find work, and although a few of these people initially seemed jealous of him because of his good fortune in receiving such an important job immediately after the war, eventually most came to appreciate his evenhandedness in dealing with them. Additionally, Willi was careful to distinguish between those individuals who had been political prisoners from those who had been incarcerated for crimes but who had been released or escaped when Hitler's regime fell. Even though his Communist bosses expected Willi to find work for every person regardless of his or her ability, he was thorough in trying to determine the qualifications of those he assigned to jobs. He genuinely believed people should be productive and useful in the work assigned to them. Further, he was steadfast in refusing to place criminals in positions of responsibility—a stance that eventually got him into trouble with his superiors in the Hagenow region.

For the first months of their stay in Hagenow, however, the Schmidts adjusted well to life in their new environment. Their new home on Poststrasse was in a fashionable section of town, and even though they were assigned only the first floor, the accommodations were quite nice. Willi and Hertha began socializing frequently, attending costume parties and other events with the city's new leaders. At home in Hagenow the Schmidt children enrolled in schools and went about their new life as if things were returning to normal. They even enjoyed occasional visits to the movie theater. They were finally able to get some special care for Einhard, who was suspected of having tuberculosis. He was sent to a summer camp on the Baltic, where doctors confirmed that he had a spot on his lung.

Of course, even for the families of those who had been fortunate enough to land a good job in government service, living under Soviet domination was anything but "normal." No doubt the Schmidts and some of their neighbors in Hagenow had some misgivings about the new regime, but they were careful not to voice their concerns in public. The idea that one could be told where to live—and when to move out to accommodate another family who had greater status in the supposedly democratic and egalitarian society—seemed a bit strange. But the Germans had just come through a war in which they were once again the losers. They knew that, for their own safety, they would have to suffer in silence under the rule of the Russians who relished every opportunity to inflict additional inconvenience and even suffering on the conquered population.

As they had learned in Flecken Zechlin, the Schmidts found in Hagenow that not all Russians were evil. During their first winter in their new home, they were strapped to find any dairy products for their younger children. Omi and Opa Dittmann were still keeping cattle, but they were far away now, and besides, they were now forced to turn over all their milk to the government for redistribution or use by the occupation force.

When things looked most bleak, a few kindly Russian officers brought milk to the Schmidts and other families with infants. Joe and Barb were the immediate beneficiaries of these acts of kindness. One of the officers took a special liking to the baby girl, holding her on his knee and saying, in broken German, that she reminded him of the daughter he had left at home. As time passed a number of the Russians became friends with the Germans they had come to terrorize. When they were finally ordered to redeploy back to Russia, they cried openly and sought out their new friends to say goodbye.

Like the Allied Powers in the other zones of occupied Germany, the Soviets tried feverishly to get the school system up and running again as quickly as possible. Before the war the German school year began in the spring, but in 1945 the opening of the year was moved to the fall, and remained that way afterward. What Rolf was experiencing at the school he went to was repeated in the institutions attended by his brothers and sister. The curriculum was revised, as the Russians and the new East German government wanted to remove all references promoting National Socialism. There were no textbooks, since those that had not been destroyed in the war were considered unsuitable for use in schools committed to indoctrinating the children in Communist ideology. There was not even paper for note-taking.

In some instances, children ended up cutting the edges from old propaganda publications to use as clean paper for assignments. The technique of memorization, always a hallmark of German education, became a necessity if one wanted to retain anything. Whereas before the war students may have opted to study French or English, everyone was now forced to study Russian. Additionally, because so many school buildings had suffered damage from bombings and artillery fire, grades were often combined to make use of all available space. For the next four years, the Schmidt children were bounced from school to school, and what they learned was inconsistent, fragmented, and seemed of little practical value.

Conditions in school may have been dismal, but they paled in comparison to the general economic situation in the country. What had been bad during the last years of the war seemed to worsen under the Communists. Willi's new position provided a salary, but there was little the family could buy with the money he earned. The entire region continued to operate on a "barter" economy, with a thriving black market everywhere.

During their first year in Hagenow, Willi and Hertha watched with quiet dismay as the Soviets went about establishing a Communist-style government in the region of Germany under their control. In the spring of 1946, in a move intended to demonstrate to the outside world that the Soviet zone was even more free and democratic than other sections of Germany, the Soviet-imposed central administration called for elections in all communities and states. What happened is an object lesson in the Communists' desire for controlling the outcome of anything Party leaders authorize, and at the same time led directly to Willi Schmidt's first run-in with his Soviet masters.

For a time before the war, some of the old political parties had been kept alive despite Hitler's attempts to quash them. Almost immediately after the war ended, several of these, including the Christian Democrats and the Social Democrats re-emerged and began clamoring for the restoration of some form of republican government. The Soviets were not at all thrilled to have Western-style democracy operating in their zone. At the time, however, they were forced to share the governance of Berlin with Britain, the United States, and France, so they could not take open steps to quash all parties opposed to Communism. Ironically, the other Allied Powers were not particularly keen on seeing political parties restored to power so quickly, but there was a growing sense among them that if Germany were to recover from the ill effects of Nazi domination, normal political activities would have to begin before too long.

What the Soviets wanted, naturally, was to have everyone in their zone happily embrace the Communist Party. They were willing to let the German people come to that conclusion on their own, though, and they saw that among the old parties they had some natural allies. For example, the *Sozialdemokratische Partei Deutschland* (SPD), a leftist coalition that had been antithetical to the National Socialists before Hitler assumed absolute power, seemed acceptable. The much weaker German Communist Party also became a viable political force again, but it attracted few new members.

Quickly the Russians discovered, much to their chagrin, that neither party was willing to slavishly follow the dictates of Moscow. When it was clear the SPD was gaining membership and the hard-core Communist Party was being ignored by the Germans, the Soviet authorities and their handpicked leaders in the German government decided to take matters into their own hands.

In April 1946, the SPD was forced to combine with the Communist party in the eastern zone of Germany to form the *Sozialistische Einheitspartei Deutschlands*, or SED. Inside the new consolidated organization, the hard-line Communists began exerting the kind of influence the Party had in Russia and other Soviet states. As Hertha observed in looking back on this period, "Democracy was effectively eliminated. The Communists 'faked' to the outside world that the country was still democratic, but the SED ruled in any way they wished."

When they had control, Soviet authorities exercised it absolutely, working through surrogates such as Ulbricht, Sobottka, and others who had trained in Russia before and during the war. Many mid-level leaders had been placed in key positions within regional and local governments, assigned positions such as deputy mayor or chief of the criminal police.

These leaders became adept at appealing to the lowlifes in the community. Germans who had been marginally productive—or even criminal—during the decade or more prior to the war were now placed in positions of authority. They strutted around proudly, wearing distinctive armbands, symbols that they were in some ways above the law. Under the tutelage of the Soviets, these East Germans became particularly creative in finding ways to control their neighbors. In fact, the Soviet system of spying on one's friends and family was being perfected in the hands of the East Germans who would eventually establish Stasi, the Secret Police organization that terrorized the population until the collapse of East Germany in 1989. Willi and Hertha would both find out how pervasive that culture of clandestine spying and outright fabrication could affect the lives of innocent people.

Apparently the individual in Hagenow who was keenly intent on controlling the election of the *Landrat*, the equivalent of the County Commissioner, in the fall 1946 election was Waldemer Verner, then serving as chief of the criminal police. Verner was a dyed-in-the-wool Communist and former prisoner who had fled to Sweden when Hitler came to power. Early in his life he had trained in Russia, readying himself to be a leader in any post-Nazi government. Perhaps because he was himself of Jewish descent, when Verner returned to Germany after the war, he was bent on punishing any German who had supported Hitler. Further, he was eager to please his Russian masters, and was accustomed to a system in which those in positions of power would receive special privileges—including the privilege to set up side deals allowing them to amass personal fortunes through schemes that were questionable at best, and in many cases downright illegal.

Because of their respective positions, Willi Schmidt and Waldemer Verner had worked side-by-side for months. For his part, Willi had come to view Verner as a scheming opportunist. At the same time, Verner may have become concerned that the Russian overseers in Hagenow and Schwerin might be impressed with the way Willi Schmidt was handling his duties as head of the administrative police and would decide that Willi would be a good candidate for the position.

There is no direct evidence that Willi Schmidt intended to stand for election as *Landrat* for Hagenow. Hertha remembered, however, that a number of their friends and a number of his professional associates had encouraged him to run for the office. What is certain is that Willi did not stand for election. By the summer of 1946, he had become increasingly concerned because he knew Verner and his cronies were running an illegal operation to steal cattle intended for State use and sell them for personal profit. He knew about the operation because Verner had approached him and offered to cut him in on the profits in exchange for facilitating the scheme.

Verner thought Willi could be a great help to him, since Willi could use his knowledge of logistics and his position as chief of the administrative police to further the theft. For his part, Willi had no intention of participating in illegal activities, and he let Verner know that not only would he not become a party to this criminal activity, he would report Verner to the regional authorities in Schwerin if the thefts persisted.

Verner decided he needed to do something to keep Willi from exposing his scheme, so he began digging into Willi's past. No doubt he had significant help from the Communists who were as eager as he was to keep control of key government positions throughout the country. He certainly could not get rid of Willi simply for refusing to go along with the conspiracy to sell off government property—that would certainly expose the scheme!—but he could accuse him of that crime if he had something else that would allow him to discredit any countercharge Willi might bring against him. And that's when news of Willi's past became valuable to him.

Somehow Verner learned of Willi's position at the labor camp. How he did so is not clear. There can be little doubt that he sought out information to use against the man he considered his rival. Since a network of informants was already being developed in the Soviet zone, he had access to resources to help him in this task. He may have spoken to former inmates at the camp; a number were living in and around Hagenow at the time.

Willi may have contributed to his own downfall. He got drunk easily and became talkative whenever he had consumed too much alcohol. At one of those moments—and there were probably quite a few, as the Russian commandant in Hagenow frequently arranged gatherings for the local officials—Willi may have expressed his disdain for the Communists. It is also possible that Christine Herrlinger, Willi's secretary and former "housemate," tipped off Verner to Willi's true role at Rechlin during the war. The opportunity to exact retribution on the man who had gone back to his wife would certainly have been tempting to the young lady.

It may be hard to understand why a soldier who had no active role in persecuting the inmates at the labor camp could be a marked man after the war. But in the eyes of the Russians, any German who wore a uniform was immediately suspected of having been a Nazi, and therefore guilty by mere association with the organization that perpetrated such atrocities on the Jews, Czechs, Poles—and the Russians, of course.

By proving Willi had worked at the labor camp, Verner could simply assert he had been a Nazi—or even worse, a member of the SS. The camp guards had been SS troopers, and any suggestion that Willi might have been a member of that group was sure to send alarms through the Russian military officials who were still responsible for ferreting out former Nazis and punishing them for their war crimes. Now if Willi were to claim Verner was involved with any illegal activity, Verner could counter that Willi was simply trying to smear the reputation of a loyal Communist—something that might be expected, Verner could argue, from a Nazi who had participated in the horrors of the concentration camps.

Willi was trapped. His "crime" was reported to the Russian military authorities, who sent a detachment to his office, taking away his papers and hauling him off to an undisclosed location for further processing. A messenger was sent to Hertha to tell her that Willi had been arrested.

The news was devastating. The Schmidts were living in Hagenow in an apartment that had been allocated to them because of Willi's status as a government official. The children ranging in age from thirteen to one were still trying to adjust to life in circumstances far different from those that had existed before the war. The older ones had just begun to attend school again. Hertha was tending a toddler and a baby in diapers. All she was told was that Willi was not coming home; she was given no indication about where he had been taken or of what crimes he had been accused.

Screwing up her courage, Hertha set off to Verner's office. At first it was hard for her to believe what had happened to her husband—and to know who was behind this plot. She knew Waldemer Verner! Although the bachelor Verner had a girlfriend, he had come more than once to the Schmidts' apartment, eaten Hertha's home-cooked meals and drank wine with her and Willi at their table, and played with their children. She had thought he was Willi's friend. Perhaps she should have realized something like this could happen though, since Verner had spoken openly of his desire to "get those Germans." Hertha knew he had to be behind Willi's arrest, or at least have some idea of why Willi had been taken away.

Hertha went storming into Verner's office, demanding to know the charges against her husband. At first Verner was evasive, saying Willi had stolen the car he was driving. Hertha knew that was patently false, as Willi had papers proving the car was properly allocated for his use. Then Verner told her he knew Willi had concealed his past from the British and then the Russians, and that his role in the forced labor camp was enough to merit a long prison sentence. There was, he said smugly, nothing he could do. Hertha left furious but determined; she would exonerate her husband if it was the last thing she could do. That almost proved to be true.

When Willi was spirited away from Hagenow, his captors took him to Schwerin, the region's capital. There the Russians had established not only an administrative headquarters for their own and the German puppet government's operations, but also a Military Tribunal to deal with offenses committed against either body. The Tribunal conducted its business in the Ministry of Justice building, near the heart of the city on Demmlerplatz.

Constructed in the eighteenth century for the Princes who ruled the Duchy of Mecklenburg-Schwerin, the building covers more than a city block. A deep green lawn, crisscrossed with walkways, separates it from the street. Three stories tall, its center section and two massive wings are attached by recessed sections that give the building the look of an English manorial home built in the Georgian style. The building is white stucco, with a red tile roof. Imposing columns flank the main entrance, which consists of two sets of heavy wooden double doors, each topped with brass grillwork. It is solid, even majestic. Its very architecture tells passersby that important things happen inside.

But in the period after World War II, what went on inside was hardly justice.

Running in a perpendicular line behind the Ministry of Justice building is an Annex used to incarcerate those who were brought to Schwerin for trial. The very architecture of this an-nex suggests its role as the dark underside of the justice system. Where the Ministry building glistens in white, this structure of molded and grimy cinderblock, with its barred windows, reflects the feeling of hopelessness prisoners must have experienced when they arrived there. One has to wonder if Willi or Hertha were aware of the great irony imbedded in the building's history. It had been constructed near the beginning of the twentieth cen-tury as a rehabilitation center for prisoners. That might explain why the building has a glass and steel atrium roof that admits a flood of natural light into a central area onto which all the cells open. When they were constructed the cells had no heating sys-tem (and certainly no air-conditioning) but the authorities under the Kaiser may have permitted prisoners to have small braziers or pot-bellied stoves to generate warmth in winter. The sun beating through the glass atrium provided some natural heat as well—a blessing in winter, perhaps, but hardly welcome in summer, when cells became unbearably hot. Included in the original construc-tion on the top floor was a small but very inviting chapel.

Unfortunately, the Annex did not serve its original pur-pose for long. Hitler's government used it as a prison, not a halfway house. The Soviets continued the practice of their Nazi predecessors and went one step further; not only was the cha-pel turned into administrative offices, but the basement became a torture chamber. The original cell doors may have had open bars, but either the Nazis or the Soviets made sure prisoners were locked behind solid steel doors that kept out the light and restricted prisoners from seeing anything outside their cubicles. When Willi Schmidt arrived at the Ministry of Justice Annex, he must have known he was entering a detestable hell-hole from

The Ministry of Justice Building in Schwerin. The beautiful façade masked the horrors carried out inside by the Russians and the Germans recruited as part of the puppet government that would become the East German State. (photographed 2006)

The Annex of the Ministry of Justice Building, Schwerin. Although designed as a rehabilitation center, the Russians and East Germans used the building to hold political prisoners like Willi Schmidt until they could be brought to trial. (photographed 2006)

which few were released without some form of physical or psychological scarring.

Willi was held in the Annex for several months before he was brought to trial. Though he later made only oblique comments to his family about his time in prison, other sources have provided ample documentation regarding what life was like for those unfortunate enough to be spirited away by the Soviets and their East German toadies. The cells in the Annex measure approximately ten feet by twelve feet (possibly smaller in some cases). There is some evidence to suggest they were originally intended to house two prisoners. Individual cells contained no toilets or facilities for washing; no doubt the first occupants had washbasins and chamber pots. A single shower room containing indoor plumbing and including a shower and sink had been constructed

View of the inside of the Ministry of Justice Annex. Cell doors are visible along the iron walkways. The atrium that let in sunlight can be seen at the top. (photographed 2006)

Typical cell inside the Ministry of Justice Annex. Originally designed to hold two prisoners, under the Russians and East Germans these 8x12 foot cubicles served as holding cells for as many as twenty prisoners. (photographed 2006)

on each floor. Presumably, prisoners were escorted to this facility at regular intervals. Though even the conditions may have seemed primitive, the original inmates had engaged in regular rehabilitative activities that took them out of their cells, as they learned trades and readjusted to life in society outside of prison.

Neither the Nazis nor the Soviets had much concern for their prisoners' personal welfare, however, and by 1946 it had already become commonplace to stuff a dozen or more prisoners into a single cell. There were no activities for prisoners, and none ever got to see a lawyer, even if one was assigned to represent them before the tribunal that would eventually hear their cases. Some passed the time by making crafts from any materials they could get their hands on—straw, matches, handkerchiefs—but most simply sat in a stunned stupor waiting to be called from the darkness of their cells into a courtroom where only the sentence, not the verdict, was in doubt.

In 1946, conditions in the cells were hellish. Doors installed on the cells were made of thick steel plates, with an aperture wide enough to slide in trays of food and a peephole through which guards could check on the inmates. A single bucket served as a chamber pot for a dozen or more prisoners. It did not take long for it to become filled and overflow onto the cell floor. To make matters worse, there was no toilet paper. Rags were used for cleaning oneself and for wiping down the floors. Sometimes the rags ended up in the buckets, filling them up even faster. The cells reeked constantly with the stench of human waste.

The guards, often selected for their fierce hatred of the Nazis and their willingness to inflict hardship and pain on others, took pleasure in tormenting the captives, often trying to pit them against each other and create animosity among cellmates. One of the guards' favorite forms of entertainment was *kübeln*, or "bucketing." Normally, when the slop bucket in the corner of the cell was filled and the waste began to spill over onto the floor, one prisoner was designated to take the bucket to the shower room, where the contents would be poured down the sink—the same one at which prisoners were supposed to wash. Often bored with the routine of prison life, however, the guards made a game of this process. They would stage "bucket races," betting among themselves that one inmate could empty a bucket faster than another. The guards would identify at least two cells with full slop buckets and designate the prisoner who was to participate in the "race." The prisoner would have to stand still, holding the bucket next to him, until given the signal to run. The prisoner would then race to the sink, empty the bucket— often splashing the contents over the sink onto the floor—and then race back. More often than not, the loser would be made to clean up the mess by the sink.

Years later, Willi related to his family some of the details of the interrogations he was forced to undergo. On more than one occasion he was taken from his cell and thrown into a dark room, where a single light was shone into his face. He never saw his interrogators. From the dark the voices of these officials hounded him to provide information about his involvement in the scheme to appropriate livestock and materials for personal gain, and about his work for the Nazis. And of course, they prodded him for names—names of others involved in the "conspiracy," names of others who might be spies for the Allied Powers or the German government in the West, names of anyone who might be profiting at the expense of "The People." Above all, it seemed, they wanted him to name names.

Shortly after he had arrived in Schwerin, Willi sent a note to Hertha through the prison administration asking that she obtain a lawyer to represent him. He also asked her to gather statements from a former camp official living close to Hagenow who could testify that Willi had not been a guard in the labor camp. Hertha decided to take matters into her own hands. Entrusting the smaller children to the care of Lori and Rolf, and to a refugee girl staying with them at the time in exchange for room and board, she began traipsing around the countryside, hitchhiking from town to town, sustaining herself by begging for a slice of bread or a sandwich from those who were fortunate enough to have food. Eventually she obtained documentation from former prisoners that Willi had actually tried to improve the lives of the camp's inmates, especially the women and children, by getting them extra food and supplies. She also verified that Willi had not stolen the car he had been driving.

Once she had assembled all her documentation, Hertha went back to Verner's office. Verner reviewed the documents casually, but was unmoved. Instead of agreeing to see that Willi was freed, he instead assured her Willi would go to trial for his crimes. She and her family would be left to fend for themselves—unless she agreed to "cooperate."

"Cooperate?" she asked.

"Look," he told her. "If you get a divorce from your husband, we'll care for you and your children. If not, we won't!"

Hertha was shaken. It was apparent that the "law" under a Communist regime bore little resemblance to the one she had known before the war. It was also clear to her that Verner's plans for taking care of her family included some kind of arrangement that required her to spend some "private time" with him.

It was difficult to find a lawyer courageous enough to defend Willi against the Communists. The one Hertha finally hired was old and unaware of the power the Party had within the courts system. Both he and Hertha thought the Communists were simply mean-spirited. His efforts would prove futile, and Hertha soon learned she and her husband were dealing with people more sinister than they had imagined.

When Willi was finally scheduled to appear in court, Hertha took Rolf with her to Schwerin to witness the proceedings. Just being in the city heightened Hertha's sense of apprehension. Although Rolf had been to Schwerin before with his

Courtroom inside the Ministry of Justice Building, Schwerin, circa 1946.
Willi Schmidt's "show trial" was conducted in this room.

father when Willi had gone there as part of his official duties,
no one in the family had ever spent any appreciable time there.
Hertha could see immediately that Schwerin was a most dismal
place. Even though it had escaped Allied bombing, residences
and office buildings were starting to show the decay that would
worsen during the next four decades of Communist domination. There was no paint to freshen up facades, and the poor

quality whitewash used as a substitute quickly turned gray, giving the city a uniformly ashen appearance.

And, of course, there was no hotel in which they could rent a room. Instead, they found overnight accommodations for two nights in an old arsenal that had been converted into a dormitory. It was being used by the homeless, by derelicts shunned by the authorities, and by a number of unfortunate folk like Hertha and Rolf who were coming to the capital to witness proceedings of the Tribunal. The atmosphere in the building was nightmarish. The structure was dilapidated. The bedding smelled abominably, and was certainly infested with lice and other vermin. Outside the windows, Rolf could see rats the size of rabbits scurrying about in the alleyway. Everywhere about them the people had a look of despondency and despair.

Willi's trial took place inside the courtroom in the Ministry of Justice. Like the building's exterior, the courtroom's décor bespoke the serious nature of proceedings held there. From the oak floor, paneled walls and tall columns rose nearly thirty feet to a ceiling scalloped in various rectangular shapes and bordered by braided molding. A massive chandelier suspended from the ceiling loomed over the tables where the defendants sat with their lawyers and where government prosecutors presented their evidence to a panel of judges seated on a raised dais. Spectators could come in through doors on the second floor of the building and sit in a gallery that gave them a view of the trial. Participants in the trials entered on the ground floor through wooden doors some ten feet high. Willi and his fellow prisoners were brought from the Annex into the Ministry of Justice building by an inside door that connected the two structures. By this means, the Soviets were able to keep prisoners out of sight during the entire time of their incarceration and trial.

Willi's was a show trial, of course. He did not offer any information about his work at the concentration camp, but he did not deny his association with the facility when he went before the judges. In a somewhat surprising turn of events, though, former prisoners from the labor camp testified about Willi's efforts. There were other character witnesses as well. Then there were some who told of his role in the profiteering scheme (which he had uncovered, of course, but not participated in).

Under questioning, these witnesses did not seem particularly credible. Hertha thought the Tribunal was inclined to let Willi off, since there was no strong proof of his guilt on any of the charges. She recalled later that one judge had even informed her that Willi would be released into her care, since he had apparently become weakened during his long pre-trial confinement. Hertha arranged for transportation to bring Willi home. But if Hertha was expecting justice, she was bitterly disappointed. Verner intervened again, pointing out the traitorous nature of Willi's deception regarding his role in the forced labor camp. That was all the members of the Tribunal needed to hear.

Willi was branded as an opponent of Communism and sentenced to two years' imprisonment. He was taken from the courtroom without so much as a chance to say goodbye to his loved ones. Since the Annex was principally a holding center and not a place for long-term incarceration, the authorities arranged to send him to another prison outside Schwerin. No doubt he was spirited away from the city in the dead of night so no one could see how he left or learn where he was going. Demoralized and in tears, Hertha Schmidt returned to Hagenow. But if the Soviets thought she was beaten, they were sadly mistaken. She had not yet begun to fight.

Life "In Exile"

(1946-1949)

❧

When Hertha learned Willi had been taken from Schwerin, she returned home to care for her children. Now they would need her more than ever. She would have to be both mother and father to them. She would have to find some way to feed them. She had no idea if she would be permitted to remain in the nice home where the family was living or be forced into less commodious facilities. She hadn't a clue about where she would get money to purchase necessities. But none of these obstacles deterred her from the commitment she made to herself when her husband was led from the courtroom in Schwerin. She vowed then to find out where he had been taken and get him released, no matter what the cost.

Hertha knew that to obtain Willi's freedom she would undoubtedly have to appeal to a higher court. But first she decided to make another appeal to Verner. Almost immediately after returning to Hagenow, she marched down to his office to plead her husband's case. She argued that Willi had been a model government servant after the war; she pointed out how he had helped Verner on more than one occasion. She pointed out, too, that sympathetic neighbors and friends were concerned that with Willi in prison, there would be no way for Hertha to care adequately for the couple's eight children. Did Verner want that kind of bad press?

Verner scoffed at her pleas, telling her he would keep Willi in prison no matter how many lawyers Hertha hired to try to get him released!

By this time Verner had concluded that not only was Willi someone who needed to be eliminated as a threat; Hertha, too, was dangerous. His first step against her was to order the immediate removal of the family from Hagenow to the village of Vellahn, a farming hamlet twenty kilometers to the southwest. Here they would be isolated from major population centers, thereby reducing Hertha's chances to create more problems for him until he could find a more permanent solution for dealing with the entire Schmidt clan.

A truck came to the Schmidts' home on Poststrasse and a group of movers piled all their possessions inside. When the family arrived at their new living quarters in Vellahn, they received instructions not to unpack too much; they would be staying there only until Verner arranged for their removal to yet another village even farther away. Hertha was sure he would send them to an area that had been overrun by the Russians in their rush to Berlin—probably somewhere in the far eastern section of Germany, where villages and towns had been devastated and some places virtually abandoned in the months before the war ended. Verner wanted there to be no communication between Hertha Schmidt and her husband or between her and any officials in Hagenow who might be sympathetic to Willi's case.

Anyone who knew Hertha Schmidt then or later in life would not be surprised that she did not react meekly to this news. Insisting she wasn't going any farther, she settled her family into their new quarters in Vellahn and immediately began her crusade to obtain Willi's release from prison. She hitched a ride back to Hagenow and went to the office of the current Landrat, whom Verner was to replace shortly, and appealed to him. Both Hertha and Willi had known the Landrat for some time, and Hertha thought he was a man who would listen to reason.

He knew Willi was not guilty of any crimes. She reminded him that he would be embarrassed if Hertha made a public spectacle when forced to move again. She was willing to stay in Vellahn, but would go nowhere else.

Nevertheless, the official was evasive, indicating there was nothing he could do for her. Apparently he, too, was learning about the power of the Communists to retaliate against citizens—even public officials—who chose to cross them. He wanted to keep his record clean, especially as he was going out of office soon. Hertha reminded him sternly that he was still in office, that he had worked with Willi in the past and claimed him as his friend. "I demand that you help me!" she insisted.

Whether this appeal was the reason Hertha won a temporary victory, or whether Verner simply felt he did not want to deal with further complaints from her, the outcome was modestly favorable for the Schmidts. They were allowed to stay in Vellahn, and they were put up in a building the Party had commandeered.

Life in Vellahn was hardly the same as it had been in Hagenow. Located in the midst of farming country and stretches of woodland, connected to larger communities only by roads of cobblestone or hard-packed dirt, the tiny village was virtually isolated from any population center. Its inhabitants, numbering no more than three hundred, were mostly farmers or merchants who catered to other locals; there was not much traffic with the "outside world." There was no industry and no real prospects for anyone not already immersed in village life. The small farmers were being squeezed by the government, whose new chief of administrative police had strict orders to extract quotas that would eventually be impossible to meet. In this way the State would have a reason to confiscate the small farms and create larger conglomerates. The system forced the farmers to hide livestock and foodstuffs, and made life for all the villagers a living hell.

But at least the Schmidt family was together, they had a roof over their heads, and there were opportunities to obtain food and clothing as long as they remained resourceful. Their new home was on the ground floor of a two-story brick structure at Wittenburgerstrasse #6, a main thoroughfare through the hamlet stretching from the Lutheran church and community center on the northeast end of town to the marketplace on the southwest side. Naturally they shared their building with others. Doctor Helmke, a retired army surgeon, lived above them and had his office in one room on the ground floor. Also on that level, with a separate entrance to the street, was a dilapidated tailor shop. Its owner, who was constantly drunk and had been brainwashed by the Communists, saw no value in being nice to his customers or accommodating their needs. In fact, people in the village were sure he was an informer for the Soviets and later for the East Germans.

The Schmidts' apartment was hardly spacious, but the family managed to make do. The living room, immediately inside the front door, became Hertha's bedroom. The children occupied two bedrooms immediately behind the living room. A kitchen was located at the rear, with a window looking out on a tiny yard which contained a long outbuilding that had once been used as a stable. Rolf set to work constructing cages in one of the abandoned stalls in the outbuilding so the family could raise rabbits for food, and the other siblings organized scavenging parties to raid the nearby woods and fields to put food on the family table. Inside, Hertha demonstrated her refusal to be cowed by the authorities; she set about cleaning the house immediately, and every week she scrubbed the tile floors until they shined.

Hertha's most immediate concern was being able to feed her family. The practice of rationing was in effect once more, but the Schmidts' allocation procured barely enough food for two weeks each month. Hertha did what she could to stretch out

The building on Wittenburgerstrasse in Vellahn where the Schmidts were relocated when Willi was arrested for the first time. Their quarters were on the ground floor on the right; a shop is on the left of the photo. (photographed 2006)

the food supply, but frequently the children would have to do without breakfast. Hertha and Rolf would go out late in the evenings to see what they might obtain by foraging. During the days the younger siblings would try their hand at swapping chores for food. Often Wölfi, Lori, and Eini would stop at neighbors' homes on their way to school, hoping to get a slice of bread. The two older siblings soon discovered Einhard was especially good at "touching" the local farm women. "He looked so pitiful," Wolf recalled, "that none of the old ladies could turn him down!" Sometimes he even managed to get each of them a sandwich or an egg.

Hertha recalled much later in life that Lori and Wolf were particularly accomplished "gatherers." The two would travel to the woods and fields outside of Vellahn with a villager who owned an old truck fitted out with an engine that ran on wood chips. The two Schmidts would ride out with neighbors, gathering fruits and nuts in large buckets. The truck owner would take some of their harvest as his payment. The rest would end up on the Schmidts' table. What they brought in was always welcome, but Hertha was constantly distressed by the knowledge that this source of food was highly unreliable, depending as it did not only on the initiative of her children but also on the numbers of people picking over the dwindling crops growing naturally in the forests and fields outside Vellahn.

On occasion, the constant lack of nutritional foodstuffs was cause for squabbling and underhanded behavior by one or another of the children.

Once a month a man would travel to Vellahn with a small projector and reels of old movies that had not been confiscated by the government. He would set up his operation in the loft of a local restaurant, and the villagers were welcome to come view these movies for free. The evening could often be long, of course, as the man had only limited equipment; "moviegoers" might spend several minutes waiting for him to change reels, repair broken film, or rewind the segments so he could complete the screening. On an evening when Hertha took the children to see one of these movies, Einhard snuck away from his brothers and sisters and returned to the house to steal some of the bread his mother had baked just before leaving. It was a short-lived pleasure, however, as Hertha quickly discovered not only the loss but the culprit, and a strong whipping was quick to follow. But deep down, Hertha must have understood her child's motivation; all of them were suffering from the constant privations.

Keeping the family clothed was another major problem. An accomplished seamstress, Hertha made clothes for the children out of what she had available. More often she was reduced to mending the worn-out shirts and pants the boys and girls were wearing. Hand-me-downs were a fact of life for the younger ones. Though the children had wooden shoes, warm socks were hard to come by so they would be repaired whenever holes appeared in them. Before long, the socks contained more darning thread than original material. The Schmidts began to look like vagabonds.

In 1946, four Schmidt children began school in Vellahn: Lori, Wolf, Einhard, and six-year-old Bill, who enrolled for the first time. Somewhat surprisingly, Rolf was permitted to continue in school at Hagenow and retain his place in the dormitory. But he knew his mother needed him as well, so on weekends he would travel back to Vellahn, taking the train to Brahlstorf, the nearest station located three kilometers south of the village, or hitchhike—a practice that once caused him considerable consternation when the drunken Russian soldiers who picked him up refused to stop the truck to let him off!

In Vellahn, scrounging for food became a way of life. There was one grocery store in the village, but the shelves were almost always empty. The farmers in the region had nothing to sell either, as they were also required to relinquish to the government most of their crops and much of their livestock, which was then sent to the cities or shipped off to Russia as reparation payment for what the Soviets considered war crimes committed during the Germans' invasion of Russia in 1941-43.

As a consequence, the Schmidt family had to rely on their instincts and some hard work just to put food on the table. The children would spend days on the ground during harvest, picking up husks left lying in the fields after the farmers had hauled away the sheaves of grain. Inside these husks there might be a few kernels, which could be carefully extracted and bagged until the family had enough to fill a sack, which could then be used for barter with the man who operated the local grain mill.

One summer Rolf worked the entire season on a local farm on the other side of the village—a large one for the region, as the farmer had two horses for plowing—on the promise that he would be paid with a sack of grain. He was hoping for a 50-kilogram sack (approximately 100 pounds), but when harvest time was over he got a sack so small that he could carry it home easily in one hand. But he knew the farmer had to turn over a good portion of his crop to the authorities, and this pittance was all he could spare.

The mill owner could not grind such a small amount of grain immediately, so he worked out an exchange for the Schmidts—as he no doubt did for other families—giving them a sack of flour already milled; he would accumulate small sacks such as the one Rolf gave him until he had enough for another milling, and the process would continue.

The lack of supplies made for some strange kinds of bartering. The family usually got their cooking oil from the local pharmacist—when he had it on hand, and when they had something to trade for it. On one occasion when Hertha was visiting his shop, the pharmacist proposed an unusual swap. He had received a large supply of saccharin—a wonderful sweetener that added flavor to the bland diet was being set out on most Germans' tables in those days. Did Hertha want some? Of course she did, but she had nothing to trade—or so she thought. The pharmacist told her that he and his wife had lost everything during the war, and as his wife's birthday was coming up, he wanted to do something special for her. Would Hertha consider parting with a piece of silk lingerie in exchange for the saccharin? It didn't take her long to go home and return with a nice silk slip. For sometime after that, the Schmidt children had sweetened foods at their meals; presumably the pharmacist's wife had a wonderful birthday, too.

More often than not, there was little variety in the family diet. Hertha used everything edible to try to provide some mix of greens and starches: stale bread, potato peelings, nettles collected along roads and beside fields. Sometimes handling these products required exceptional skill. Nettles, a common plant, grew wild in the area. These could produce painful stings if grabbed while it still in the ground, but when wetted down they could be handled without fear of injury. Once these were cooked they tasted like spinach and were very nutritious, especially in summer when they were especially tender.

Hertha also became inventive in cooking rutabagas, occasionally frying them in ersatz coffee so they would turn brown. Frequently she made soup from the foods she and her children scavenged in order to stretch her supplies. One winter the family survived on turnips. Day after day Hertha set before her children dishes of boiled turnips, tureens of turnip soup, or bowls of turnip stew. On Sundays they would have "steak"—fried turnip slices!

Occasionally Rolf would manage to pilfer an egg or two from the farm where he worked in the summer, placing his stash gently in his pocket for the trip home. Hertha would use the eggs to flavor dishes of potatoes or other staples. When the children brought home wild mushrooms from their treks through the woods, Hertha would prepare them on the same day they were picked. The fragrant aroma of simmering mushrooms filled their small apartment, letting them forget for a few moments the tragic circumstances in which they were living.

Naturally the children learned to eat everything on their plates. Some even came to like what they got. Mike became fond of his mother's potatoes, which she spruced up with bacon drippings and gravies made from whatever she could get her hands on. Lori became a fan of rutabagas, which she learned to cook and continued making long after the family settled in America. On the other hand, Joe remembers that, as a little boy, he thought the food was terrible—but he ate it anyway.

Turnips, potatoes, rutabagas, and beets could be obtained by exercising a little subterfuge—and turning a blind eye toward property ownership. During the fall in Germany, farmers would harvest these crops and pile them into long rows, covering over the vegetables with straw and dirt to keep them from freezing. The aim was to have a ready supply of these staples for the farmer's livestock throughout the winter. But it did not take long for the Schmidts to discover and raid these caches. They would sneak out to fields often covered with snow, crouching beside an underground silo where they knew they could reach something that would make a meal for them. All they had to do was to dig a small hole through the material covering the vegetables, reach in, and pull out dinner! When they had extracted a couple of items, they would cover the top of the hole so their theft would go undiscovered.

During their first winter in Vellahn, however, Rolf was the only one whose arm was long enough to reach far enough into the hole to grab a turnip or potato, so he was always part of the raiding party. The scheme worked well for some time, but on one cold day in mid-winter, Rolf carefully pushed back the straw and dirt from the hole and stuck his arm deep inside—only to emerge with an arm covered in cow dung! The farmer, who had discovered the boys' scheme, finally got his revenge.

When they lived in Vellahn, the Schmidt children did a good bit of "potato harvesting" in the spring as well. After the war, farmers in the eastern regions of Germany were growing large crops of potatoes for the Russians, who exported much of the produce back to their homeland and used the remaining part of the crop to make vodka. Peelings from potatoes used by the Russians were fed to the animals being raised for them. But Germans could not get their hands on potatoes very easily.

Nevertheless, the Schmidts found a way to gather in some potatoes—in a manner of speaking—which their mother could prepare for an occasional special meal. In the spring, farmers would cut up potatoes that had been stored over the winter and plant the pieces, ensuring there was at least one "eyelet" that would sprout to produce a vine for new potatoes. No insecticides were used to treat these "seed potatoes," so they remained edible. During planting season, the Schmidt children would go out and hide in the hazelnut bushes and watch the farmer planting. When the horse disappeared over the horizon, they would race out into the field and dig into the holes where at least two seed potatoes were placed, and they would take out only one. As the farmer came back, the children would race back to the hedges—a real challenge at some times! The children were fearful of being caught. But having two or three small potatoes was considered a feast!

For a brief time, the Schmidt clan also found another way to obtain potatoes for their diet—at the expense of the Russians living in the area, making this an especially sweet escapade. Officers of the Red Army had directed one of the local farmers to raise rabbits as meat for the soldiers. The Schmidts knew the farmer was feeding these rabbits with "food balls" made up of boiled potato peelings mixed with greens. They would be lucky to have such food for themselves! So they came up with a plan to steal these food balls without being detected.

They would sneak off to a field filled with dandelions, food rabbits found especially tempting. Filling a sack full of dandelions, they would return to the farmer's property and swap these flowers for the food balls. Since the rabbits ate the dandelions readily, there was no evidence that the more nutritious food was being stolen. Their scheme was finally halted during the winter, however, when the farmer noticed the children's footprints in the snow. Fortunately for them, he did not say anything to the Russians; instead, he spoke to Hertha, encouraging her to get her children to stop. He was certain that if they were caught stealing, the Russians would simply shoot them.

Ironically, the hard life in Vellahn led to some strange adventures for the family. Once, several of the boys were hired to bag potatoes for a nearby farmer. In exchange for their labor, they were given a sack of potatoes to take home. As they were pulling their little wagon through the woods back toward Vellahn, they came across the carcass of a burned-out car, leaning on its side; the tires had apparently been stolen. Rolf decided that the car would be a great "toy" for them to play in—if only they could right it. In the process of rocking the chassis back and forth to tip it over, however, the boys managed to push the car onto Rolf, whose arm became pinned underneath it. He managed to extract his arm, but the pain in his wrist was excruciating. Hurrying home, the boys sought out Dr. Helmke in his office. The surgeon examined Rolf's wrist with a fluoroscope and determined it was, indeed, broken. He placed it in a cast, which Rolf had to wear for several weeks. Not only did Rolf find the cast inconvenient; it severely limited his ability to help his brothers and sister scrounge for food! Hertha was no doubt distressed, as she was coming to depend more and more on Rolf to take the place of her absent husband in managing her increasingly impoverished family.

During the war, the Schmidts had been able to turn to Hertha's parents for a little help with food supplies, since farmers were never subjected to rationing in the same way city dwellers had been. The only "collective" efforts had been managed for the convenience of the farmers. For example, on visits to his grandparents, Rolf would often carry large canisters of milk to a central collection point so it could be redistributed to other locations. The only hardship was that the collection point was on the northwest edge of the town, which meant that Rolf had to huff and puff his way uphill from the marketplace where the Dittmanns lived. Under the Communists, however, farmers were told that everything they owned and everything they produced belonged to the State. Quotas were established, binding farmers on pain of arrest to provide certain amounts of livestock and produce for distribution throughout the country.

This kind of redistribution would have been bad enough had farmers been required to provide a portion of crops or livestock they had traditionally raised, but the new government, in-spired by Marxist ideals of egalitarianism, frequently demanded that farmers provide animals they did not raise or grains they did not grow! As a consequence, small farmers like Willi and Marie Dittmann spent as much of their time bartering with other farmers as they did working their fields. They would trade goods they produced with those who had items they did not have or could not grow, giving them in exchange items other farmers needed to meet their quotas. At this time, they were providing for Hedwig and her family, too, as Hertha's older sister was gradually weakening with the cancer that would lead to her death in 1950.

Shortly after the Russians had established their agricultural system in eastern Germany, the government took a strict inventory of livestock. What was not used to work the fields was almost always designated as available for confiscation under the oppressive quota system. As a consequence, if the Dittmanns and other farmers wanted meat for themselves or to use for bartering, they had to raise some livestock in secret.

Each year the Dittmanns managed to keep one pig hidden from government inspectors. When the pig was ready to be slaughtered, a professional butcher would come to the farm to kill the animal, and then Marie, her daughter Hedwig, and her granddaughter Margarete, would spend two days frantically curing the meat and making sausages. This was one of the few times there were special meals at the Dittmanns, as Marie was able to make scrumptious sandwiches from the ground-up bacon scraps.

This kind of secrecy was necessary because the tariffs on farmers were exceptionally high, while the means of production were steadily deteriorating. Equipment was aging, and there was no way to replace it. Horses used for plowing and hauling were often run-down and ill-fed. Fertilizers were unavailable. Small farmers like Willi Dittmann were still using horses to pull the machinery used for harvesting, and still needed to use scythes for gathering other crops. All this combined to make it almost impossible for them to satisfy the government's demands.

On at least one occasion, Willi Dittmann was arrested and jailed for failing to provide his quota of products. Eventually the government seized all the small farms and combined them into collectives, making the same farmers who once worked this land for themselves toil as laborers for the State. Needless to say, living so far away and feeling the pressures imposed on them by the authorities, there was no way for Hertha's parents to help her and her brood of growing and needy children.

Even while she was running her household and struggling to keep her children in food and clothing, Hertha was working incessantly to get her husband released from prison. Initially her efforts were targeted at learning where he had been taken. She finally discovered he was incarcerated in Bautzen, a former Nazi concentration camp re-opened by the Soviets during the late summer of 1945 to house political dissidents. Hertha was determined to visit Willi there so she could help gather information she would need to help Willi mount an appeal.

Knowing she would need permission from the Russians to see her husband, Hertha decided to go to Hagenow to visit the local offices of the Soviet administration, the GPU. Often thought of by the Germans as the Secret Police, the GPU actually oversaw political operations in occupied Germany, supported by the puppet German government and by Red Army soldiers who helped enforce the law—or the whim of political officials. When Hertha visited the GPU office in Hagenow to inquire about procedures for visiting her husband, she discovered, much to her chagrin, two important truths about the Communists: not only were they scrupulous in controlling their prisoners, they kept detailed records of everyone who was even remotely associated with a person suspected of being an enemy of the State. Unwittingly, Hertha had given the authorities plenty of evidence they could use against *her*.

What had happened was that before Willi's trial, Hertha had visited him several times in the Ministry of Justice Annex. Each time she brought presents to Willi, including loaves of bread, from which she would remove the center and insert letters and notes to encourage him to remain optimistic about his future. In her notes Hertha reminded Willi that he should keep his head up; he was no criminal, and some day he would be exonerated. She wrote, too, that there were others who did not like the SED and the Communists, and that Verner was becoming ever more unpopular. She told Willi that things were getting worse in the region, as young people were taking to the streets, drinking and singing protest songs.

No doubt Hertha thought her notes would give her husband hope, but Willi never saw these letters. As a matter of routine, prison officials had confiscated the bread Hertha brought, and her notes were discovered. Immediately the authorities decided Hertha and Willi might be more dangerous than they had originally thought. As soon as she showed up in the local GPU office in Hagenow to learn where Willi had been taken, the Soviet officials called the local German police and Hertha was arrested. Like her husband, she was carted off to Schwerin. She barely had time for a word with Rolf, who had come with her to the police station. She remembered years later that, for the first time, her eldest son looked close to tears. She was so proud of the way he had matured quickly during the past six years, and although he behaved like a man at thirteen, the thought of his mother being imprisoned was almost too much to bear. Hertha could see the fear and concern in his eyes, but she told him to go home to care for the younger ones, and to seek help from Vellahn's *Bürgermeister* (mayor) if the task became too hard to handle.

Hertha was given no reason for her arrest. On the way to Schwerin, she asked the GPU officer escorting her where she was being taken and why she had been detained; he said he did not know. Hertha suspected he knew full well where they were headed but had instructions to say nothing to her. Nevertheless, the officer was nice to her. Hertha began to hope that not all GPU officials were evil, just as she was aware that not all who fought for Germany were genocidal maniacs. In fact, this officer seemed genuinely sympathetic. He inquired about her children. He had a look on his face that suggested he pitied her.

Hertha knew when she arrived at GPU headquarters that she was not going to be released immediately. She was first made to wait for hours. Alone, unsure of her fate, knowing the rumors that the Soviets under Stalin had eliminated millions of dissenters in their own country, Hertha finally broke down, crying; she was unable to talk. Later in the day she was brought before another GPU officer for an interview. He pretended not to know German, so he brought in a translator who seemed not to like Hertha. For her part Hertha was certain she did not like them! After some initial questioning and apparently some bullying, the chief interrogator replaced the first translator with another one, a woman who seemed more sympathetic. Hertha thought this woman translated her responses more truthfully.

The GPU interrogator asked for names of the people Hertha had identified in the letters they had confiscated. For the first time Hertha learned what had happened to the correspondence she had tried to smuggle in to her husband. The Soviet official asked what she thought the protestors she had alluded to in her letters to Willi might do to make life better for themselves and others in this "new" Germany. Perhaps to throw her off balance, he also asked how old her baby was. She told him Barb was sick due to nutritional deficiencies; the family was afraid she might die. From that point on the official seemed to be more sympathetic.

When he learned she had six boys, he asked how she would like them to grow up. At this point Hertha became expansive in her responses. She told the interrogator that no mother can give life to six boys and wish for them to be killed in war. "You don't give birth to children just to be killed!" she exclaimed. She told him she wanted her children to grow up to be useful members of society. She mentioned she had met Russian soldiers who were humane and caring. She had seen some Russians treat their German enemies as human beings.

She recounted the family's experiences with young Russian soldiers in Flecken Zechlin who had given the family food for the younger children, and about how these Russians seemed to delight in playing with the youngsters. Boldly she told her interrogator that the Russians should be smarter in dealing with the populace, because if they wanted to be strong in East Germany they would need to win over the hearts of the people. They could do that, she said, only by treating them humanely.

The GPU officer terminated the interview. After he left the room, the woman translator told Hertha she believed Hertha was a good woman, but that she should never write letters like that again—doing so could be dangerous!

Hertha was kept in Schwerin for ten days. She did not sleep in the Annex where Willi had been held, but instead was transferred to the police station, where she slept in a prison cell. Fortunately, when hitchhiking to see Willi, she had gotten in the habit of carrying bread for her own use, wrapping the loaves in a towel. Since she still had the towel with her, she was able to use it as a pillow. Of course, she had to sleep in the same clothes for ten days. She was allowed to wash her face and hands, but not to bathe. Occasionally, she was forced to share her cell, once with a drunken woman.

Hertha was sick with worry about how Rolf had fared when she sent him home, and whether the children were being cared for. She ate the bitter jail food as best she could, although she could not get much of it down. To her good fortune, the police at the local jail had become accustomed to locking up people who were not criminals, so they took pity on her and occasionally gave her a sandwich.

On the tenth day of her incarceration, Hertha was told to gather her belongings. She was taken back to GPU headquarters where the same officer appeared for what Hertha thought would be another interview. Instead, he asked her if she would consent to spy for the Russians. Among the bribes offered to encourage her to spy for them was a promise that, after a time, she and her family would be taken from Germany to Russia, where she would live luxuriously and be given a generous allowance to raise her children.

Hertha was not going to be fooled by what she knew were empty promises, and she would not betray her friends at any cost. Thinking quickly, she began pointing out a series of difficulties she foresaw with the Russians' offer. First, she noted that her husband had been arrested for political reasons, which meant he was considered a risk by the Communists in the East German government. How could she be effective as a spy? Besides, she said, if Willi were not in his former position as a government administrator, how could she learn anything that would be of value to them? And further, she had no transportation, so she could not report to anyone outside of Vellahn. None of her excuses seemed to matter. The officer told her not to worry; he would send someone to get the information. Hertha finally said she would not spy on someone and have that person sent to a concentration camp. Then she delivered the *coup de grace*.

"I have eight children to raise without a husband!" she exclaimed. "How do you expect me to find time to spy?!"

The interview was over.

Before she would be allowed to leave, however, Hertha was told she must sign a form promising not to tell anyone what had happened at GPU headquarters. Once she did so, she could go back to Vellahn. She nearly broke down again, knowing she was going home. It took her half an hour to compose herself sufficiently so she could sign the form. Despite her discomposure, she didn't cry this time. She wasn't going to let them think they'd beaten her.

Apparently the Russians had decided Hertha was of little value to them, but they were not sure how to dismiss the charges against her without creating ill will between themselves and the German officials who had demanded her arrest. She was released quietly, and she headed back home, catching rides on farm vehicles and even on Russian trucks. Upon her arrival, the refugee girl who had been living in the apartment with the family screamed in surprise! She told Hertha the Volkspolizei—the local police—had instructed her to look for other lodgings; Hertha wasn't coming home again, and the children were to be placed in foster homes. Mother and children were reunited amid tears and laughter. Yet despite her joy at being with her family again, Hertha remained greatly shaken by her experience. For months afterward, every time she saw a Russian, she shuddered to think he might be coming to get information from her.

Hertha did not let her fear get the better of her, however. She continued her crusade to have Willi set free. Somehow she managed to get permission to visit him in Bautzen. The trip was arduous, several hundred kilometers to the east of Vellahn. She went there only infrequently, taking Rolf with her once for company. The man Hertha saw at Bautzen was a pale shadow of the vibrant, carefree spirit she had married only fourteen years earlier. Willi was emaciated and sickly, but even worse, his spirit seemed to have been broken. He gave her a glimpse of the horrors of prison life; he hinted that he had thoughts of committing suicide. Hertha became fearful for his safety and sanity. She knew if Willi were to survive at all, she would have to do something to get him out of prison and back home with the family.

Hertha began traveling back and forth from Vellahn to Schwerin, hounding any official who might be able to help her. One day her appointment was with a former camp inmate who had apparently joined the SED after the war and was now working for the German government.

As she entered his office, he gave her a hostile stare and exclaimed, "Why are you out of jail? We wanted you in a concentration camp!"

On his desk he had a copy of one of her letters that had been confiscated by prison authorities. Some of the sentences were underlined, and next to some of the names in the letter was the annotation "Fascist."

The official was amazed and angry that the GPU had released Hertha instead of putting her far away. The incident reminded Hertha that the SED could eliminate any trace of people who crossed them. She would have to be very careful in her attempts to have Willi released, or she too might disappear.

Then her luck changed. On a trip to Schwerin, she saw a Dr. Herbert, now serving as a judge for the new government. Apparently he had been on the bench in Mecklenburg before the war. When hostilities broke out, he resigned his judgeship and accepted a commission in the German army. Now he was again part of the judiciary system, and since the Schmidts had known him before the war, Hertha appealed to him to use his influence in getting Willi released. He promised to do what he could, but nothing came of this first encounter.

Hertha discovered some time later that Dr. Herbert was scheduled to visit Mirow as part of a commission visiting from Berlin. Doggedly she set off on the 120-kilometer journey to the place where her family had enjoyed so many happier days. There she found Dr. Herbert at the courthouse in conversation with one of the delegates from the SED in Berlin. Hertha approached the men and again sought Dr. Herbert's help. He in turn spoke briefly to the Berliner out of Hertha's hearing. When he came back to her he said simply, "Your husband can go home tomorrow." Hertha broke down and cried on the steps of the courthouse. After nearly two years behind bars, Willi Schmidt was once again to be a free man—in a manner of speaking.

The man who came home from prison was not the same feisty idealist who had been carted away nearly two years earlier. Willi Schmidt was physically emaciated and emotionally exhausted. His wife had to be both his nurse and his psychologist, feeding him from the meager stock she could assemble from begging and urging him to get on with his life—which included fulfilling his paternal responsibilities to eight children.

Almost immediately after arriving in Vellahn, Willi contacted Dr. Herbert to let him know he intended to have no more contact with the SED. He asked if he could file suit against the party for false imprisonment. Dr. Herbert's reply was both demoralizing and ominous. He said he was himself serving only temporarily at the pleasure of the Russian occupation forces because they needed people who spoke German in judgeships. He was certain he would not be in his position much longer. He suspected that as soon as the Soviets had competent judges who shared the Communist philosophy, his Russian bosses would turn on him and use his past as an officer in the *Wehrmacht* to discredit him and remove him from the bench.

When Waldemer Verner learned that Dr. Herbert had arranged for Willi to be released, he was furious. But others were ready to have Willi return to some position in which his administrative talents could be of use. So the SED sent word to him that if he would publicly confess his wrongs, he would be forgiven and reinstated in government service. But this time Willi had had enough of this gang. He told the delegation that he thought the whole party was a bunch of swine, and that one would have to be incredibly stupid not to see through the whole sham the SED was practicing on the population.

Unfortunately, having rejected any chance of being rehabilitated by the Communist Party, Willi Schmidt faced quite a dilemma. As a convicted criminal, his options for work were limited. He could, of course, return to some form of government work simply by admitting his guilt. If he stuck to his claim of innocence, however, there would not be many opportunities for employment. He simply did not think like his comrades in the East German government. Yet he was determined to find some way to support his family. Being naturally resourceful, he discovered that he might be able to use his skills to set up a kind of "cottage industry" using castoff straw to make floor mats, sandals, purses, shoes, and other useful household items. With the blessing of a neighbor across the street, he set up his shop in an outbuilding behind the man's home.

His most sought-after product was the new type of shoe he assembled. During the last years of the war, and for some time afterwards, many Germans had been forced to make do with wooden clogs. Often these were not sized properly; people were forced to buy shoes larger than their feet, and stuff cotton or paper into the toe to keep the shoes from sliding. Willi scrounged among trash heaps and garages to find old inner tubes, which he cut into strips and attached to three pieces of board cut into the shape of soles, producing a shoe that was considerably more flexible than most being manufactured at the time. He used old belts and other discarded leather to fashion the top straps.

Willi's design allowed him to make several different sizes easily, and to customize the designs—even at one point making "wedge" shoes for women to use when they wanted to dress up. At times he would cover the tops with scraps of felt or leather from old hats and gloves. While primitive, these shoes were a notable improvement over the old, one-size-fits-all clogs, and he was soon receiving special orders. Since there were no factories manufacturing such goods, Willi began making other items as well.

The family helped out also. Hertha worked at the shop when Willi needed her. When he was home from school, Rolf tended the kitchen and helped watch the children. Eventually other villagers joined Willi in the shop. Of course, this was not a "business" in the sense that Westerners understand the term. Under the Communist regime, no form of capitalism could exist. People were allowed to work in order to produce what they and others needed. The concept of "profit" was strictly banned. Willi was more like a manager than an owner. People who came to work there did so in order to share in the meager earnings the sale of goods provided, and to be able to take home some of the shoes and mats for themselves and their families.

While Willi and Hertha worked, several of the Schmidt children attended the small school just down the block across Wittenburgerstrasse. Joe and Barb were too young for school, of course, so Hertha had to leave them with Rolf or Lori while she was across the street helping him in the shop. Normally that arrangement worked out reasonably well, but the family got a real scare when Barb decided to wander across the street to the farmer's yard.

The farmer kept a large German Shepherd as a guard dog for his property. All of the other Schmidt children knew enough to steer clear of the animal, but Barb, oblivious to the danger, crawled into the German Shepherd's dog house! Fortunately, the dog did not harm her—but none of the older children could get close enough to get her out! The exasperated farmer finally saved the day by rescuing her and returning her to her distraught mother.

While Willi and Hertha Schmidt suffered in Vellahn, Willi's parents continued to live in relative comfort in the West. Apparently both Willi and Hertha thought it would be to their advantage to remain in contact with the elder Schmidts, so sometime after Willi returned to the family, they decided to let Rolf make a trip to his grandparents' home in the west. His experiences there provided yet another example of the self-absorption and self-centeredness all of the Schmidt children saw in their paternal grandmother. Rolf left for his grandparents' in a homemade new gray suit made of moleskin, a cotton fabric that looks like suede. Carefully he slipped across the border and made his way to the North Sea village of Horumersiel.

Rolf had planned to stay with his grandparents for two weeks, but he soon found Wilhelm and Paula Schmidt were not interested in feting their grandson—only in exploiting him. His Oma Paula greeted him by saying: "Glad you came! Tomorrow, you can help dig the garden!" He was given a place to sleep on the veranda, not in the house. The next day he began the back-breaking task, one made more difficult by the condition of the North Sea soil, which was marshy and mucky, thick and heavy —not sandy, as one might have expected. Turning it was such a bear! Worse, Rolf had to fertilize the soil as he went along. The fertilizing process was sickening, largely because he had to retrieve and prepare the fertilizer himself—from the human ex-crement that had collected in an open bucket beneath the make-shift outhouse affixed to the side of his grandparents' home.

Rolf initially thought he would work on this for a couple of hours, but he came to realize that his grandmother expected him to turn over the entire garden. His surprise and dismay at having to work on this project for days was reinforced by Oma Paula's seemingly highhanded behavior in a number of other ways as well. At breakfast one morning, she prepared five eggs. Great, Rolf thought! At least he'll eat well. He was sorely mis-taken. He got one egg, and grandfather got one; Oma Paula got two, and then set one aside for the next day. She did the same with cake: She served Rolf one very thin slice of a very nice cake, then quickly put away the remainder for future days.

Her selfishness seemed to know no bounds. Shortly after he arrived, Rolf found *The Bible of the Gardener*, a book in which var-ious garden tasks were described on individual pages: how to plant beans, how to tend soil, how to distinguish among various crops. Rolf knew that, living where they did, his grandparents could not grow most of the plants and foodstuffs described in the book, so he asked if he could take *The Bible of the Gardener* home with him.

"No," Omi Schmidt said sternly. Disappointed, he be-gan copying the book.

Shortly thereafter, his grandmother came in and asked: "Are you done?"

Assuming she was talking about his efforts to transcribe the book, he told her No, he had more to copy.

"No, no!" she thundered, "Are you done outside?" She wanted him back out working the garden! He ended up copying only a few pages.

Even these displays of selfishness could not match the final humiliation Oma Paula inflicted on her grandson before he left. Rolf had noticed that his grandparents stored apples in their basement. He was quite surprised when Oma Paula told him he could go into the basement to get one. Downstairs, he found hundreds of apples. But Rolf saw a particularly nice one on a shelf, still fresh from recent picking; excitedly he began eating it. He was not yet finished when his grandmother saw him and screamed, "You didn't take that one!"

She had wanted him to take one of the older ones that had lain in storage for months, and were almost ready to spoil. When he left to return to Vellahn, Oma Paula begrudgingly gave him some older apples to carry in his rucksack. He headed back home after only a week. In retrospect, perhaps, his grandparents' treatment of him was an omen of things to come for all of Hertha Schmidt's children. This was the way many West Germans dealt with refugees from the East.

The journey back to Vellahn proved to be yet another harrowing experience, not only for Rolf but also for his parents. The trip started routinely. Rolf left Horumersiel and took a bus to the train station. He made his way by rail southeastward to the last station in the West. But the train could not cross into the Soviet zone, so all passengers were required to disembark—even though the tracks still ran toward the east. Temporarily stranded, Rolf came up with a plan that made good sense. There seemed no need to sneak back home, since he was entering rather than leaving the Soviet zone, so he marched down the abandoned train track toward Boizenburg. As he approached the border, a contingent of Russian and East German soldiers and police rushed at him.

"What are you doing here!" a guard demanded.

"Coming home," Rolf explained.

"Home! Where do you live?" one of the guards shouted back. Rolf told them.

They were incredulous. "You went out! How did you get out! Did you have a permit?"

Rolf played dumb. At that time everyone was leaving, and the guards were alerted to stop illegal crossings from east to west. They did not seem too sure about procedures for dealing with someone coming into their Zone! To win over the guards, Rolf said he liked it in East Germany and was simply trying to get back to his family.

Rolf was taken to the police station and placed in a holding cell with about thirty people—all of whom had been arrested for trying to escape to the West. Fortunately, he did not have to spend the night in jail. Within a few hours, his father showed up. Someone must have notified Willi in Vellahn. He was mad at Rolf, because, as he explained to his son, this incident could get him into more trouble with the authorities. He knew both he and Rolf could be incarcerated—or shot.

After Willi got a stern lecture from the authorities, he was permitted to take Rolf home. No doubt Hertha had been frantic the entire time, not knowing what might happen when Willi arrived to rescue his son. There was always the chance neither would return. After all, Willi was certainly still on the government's "watch list," even though he was not engaged in subversive activities. Nothing happened immediately, however, but the incident certainly didn't help Willi's standing with the German government or the Soviets.

Since his release from prison, Willi had been keeping a very low profile, trying hard to blend into his community. He and Rolf joined the local choir in Vellahn, which performed regularly at the community center and at the massive Lutheran Church in the center of the village.

Life at home was not always pleasant, however; in fact, Willi's return from prison brought back some of the marital tensions that had existed before his arrest and confinement. Though Willi and Hertha tried to keep their squabbles private, there were times when the children overheard them arguing. The older ones were particularly disturbed by these quarrels, as they had come to respect their mother for her heroic actions to hold the family together during their father's absence.

Eventually the situation became unbearable for Rolf. Late one evening in the early spring of 1949, he overheard raised voices coming from his parents' bedroom. Unable to lie in bed quietly and ignore the noise, he jumped out of bed and burst in on them. In an angry rage, he verbally assaulted his father, yelling at him to stop haranguing his mother.

To his surprise, Hertha snapped at him to calm down. Taking her husband's side, she directed a hostile tirade at their eldest son, demanding that he return to his room immediately. Stunned, the sixteen-year-old did as he was told. But he was perplexed. How could his mother defend that man, Rolf wondered, after all he'd done? He was as yet too young to understand fully the lessons Hertha provided by her courageous actions in attempting repeatedly to have Willi freed from jail.

Sometimes Willi would explode at his children as well. Even though his craft shop was modestly successful, he could not really provide for his family. There was money coming in, but it was virtually impossible to buy enough food in the empty markets. The children were still required to scrounge in the woods and beg their neighbors for staples needed to keep the family alive. Willi and Hertha had bartered away many items of clothing—even Willi's long underwear had been exchanged for a week's food. This must have been especially galling to Willi, who was doing what he could to stay out of trouble and fulfill his responsibilities as a father and provider.

One evening, when Willi was kneading some ground meat the family had managed to obtain (a rare occurrence, indeed!), he turned to Wolfgang and directed him to ask the neighbors for some food to go along with the meat dish. Wolf did not especially relish the idea of begging, so he suggested to his father that Willi send Einhard instead. The next thing Wolf knew, he was on the floor, his face bloodied by the back of Willi's hand. No child was going to be allowed to talk back to Willi Schmidt!

Whatever good fortune Willi and his family realized from his shop was certainly short-lived. Once the enterprise became successful, the authorities—possibly at Verner's prompting—stepped in to take control away from him. Technically, private ownership was all but forbidden in the Soviet zone of Germany. Under Communist doctrine, the workers were supposed to control the workplace. Representatives from the labor ministry insisted that Willi's workers be allowed to organize.

Willi was not in favor of this, because it meant dealing with the union, another agency of the government. Far from being a vehicle for improving the worker's lives, the unions were little more than enforcement agents for the Soviets who were systematically exploiting the German populace as a means of extracting reparations for the war. There had been instances of union leaders demanding that workers at a local plant work on Sunday—without pay—so the proceeds from that day's labor could be directed to "our great liberators, the Russians!"

Wolf heard his father tell a group of workers it was simply unfair to ask people to work under such conditions. That attitude may have endeared him to his employees, but it did little to improve his standing with local political leaders.

Eventually Willi was told his workers had the right to elect a manager. Begrudgingly he indicated his willingness to allow the election to take place. Ironically, the workers asked Willi to stay on in that role! But by that time he was fed up with the Communist way of doing things. He refused to become a leader—again—in a system that had already sent him to prison on trumped up charges simply because a powerful individual wanted to avenge a private grievance.

Arrest and Escape
(1949)

❧

*I*n the early hours of the morning on Sunday, April 10, 1949, Willi Schmidt was taken from his family for the second and final time. Four men came to the Schmidts' home in Vellahn. Willi and Hertha were asleep in the front room of the apartment, so the men did not have to knock loudly to arouse them. When the Schmidts answered the door, the men burst in and one of them, with his gun drawn, told Willi he was under arrest. The others began rifling through family papers, photographs, and memorabilia, tossing them into boxes that they took out to their vehicle.

The technique was a common one. The Communists knew if they gathered up enough materials, they could find something to use against their suspect. An innocent document, or family photograph, such as one of Rolf at a Hitler Youth meeting, would be enough to get a conviction in a sham trial where the verdict had been predetermined. Besides, by taking away all the family's documents, the Communists would deprive relatives of a chance to mount a defense or clear the defendant's name at a later date.

Willi was allowed to pack a small suitcase with some personal belongings. Apparently he made no protest—he may have sensed that doing so would only infuriate his captors and make life harder for him and his family once he was hauled away.

Hertha may have begun to complain vocally, because both Lori and Rolf were awakened by noises from their parents' room. But their mother quickly became silent, realizing her life, and her children's lives, could be endangered if she spoke out at this moment. Rolf started to enter the room where the men were holding his father at gunpoint. Both his father and mother motioned him back toward his bedroom and told him to keep quiet. Ominously, one of the men who had come for his father waved a gun at Rolf and growled angrily that he should leave.

Lori remembers seeing a light coming through the bottom of the French doors that separated the living room from the bedroom where she was sleeping. Rising quietly, she tiptoed to the doors and opened them slightly. When her father turned toward her, one of the men slapped him with a pistol. She shrunk back into the darkness and watched through the crack between the doors as the men finished packing her family's papers, noting that two small photographs had fallen unnoticed beside the couch. Later, when the officials were gone, she retrieved these snapshots.

In a few minutes, the men completed their search through the Schmidts' personal effects. Willi Schmidt was taken out of the apartment. No one in his family would ever see him again. He was rumored to have been taken first to Schwerin, then to Neubrandenburg, a former Nazi concentration camp some 200 kilometers east of Vellahn that, like Bautzen, had been reopened by the Russians. Later the family heard Willi may have been taken to Moscow. A number of East German citizens were sent there for further interrogation; most did not return.

The morning after Willi was hauled away, Hertha went to see the authorities in Hagenow. The Soviet officials feigned outrage. What made her think they had anything to do with Willi's disappearance. They certainly had no idea where Willi Schmidt had gone; perhaps he had simply abandoned his family! To claim Russian soldiers had taken him away in the middle of the night was a smear on the Red Army. She had better watch what she was saying!

Demoralized, Hertha went home. Before too long, however, the local police chief asked her to come see him. The man had been a family friend for several years, and may well have worked with Willi when Willi was the head of the district's administrative police. Hertha pleaded with him to help her locate Willi and intercede with the authorities to have him released.

The police official looked at her sadly and said, "I would have to say that you imagined all this; I would have to deny that it happened."

The chief told Hertha that, if asked, officials would simply repeat their story that Willi had disappeared of his own volition; they would insist he probably absconded to the West. Further, he confided to Hertha that he had seen the documents that would be used to arrest her again and have her children placed in orphanages. This time there would be no Dr. Herbert to whom she could appeal, no sympathetic Russian interrogators who would understand that Hertha was no threat.

"My best advice to you," the police chief told her, "is to disappear yourself."

Hertha returned to her family with a new determination: She would save her children at all costs. First, she briefed the ones who were old enough to understand the situation that they must never tell anyone what had happened to their father. Taking Rolf further into her confidence, she explained the severity of the family's situation and discussed their options, which looked decidedly bleak. Hertha had recently become convinced the Communists would be in their region for a long time to come. She had heard earlier the rumors that had been circulating of attempts to mount protests in Berlin and elsewhere in the Soviet-controlled area of Germany. Sadly, the same sources who reported on these efforts to challenge the Soviets also delivered the sobering news that all these uprisings had been squashed, and the protestors arrested or killed.

Rolf, now sixteen and feeling the responsibility of the "head of household," knew he had to help his mother care for the family. They agreed the only way to be certain the family would be free of future threats from the new German government or their Soviet masters was to leave East Germany. But they could not expect to gain official permission to emigrate. The two of them would have to arrange for the family to escape to the West.

Hertha and her eldest son developed a plan to get out of the Soviet zone. They both knew that any border crossing would be risky. Although Rolf had been back and forth between East and West, he did not recommend the kind of crossing he had made. As a single teenager, he had not found it hard to slip through the forests west of Hagenow and across the lightly-guarded border by avoiding the towers placed along its perimeter. But he did not think a family of nine could make the same trip undetected.

By 1949, all the roads heading to the west had been barricaded. A swath of land several hundred yards wide had been cleared of all vegetation, and mines planted indiscriminately throughout this "no man's land." Signs had been placed in the fields adjacent to the border, and on all roads leading to the West, warning: "NO ACCESS: Unauthorized Persons Not Allowed to Enter or Drive Through." Guard towers had been placed at 200-foot intervals along the border; armed men and dogs made sure that no one could escape this "worker's paradise" by slipping unobtrusively into the West. Clearly, the Schmidts needed another route.

Hertha had heard that, although the Russians held a stranglehold over the citizens in the soon-to-be-designated State of East Germany, it was still possible for people to travel between sectors in Berlin. The city was still a single political entity, administered jointly by the four Allied Powers. Of course, the

Russians had set up checkpoints at all roads leading into the sectors controlled by the Americans and British, but the public transportation system still ran through each sector! True, the Russians had guards at the last stops in their sector, and they continued to inspect the trains and trams. Nevertheless, people with valid identification papers—even East German papers—were allowed to pass back and forth with greater ease than in any other place in the country.

Although no time may be good for an escape such as the one Hertha and Rolf planned for the family, the Schmidts were actually fortunate they chose to get out of East Germany when they did. In 1949, the Soviet occupiers were in the final stages of turning over all operations in East Germany to their German surrogates. As a consequence, several administrative procedures were in flux, among them the responsibility for guarding the borders and supervising various checkpoints being used to cross from the Russian sector into those controlled by other nations. Hence, during the summer of 1949, those brave enough to try had a better chance of being able to leave Soviet and East German domination forever and find freedom in the West.

Later, as the exodus of citizens from the Soviet zone increased from a steady stream to a flood, the new East German government took increasingly harsher steps to keep the workers inside paradise. Barriers along the border between East Germany and her neighbors were strengthened, and guards were given authority to shoot those trying to escape. Eventually the authorities erected a massive wall across the city of Berlin—a symbol, in retrospect, of the Communists' inability to keep people in East Germany from escaping to a life which they believed would be better, and knew could not be worse.

Hertha and her eldest son decided the best way to freedom was through Berlin. Getting *to* the divided capitol was no simple task, however. Travel for those living anywhere in Russian-occupied regions of Germany was restricted, and there would be a good chance that once the family was aboard a train or bus, a Soviet or East German policeman would ask for identification and travel documents.

Wolf believes Hertha arranged with her friend, the local police chief, to obtain authorization to move to her parents' farm in Flecken Zechlin, traveling by way of the Soviet sector of Berlin to attend her sister's wedding. The story made exceptionally good cover for leaving Vellahn, since everyone would assume she wanted to be close to the Dittmanns, who could help her raise the children. The official authorization would stand her in good stead if she were stopped anywhere in the region.

The pass to visit Berlin was a further bit of subterfuge, too; one of Hertha's sisters was in Soviet-controlled Berlin, but there was no wedding to attend. Nevertheless, armed with these precious documents, she embarked on the dangerous journey.

Hertha knew that while a family of nine traveling together from Vellahn to Soviet-occupied Berlin might not be challenged, there would be little chance of such a large group getting into the Allied sector unnoticed. Consequently, she decided to make the crossing in two trips. She and Rolf would take the four oldest children first. Once these four were safely in Allied custody, Hertha and Rolf would return for the little ones.

The plan was fraught with danger and difficulty, of course, not the least of which was that some of the smaller children, especially Barbara, who was not yet four, might not understand what was going on and might do or say something inadvertently that would tip off authorities to their plan. If the family were taken into custody and their plans exposed, Hertha was certain she and Rolf would be arrested and perhaps even executed, while the younger children would be dispersed to foster homes. Nevertheless, she decided to risk the crossing.

She took someone into her trust—probably Gertrude, the refugee girl who had been living with them as a kind of domestic—enlisting her to watch the youngest members of the family while she and Rolf set into motion the first part of their plan.

Even getting out of Vellahn required some subterfuge, as the nine of them were not leaving together. Hertha went to one of the villagers in town—probably the same one whose trucks took pickers into the woods for berries and mushrooms—and made a deal. If he would cart her family to a railroad depot where they could board a train for Berlin, she would allow him to take away all the family's furniture for himself. Publicly he would say he was storing it for the family while they were establishing themselves in Flecken Zechlin, preventing looters from stealing it. Privately, of course, he knew they were never returning, and the beds and couches were his to keep. To further disguise their real intentions, the Schmidts took very little with them—only some small suitcases packed with items one might use for a visit to relatives.

No one in the family remembers the date in the summer of 1949 when the Schmidts began their odyssey from Vellahn to Berlin. Their departure may have been precipitated by Hertha's being taken into custody once again and questioned about her own loyalties. Lori remembers that, just before the family began its flight, her mother came home distraught and related to her the story of having "escaped" once again.

Apparently the authorities were still not sure what to do with her, but they solved their dilemma by agreeing tacitly to letting her slip away when no one was supposedly looking. She was questioned on the ground floor of a large building, possibly in Hagenow since there were no such facilities in Vellahn. As the noon hour approached, one of her interrogators left her and ascended to the landing above. The second waited for his comrade to reach the landing, then, speaking in a subdued voice so as not to call attention to himself or Hertha, said to her: "My colleague is going to call me to come upstairs for a moment. When I leave to join him, you head on out the door."

The plan went as arranged, and when the two men began conversing on the landing above her, Hertha said she exited
the front door of the building and headed back to Vellahn, certain now that she had to leave immediately.

What is certain is that one evening several weeks after
Willi was taken away Hertha bundled up the first group of her
travelers and loaded them into the back of her neighbor's wagon, tucking them into the straw that filled his truck bed. The
old wood-chip-fired stove that powered the truck worked well
enough to get them down to the railway station at Brahlstorf,
where they boarded a train that took them to the outskirts of
Berlin.

Lori remembered that they disembarked in the suburb
of Oranienburg, where the family picked up transportation into
the center of town. This leg of the journey, as nerve-racking as it
might have been, was not nearly as dangerous as the next step:
the trip from the Soviet sector into a part of the city controlled
by the Americans or the British.

It was late in the evening as they emerged onto the streets
of Berlin. They had seen the results of the war in Mirow and
Hagenow, but they were hardly prepared for the kind of devastation that greeted them when they reached the capital. Though
the war had been over for four years, huge piles of rubble were
everywhere, still blocking some streets and making foot and auto
traffic difficult. They would learn later that many citizens were
employed full-time to chip mortar off the bricks and stones,
which were being used to construct a new city on the foundations of the one destroyed by Allied bombing.

Once in Berlin, the Schmidts were exceptionally careful
not to draw attention to themselves. Rolf, Lori, Wolfgang, Einhard, and Bill dispersed on the platform where they waited for
the subway, trying to look nonchalant. Hertha decided to try to
cross during rush hour. Dozens of Berliners on their way to work
crowded around them as they waited for a tram. Once aboard,

they did not sit as a group. When the tram pulled to a stop at the last station in the Soviet sector, they remained aboard, hoping to be ignored by the inspectors. Fortunately for them, no one paid much attention. The tram started up again, picking up speed, crossing the imaginary demarcation line into the American sector, carrying them to freedom.

Wolfgang recalled that, as soon as they alit from the tram, Hertha marched into the first police station she spotted, herding her children in front of her.

"Here we are," she announced to the officer on duty. "We're refugees! We're tired, we haven't eaten, and we have no place to stay."

Confusion reigned! Some officers tried to explain that they could not help the Schmidts. One took Hertha off to speak with her alone.

"You can't stay here," the officer told her. "This is not how things are done! You have no papers. We will have to arrest you!"

"Fine!" she shot back with what would become a familiar refrain for her. "Arrest me—and then you can take care of these children!"

Meanwhile, other policemen had taken the Schmidt children off to find them some sandwiches, dipping into the station's petty cash fund to procure the food. After the initial turmoil subsided, Hertha learned if she wanted to stay in Berlin she would have to present herself and her family at one of the refugee processing stations in the city. She was told to go to the nearest center and formally request asylum.

Armed now with some knowledge of the process she must follow, Hertha reassembled her family outside the police station and headed off to look for the refugee processing station. Rolf remembers the family wandering along the streets in the city asking directions. Berliners, accustomed to seeing refugees in their part of the metropolis, were cooperative and sympathetic.

When the Schmidts reached the building where those seeking asylum were to be processed, they joined a long line of people there for the same purpose. Some of the siblings remember the Americans were a bit reticent to deal with the large family, but Hertha knew if she pushed her children forward, no one would deny them what they needed.

Once the Schmidts reached the front of the line, they were asked for vital statistics and for some cursory information regarding their previous residence. There was little interrogation to determine why they wanted to remain in the West. Apparently by 1949 the Americans and British were well aware of the hardships being suffered by citizens in the Soviet zone, and they were more than willing to help those Germans who desired to escape and start a new life.

The group was taken to a refugee shelter not far from the processing station. It was an old above-ground air-raid bunker which had been heavily reinforced with concrete by the German military to avoid destruction during the bombing raids on the city. This large circular structure had been divided into a number of rooms, shaped like pie wedges, all facing an open, circular space in the center of the facility. This center section was divided into office space, an area used for dining, and a place where people could get out of their rooms to relax or socialize with other refugees.

The Schmidts were assigned to a single room. Inside were several bunks placed against the back and side walls, but not much else. Sometime during that first day, they were all de-loused with DDT sprayed over them from hand-held pump sprayers. Then they were allowed to use a large shower room elsewhere in the facility. Unfortunately, the family was given only one towel, so by the time the last person got to shower, the towel was of little use for drying off.

That evening, the family ate a meal of American rations prepared communally and served to refugees in whatever plates or containers they may have had. There was cabbage soup and rice pudding with raisins, flavored with cinnamon (too much cinnamon, some of the children thought).

The Schmidts were given a few utensils and a bucket, which they filled and passed back and forth, each child taking a few spoons of food before handing it to the next family member. Despite the inconvenience, they thought the meal was heavenly. Perhaps they were relishing the idea that they could get as much as they wanted. Perhaps, subconsciously, they were simply enjoying the taste of freedom.

Although no one ever told Hertha directly, when the Schmidts were going through the processing center, the authorities implied that, because the family was seeking asylum, they could not return to the Soviet sector for any reason. By 1949 the Allies had come to fear the Soviets might be sending spies across the border to collect information on military and economic conditions in Berlin and the West. Of course, as soon as she had her older children safely bedded down in the refugee camp, Hertha began plotting with Rolf to return to Vellahn to gather up the remainder of the family.

After spending the evening with the older children in the shelter, she and Rolf set off the next day to the subway station in Berlin. They had made sandwiches to eat on the trip back to Vellahn, packing them in the small suitcases they had brought across the border the day before and were now taking back to retrieve the younger children's clothing. Unfortunately, as part of the processing routine a talcum-like powder—probably moth power, but possibly DDT—had gotten into the suitcases. The flimsy wrappings on the sandwiches came apart during the trip back through Berlin, and when Hertha and Rolf went to eat their meal they found the sandwiches covered with this powder. Nevertheless, they decided they would simply take their chances with illness in order to stave off hunger, so both mother and son dusted off the powder as best they could and ate their sandwiches cautiously.

Retracing their steps, Hertha and Rolf slipped back into the Soviet sector (there were fewer problems going east in those days), took a train to the station nearest Vellahn, and made their way back to the village for a reunion with those children who had remained behind. They spent only a night there, however, before leading this second contingent on the same journey they had made only two days before with the older children.

Knowing what to expect, Hertha and Rolf were more confident as they went through each "checkpoint" along the way. The only complication they faced occurred when they were waiting on the platform for the train to arrive. Mike got separated from the group and was lost for some time. In later years, Mike would recall that, at just seven years old, he seemed to be abandoned amid a sea of large strangers who paid him no attention as he looked about vainly for his mother and older brother. Fortunately, Rolf was able to find him and re-unite him with the party.

Once inside the American sector again, Hertha was immensely proud of her daring escape. Her family was free of the Soviet and East German terror! She had managed to elude the authorities who had taken away her husband and made her life a living hell. Proudly she marched back into the refugee center with the remainder of her brood, assuming she would be congratulated on her heroic accomplishments. Instead of receiving accolades, however, she was immediately challenged by an incredulous official at the center.

"What do you mean, you went back?" he asked her. "You were not *supposed* to go back!"

The fact that she had risked her life in evading the East Germans' security measures to rescue the remainder of her family did not seem to impress him.

Perhaps the Americans were a bit embarrassed that this woman had managed to breach *their* security system as well, traipsing back and forth at will across the border between the sectors. Perhaps they really were concerned that she had ulterior motives for her activity. At any rate, Hertha Schmidt, the woman who had risked her life to liberate her eight children from a Communist regime, was detained for questioning as a spy.

Fortunately, the official who interviewed her sympathized with her plight. Instead of returning her to the Soviet sector, he doctored the paperwork to make it look as if the second trip never happened. She slipped away quietly from the processing station to the refugee center, where the older siblings rejoiced to see their mother and the rest of the family. Now—finally—Hertha Schmidt and her children were together, safe, in the West.

After a week in the converted air-raid shelter, the Schmidts were transferred to another refugee center in what had once been German barracks in the Wannsee section of the city. In their new temporary quarters, the family was assigned space on the ground floor of a two-story building which contained individual bunks and a stove.

The Schmidts were given two rooms; each child had a bed. There was light streaming through the windows; there were fields outside where the children could play. There was a central kitchen which prepared meals for the refugees; during the day one could smell the food cooking. The Schmidts could eat in the common dining hall or take their meals back to their rooms. After four years of near starvation, they thought they were in heaven. Everyone gained weight during the next several months.

The younger Schmidts were enrolled in schools and summer camps, where they were given meals and allowed to play with other refugee children in a supervised environment. Hertha allowed them to go down to Lake Wannsee as well. At the lake beautiful public beaches were available for those who had the money to pay. Tall fences had been erected to keep out undesirables, but the Schmidt clan did not let that deter them. They managed to overcome this obstacle—literally—and join the swimmers and sunbathers who were enjoying the Berlin summer by the lakeside.

When they were not in camp or at the lake, the children roamed about looking for military convoys to see if they could convince the soldiers to part with some of the chewing gum and sweets that many of the GIs carried. For the first time in a long time, life seemed good.

Not all of their adventures were simple and carefree, however. Sometime during the summer of 1949, Hertha met a Red Cross worker whom she thought could obtain some clothing and other supplies for her family. So she sent Rolf into downtown Berlin to meet with the man at his apartment. When he arrived, he immediately became uncomfortable at what he saw around him. At sixteen Rolf was comparatively naïve. He could see there was a party in progress. The women appeared to be prostitutes and some of the men "weirdos," but Rolf was unprepared for what he saw next. . . . Men paired off with other men, and women with other women. In fact, he even saw two women kissing!

The host approached Rolf and made an attempt to befriend him, but Rolf blurted out that he had to leave to catch the last bus to get back to his family. Someone made an offer to drive him, but when Rolf explained that he lived in the refugee camp out near Potsdam, the offer was withdrawn. Happily, Rolf slipped away and headed to the bus stop.

Hertha knew Berlin would not be the last stop for her family. Her ultimate goal was to have them all transported to the western part of the divided country. While her children were playing at the refugee center or strolling around Berlin, she was off dealing with refugee administrators, seeking asylum for herself and her family and petitioning to be taken out of the capital to the west.

The British, French, and Americans, had set up a careful screening process to make certain those they took out of Berlin were not spies sent over by the Russians or their puppet government to infiltrate sections of Germany under Allied control. Each applicant for reassignment had to appear in a special court to plead his or her case.

One condition for leaving Berlin was that the individual or family had to demonstrate that they could provide for themselves once they were relocated. In this way the Allies felt they could stem what could be a flood of refugees sent over by the Soviets to burden the fledgling independent German government being established in the West.

Hertha Schmidt knew she would have trouble passing that test. She had brought no money out of East Germany. She was living in a refugee camp with eight children, and while the older ones might be able to get jobs in the West once they finished their education, she was going to be tied down at home for several more years with her younger ones. Nevertheless, she informed the Court she was perfectly willing to work now *and* in West Germany—if someone would give her a job.

Fortunately for her, the story she told of her family's plight and its harrowing departure from Vellahn touched a special group of spectators in Court. It had become customary for off-duty soldiers to attend some of these hearings, probably because it gave them a way to fill the hours that weighed heavy on them when they were not working. When the soldiers heard the Schmidt family's story, they began passing a hat to collect "relief funds" for Hertha. Before long, they'd filled the hat, and one of the GIs presented the money to her. At least she would have a small nest egg when the family arrived in the West!

Of course, leaving Berlin was not that easy in the summer of 1949. At that time, the only safe way out was by air. Since June 1948, the Soviets had been maintaining a blockade to prevent foodstuffs and other materiel from reaching Berlin by land, hoping to drive the Allies out of the German capital. In this way the Soviets planned to take over Berlin, their next step in reuniting the entire country as a Communist state. But the Allies would not give in easily to this bullying.

Under the leadership of General Lucius Clay, military governor in the American Zone in Germany, the Allies mounted a massive airlift to bring in foodstuffs and material Berliners needed to survive. For more than a year, flights streamed into the American-controlled airfield at Tempelhof and the British field at Gatow; every ninety seconds an aircraft touched down or took off. Once the supplies were unloaded, the planes were made available to refugee administrators to evacuate those wishing to leave the city.

Wolfgang, Einhard, Bill, and even Mike, who was not yet eight, were fascinated by the constant stream of aircraft droning overhead day and night, swooping into the airfields. Both Wolf and Einhard recall visiting Tempelhof and standing outside the fence atop rubble from the Allied bombing, watching the gray line of planes in the sky slowly glide toward the runways, touch down, roll off, unload, and then rush back into the air, gracefully turning westward where they would be reloaded with the precious materials that were keeping Berlin from falling into the hands of the rapacious Soviet military.

Both American and British military forces established an orderly system of departure to evacuate refugees crowding a city whose permanent citizens were already suffering from the Soviets' blockade. The supply runs had continued even after the Soviets had called off their blockade in May 1949, so administrators were able to organize outbound transportation for refugees from Berlin to the West on planes leaving Tempelhof or Gatow. As a result, when it was time for the Schmidts to leave, they were given places on one of these flights. Actually the Schmidts were among the last to leave Berlin this way; the Allies ceased operating these flights in October 1949 and resumed overland transportation of supplies along the one highway corridor designated for their use.

In early September, Hertha Schmidt was notified that her family was to report to Gatow airport for their flight to the West. Excitedly, the family began packing their meager possessions for the trip. Wölfi was at a summer camp, so Rolf went to find him and bring him home. Jubilantly, he raced away with his elder brother. The family boarded a bus at the refugee camp and traveled the short distance to Gatow airfield, where they waited until directed to climb into the belly of an empty DC-3. There were no seats, only long rows of cots attached to the fuselage where people could sit for the hour-long flight to the west. Mike remembers the plane smelling of fuel. Vestiges of previous cargoes littered the floor—cabbage leaves, coal dust—but no one seemed to mind too much.

They had never flown before, so the children stared in wonder out the small round windows as the plane lifted off and climbed into the clouds above Germany's divided capital. The plane was not pressurized, and the younger children's ears burned with pain as the plane climbed to its cruising altitude. Still, it was another adventure for them! But the older ones realized this was a serious step for the family, and their mother was no doubt teary-eyed as the cargo plane ascended into the sky. Hertha knew that she was leaving for good the life she had known in Flecken Zechlin and Mirow, and the husband who had been taken away from her only a few months earlier.

In an hour the plane touched down in Lübeck, inside the British zone. The Schmidts' life under Communist rule was behind them forever.

Refugees

(1949-1952)

❧

*T*he Schmidts spent their first few hours of freedom in the old German town of Lübeck. The city had a storied history, having been the cornerstone of the Hanseatic League in the Middle Ages. Like Berlin, Lübeck had suffered extensive damage during the war, and it still showed the effects of the devastation caused by aerial bombardment years earlier. None of that mattered to the Schmidts, though. Once they arrived in the West, a great sense of relief began to settle on Hertha and her older children. It affected them both physically and psychologically.

Reflecting on the period, Rolf observed that, "It was as if you had lived through a hurricane, and when it was over you saw that your house was still intact. You can finally breathe a sigh of relief, knowing you've survived."

Until they had reached West Berlin, Hertha and Rolf had been consumed by the idea of "freedom." There had certainly been no freedom—not to live where you wished, nor to travel where you would like to go, nor especially to say what you wanted to say. Instead there had been everywhere the presence of "authority" controlling the schools, the media, the workplace. And that authority had been corrupt, as the Schmidts had witnessed first-hand. By contrast, in the West they were free from the "rules" that governed everyday life under the Communists.

Unfortunately, the picture was not as rosy as Hertha might have wished. The region that would become the new nation of West Germany just five years after their arrival was awash in refugees. Millions had fled there in the final years of the war, and millions more had poured in since 1945 hoping to escape the Communists. As a result, more than nine million people—one-fifth of the population living in West Germany—were *Flüchtlinge*—refugees. Since most had left behind everything they owned, they were dependent on the occupying powers and the new German government for virtually everything: food, housing, education, and employment.

This did not sit well with the citizens of cities and towns in the West. They resented these newcomers whose demand for support was overtaxing the millions still suffering from the ravages of the war. After all, those born in places like Frankfurt or Mannheim or Cologne had seen their cities leveled by Allied bombs. There was already a serious shortage of housing, and these émigrés were only making things worse.

To the lifelong residents of West Germany, it seemed that people from the East were getting preferential treatment in meeting their needs, displacing long-time residents from homes, causing serious overcrowding, and slowing the pace of recovery. No wonder they felt deep animosity toward this brood of interlopers, and as a consequence treated them disdainfully.

The plight of the refugees was aptly summed up by the United States High Commissioner for Refugees in his 1950 Report to Congress. Most of the refugees, he noted, were badly housed in overcrowded dwellings; they were experiencing higher unemployment rates than the general population; they were largely unassimilated into their new communities; and everywhere they suffered serious discrimination. This was certainly not the paradise Hertha may have dreamed about when she smuggled her children out of the Soviet Zone of Occupation.

The Schmidts presented a particularly vexing problem for relief workers and refugee administrators. A mother and eight children, the oldest sixteen and the youngest just four, were a great burden on the system. Beginning in the summer of 1949, the family moved through three relief camps before finally landing in a permanent "home." Frequently they would see other, smaller families come and go, getting resettled in more permanent settings because they were easier to place.

The Schmidts did not stay in Lübeck for very long. The British had set up an efficient system for moving refugees from the airport to reception stations in other parts of the country. Hertha and her children were hustled to a train which took them south to a refugee processing center outside Wipperfürth, a city some 60 kilometers northeast of Cologne—and just 30 kilometers southwest of Wuppertal, where Hertha had first met Willi nearly eighteen years earlier.

In this overcrowded camp that had once been a German *Luftwaffe* barracks, the family shared quarters in a large room with 30-40 other people. Double or triple bunks were assigned to the refugees, who were not expected to remain there long. The refugee administrators were moving families out quickly to commandeered homes and apartments in the region, where they would be housed until permanent quarters could be found. As in Berlin, the family had to scrounge for utensils and serving tools. It did not take the Schmidts long to acquire implements for eating, though, and they fared well enough by resorting to old habits to supplement their rations. The older children went out into the meadows around the camp to pick wild mushrooms or other tasty goodies.

From Wipperfürth, the Schmidt family was packed off to Solingen, a manufacturing town world-renowned for its cutlery and steel products. Large factories produced the raw materials for these products, but most of the finished work was done by highly skills craftsmen working in small shops scattered throughout the city—the epitome of the "cottage industry." During the war the city's foundries had produced materials for the German armed forces, and its railhead had been an important junction

for movements of troops and supplies. Not surprisingly, Solingen had suffered heavily at the hands of Allied bombers.

The family has no records indicating why the Schmidts
were sent to Solingen. Their journey could have easily taken
them to any one of a hundred towns or cities in the western
area of Germany. But once again fortune had smiled on them,
although one might not have thought so if one visited Solingen
in the fall of 1949.

The city was still largely in ruins, its downtown having
been bombed into rubble at the direction of the British air commander who was frustrated at the Germans' stubborn unwilling-
ness to surrender. Many of the factories that had supplied raw
materials for the cutlery industry had been converted to producing war machinery; now these were little more than piles of
brick and mortar. Dirt and dust stirred from the pavements, and
grime was everywhere. And of course, even before the war, the
industries which had made Solingen famous had contributed to
the generally unhealthy conditions, producing smog and poisonous fumes that made life uncomfortable for rich and poor alike.
Housing was scarce, and the citizens of Solingen were not all re-
ceptive to the idea of having refugees relocate among them. That
attitude would manifest itself in the coming years as Hertha and
her children began to establish themselves in the community.

Despite these drawbacks, Solingen offered many advantages. The city was quite cosmopolitan. Many of its citizens
spoke a second language, and years of trade with other countries
had given the residents a much broader perspective on the world
than that held by many of their neighbors—such as those from
Bavaria, for example, who frequently looked upon the people
in the north of Germany as little more than "dumb Prussians."
Living in Solingen not only provided the Schmidt children with
a chance to learn a valuable trade; it also helped them ready
themselves for adapting to other cultural environments, a skill
that would prove exceptionally useful in the coming decade.

Whether Hertha was thrilled at being relocated in Solingen, she did not reveal. But she must have felt it was time for her family to settle somewhere so her younger children could be enrolled in school and her older ones get on with apprenticeships that would lead to gainful employment and eventually self-sufficiency. There was one more stop along the way, however—one that would be imprinted on the memories of all the children and become the site of some of their most memorable adventures.

On September 13, 1949—Einhard's eleventh birthday—the family arrived outside Solingen and were given quarters in Burg Hohenscheid. Sitting atop a hill that gave its occupants a view of the countryside for miles in every direction, the stone structure dated from the Middle Ages. In all probability it was erected as an outpost for Schloss Burg, a major medieval ducal seat several kilometers to the north.

During the later Middle Ages, it may have been used by rogue knights as a refuge from the authorities, a place to store treasure looted from travelers and nearby villages. A single tower stood several stories tall, topped with a flat roof from which the first inhabitants could survey the hillsides sloping away from the fortification. A shorter section, no doubt intended as living quarters, was attached to the tower, and a raised stone walkway extended from the tower entrance for about 15-20 feet, where it ended at a small outbuilding, also constructed of stone, that was originally intended for storage or stabling horses.

In front of the castle was a cobblestone courtyard, in which stood a tall beech tree. On the side of the courtyard opposite the elevated walkway and storage shed was a large farm.

Before the Schmidts and other groups of refugees arrived at Burg Hohenscheid, the current owners of the castle were attempting to restore the place so it could once again be a tourist destination, as it had been before World War II. Part of the renovation plans included the creation of an upscale restaurant. Unfortunately, the owners' intentions were stymied when

The bombed-out city of Solingen as it appeared in 1949, the year the Schmidt family arrived. (photo courtesy of Solinger Stadtarchiv)

Burg Hohenscheid outside Solingen, circa 1950. The Schmidts occupied rooms in the tower for nearly three years.

the new government in West Germany decided to requisition parts of the old castle to use as temporary housing for families waiting to be placed permanently somewhere in and around the city of Solingen.

Because the Schmidt family was so large, they were assigned an entire floor in the tower—not particularly spacious, and not well appointed. There was no indoor plumbing, In fact, water had to be hauled up two flights of stairs into the apartment, so the entire family was careful about using this valuable resource. The children bathed only once a week, often in the same water. By the time the last ones got into the makeshift tub, the water was barely lukewarm and certainly a bit discolored. In the kitchen a wood-burning stove provided the only heat as well as the only source for cooking and boiling water. The Schmidts were allocated a space in the basement to store coal and potatoes. These were minimally adequate accommodations, but as temporary quarters, they were acceptable.

For three years, the Schmidts remained at Burg Hohenscheid, watching as other refugee families were relocated to permanent housing down in the city or in adjacent towns and villages. Their continuing presence deeply chagrined government authorities, who were required to provide for them from public funds. It was also vexing to the owners of the castle, who wanted to proceed with their plans to open a restaurant and guest house; they could not renovate the tower until the Schmidts moved out. But Hertha was insistent that she be given permanent housing adequate to her family's needs.

Hertha's travails in dealing with the West German bureaucracy started within weeks of the family's arrival in Solingen, and they were not limited to battles over housing. Individuals on welfare were entitled to receive from the government a certain amount of coal and potatoes each fall, so they would have heat and minimal subsistence through the winter. At that time shoes were still expensive, and the government was providing welfare recipients one pair of new shoes annually. Once her children were in school, Hertha went to the authorities to obtain vouchers for all three commodities. But she was told the Solingen office did not have the funds to provide her family coal, potatoes, and shoes at the same time; she would have to decide which was the most important.

She wasn't going to do anything of the sort! Her family needed all of these items, as winter was approaching. After several weeks of wrangling that was getting her nowhere, Hertha dressed the entire family and took them with her to the welfare office. Sitting them down in the waiting room, she entered the office of the administrator who managed programs for refugees. Once again, she employed a threat that had worked in the past.

"Okay," she said to the hapless official, sitting on the corner of his desk. "I'm here for my vouchers, and I'm not leaving until I get what I want. If you deny my request, I am walking out of this building *alone*. My children are in the waiting room outside. You will have to take care of them."

"If you walk out," the administrator retorted, "we'll have you arrested for abandonment!"

"Fine!" Hertha shot back. "Then you'll have to feed and clothe me and the children!!"

Needless to say, vouchers were provided to the Schmidts for coal, potatoes, and new shoes.

While their mother may have been frustrated with the conditions at Burg Hohenscheid for so long, the Schmidt children—especially the younger ones—found their stay in the castle a time for building great memories. Although she was younger than Joe, Barb was often the leader in their escapades, displaying a daredevil attitude and a spirit of adventure that must have made Hertha think of herself when she was a child.

When tourists began visiting the castle again, Joe and Barb would sneak out and retrieve gum from the bottom of the bench beside the beech tree in the courtyard. The younger boys would play amid several open arches that appeared enormous to them at the time. However, what was fun for small children could be a cause of heart-wrenching worry for their mother. The two youngest had a habit of racing across the bridge connecting the castle's turret to a storage building. While playing there on one occasion, Barb got in a scuffle with the daughter of another refugee living in the castle, and in the fracas fell on cobblestones below, suffering a serious head injury.

At another time, Barb was playing in the hay inside the barn, jumping recklessly into the large stacks, and managed to hit a stone resting just under the surface, cracking her collar bone. Frequently, she would climb the tall willow trees near the castle, refusing to come down until after dark. Once she decided to take a nap inside the large laundry basket piled full of dirty clothing, causing her mother to launch a frantic search inside and outside the family apartment.

Joe may have been an even greater headache for his mother. He was constantly stealing apples from the orchard managed by Herr Birschel, who owned the farm adjacent to the castle. When he was caught he had to answer for his mischief to his distraught mother, who gave him a good whipping, of course!

On another occasion, Joe broke out all the windows in one of Birschel's outbuildings. To make matters worse, when the farmer appeared on the scene, Joe panicked and climbed the tower to the highest point of the castle. When he heard someone emerging from the doorway below him, he sent down a wattle of spit. Perfect aim! Right on top of the head! But it wasn't the farmer. It was his mother, coming to retrieve and discipline her errant son. It took quite a bit of coaxing from his older brothers to get Joe to climb down to face the music.

The farmer wanted Hertha to pay to have all these windows repaired. Fortunately, Opa Schmidt came for a visit and replaced all the panes, saving the family the cost of labor.

On another occasion, Joe wandered off with a busload of tourists who had come to the castle for lunch and then took off on a leisurely stroll through the woods to a nearby village. When they discovered he was not part of their entourage, Hertha was notified and asked to come retrieve him. Poor Rolf was designated as the "rescue party," and he dutifully trudged over to the village to retrieve his little brother.

For a time the winding road that passed from Solingen through the tiny suburb of Hästen to Burg Hohenscheid doubled as a "scooter path" for the Schmidt brothers. They outfitted a scooter with a "bucket seat" so two of them could careen down the steep hill between the outskirts of Solingen and the Hästen schoolhouse, oblivious to traffic, often veering off into the school yard, using the dirt and sand there in much the same way that truckers in the USA use emergency ramps to slow themselves and prevent runaways on steep mountainsides.

Occasionally, Hertha led her family on long walks to Schloss Burg, traveling down the mountainside from Burg Hohenscheid into the Wupper River valley. Leaf- and needle-covered trails under the canopy of dark evergreens and beeches shaded their walk, as they took visiting friends to see the region's most historic site, the famous *Müngstenerbrücke*. The Bridge at Müngsten, a towering railway trestle, spanned the valley between Solingen and the city of Remscheid on the hills overlooking the eastern bank of the river. Such excursions were no doubt rare, but they were certainly welcome. Hertha was determined her children would enjoy a normal life, doing the things other German children did for fun and education, not held back simply because the family did not have much money.

One by one, as they finished their secondary education, the Schmidts began preparing for careers. There was no chance of any of the Schmidts attending university. There was, of course, no legal prohibition against them doing so. But in the class-bound society that had existed before the war, they were considered "unfit" to be educated at the gymnasium, the second-ary school that prepared people to enter Germany's institutions of higher learning. The unwritten rule was that those born into the lower classes should keep their place; even in democratic post-war West Germany attitudes of privilege ran deep in those born into the upper classes.

It was unthinkable for any of the Schmidts to aspire to becoming a "doctor"—which in turn would limit their ability to rise to the executive levels of any business as long as they remained in their native country. Hertha was insistent, however, that every one of them learn a useful trade, telling them if they could work with their hands, they could always find employment. Having suffered serious deprivations for so long, she did not want her children to spend a lifetime in poverty, dependent on the government for their subsistence.

Not surprisingly, almost every one of them entered trades supporting the manufacture of materials for cutlery and steel implements. The apprenticeship program in Germany was demanding; as many as 8,000 hours, or four years, could be spent learning a highly technical trade, and apprentices earned only a modest stipend while completing their training. Yet as each one entered his or her apprenticeship, the financial burdens on the family began to ease up. Every one of them contributed a portion of their earnings to the common "pot."

As soon as the family arrived in Solingen, Rolf reported to the local agency charged with placing young men in apprenticeships. He had considered asking if he could become a watchmaker or doing some other fine-tool work. But there was no demand for those kinds of jobs, he was told by an overweight clerk who seemed little concerned with Rolf's preferences. Instead, he was placed at a hot-forge across town.

Rolf would leave very early in the morning, walk two kilometers to the first trolley stop in Hästen, ride across the city, then walk another three kilometers to his employer's. Fortunately, he was placed under a skilled and sympathetic master, Alfred Köhler, who taught him the painstaking and exacting process of using machines (many of them very old) properly and safely. He also taught Rolf the art of smithing. Köhler even located a set of tools for his young apprentice, knowing Rolf could not afford to buy them. Later, Köhler would be a strong supporter when Rolf decided to leave Germany for America. He was one of those rare exceptions in the West German populace: He thought it only right to help an aspiring young man to better himself—even if that young man *were* a refugee.

Lori spent an additional term in school in Solingen, repeating the last year of studies she'd already finished while in Vellahn, then began an apprenticeship in the hotel and restaurant industry. At age fourteen, she moved away from the family to take a position at the Hotel Schwerthof in Solingen.

Unfortunately, Lori and seven other young women living in the dormitory learned few of the skills that would make them managers someday. Instead they were little more than ill-paid drudges for the unscrupulous hotel manager. They rose each morning at 4:00 a.m. to begin their work day and were lucky to get to bed before midnight. For these long hours they received little more than pocket money—and threats of reprisal if they informed their families about their working conditions. But someone must have had the courage to say something. Within a few months after Lori arrived, the manager was arrested for his fraudulent activities. Lori went back to her family and eventually landed a job at a factory producing razor blades.

Wolf, Einhard, Bill, Mike, and Joe enrolled in school up the hill from the castle in Hästen. Barb was as yet too young for school, but she accompanied Joe every day along a dark path through the hilly woods where hoot owls sounded eerie calls that could frighten youngsters traveling through the dark forest. Barb would sit outside the school under a tree while Joe was inside, waiting to walk home with him at midday. Unfortunately

Joe, who was small for his age and had suffered from malnutrition for a long time, did not adjust well to the school routine. When it was clear he was not ready for the experience, Hertha withdrew him and waited until the family moved into the city of Solingen to have him start his formal education.

Although the period of near-starvation was over, the Schmidts still had to "make do" with meager supplies and foodstuffs. The family received a very small allocation of coal for heating and cooking, so they supplemented their fuel supply by collecting firewood from the surrounding woodlands. The younger children would travel through the woods on their way home from school to pick up sticks and branches lying on the ground.

The woodland immediately adjacent to the castle was owned by Farmer Birschel whose property abutted Burg Hohenscheid. He did not seem to mind the removal of stray branches and fallen trees. The Schmidts' need for wood was voracious, however, and it did not take long for the ground to be picked clean. That did not stop the enterprising Schmidt brothers; they just took out an axe and "created" some fallen trees and branches. Rolf even resorted to chopping up Birschel's fence posts.

One day Rolf and Wolfgang were out felling a green tree when Birschel spotted them. He rushed into the woods and confiscated their axe. The boys went home and sheepishly reported what had happened to their mother. The next day Hertha went down to see the farmer to retrieve the axe. He said he would be only too happy to return it—if Hertha would promise her boys would not cut down any more live trees. She couldn't, she said. Certainly she would encourage her boys to look for fallen timber whenever they could, but her family needed to cook, and they needed heat, and if felling trees were the only way they could supply themselves, so be it. Reluctantly the farmer handed her the axe, and it was not long before he was designating trees the family could cut for their firewood.

The Schmidts weren't the only ones cutting down trees on other people's land. After the war thousands of people all over Germany were doing the same thing, starting in the harsh winters of 1945-46 and 1946-47. Many of the stately trees that had lined city streets and country roads for years in the East and the West disappeared—gone "up in smoke" literally, as people who had no other materials to generate heat grasped whatever source of fuel they could find to help keep them warm and pre- pare their food. Government allocations of coal and stocks of wood were hardly adequate to keep a large family supplied with even minimal amounts of fuel needed for heating and cooking. Hertha Schmidt was not one to condone theft—but she had to make hard choices when it came to obtaining what the family needed to survive.

Once Rolf began his apprenticeship, he was able to sup- plement the welfare payments Hertha was receiving with his *Un- terstützung*, the monthly stipend of DM 70-75 he received while he was learning his craft. The other children found ways to help out as well. Lori and Wolf spent time picking flowers for sale to fami- lies and local markets. They became so adept they had customers as far away as Wuppertal, which they visited by train periodically.

Einhard and Wolf combined to manage a paper route. Several of the children helped neighbors till their small garden plots, and some of the boys assisted a local grocer who could always use a hand loading and unloading delivery trucks. Since it was customary for people to store large sacks of potatoes, ap- ples, and other staples in their basements during the winter, the Schmidts found there was ready employment for anyone want- ing to take on the backbreaking task of filling 100-pound sacks. They were often paid for their work in fresh vegetables and fruits. When the children received cash for their labor, as they often did for stocking people's basements with soft coal before winter set in, they would use the money to purchase necessary clothing, coal, or food for the family.

The boys and Lori also worked the potato and beet harvests, picking the vegetables and stuffing them into 100-pound sacks. This was hard work, but the good news was that during the two weeks they worked at harvesting, they would receive three hearty meals a day—a rare treat! Their formal "payment" for two weeks' work would be a sack of potatoes or beets, which they valued immensely.

The only vegetable in reasonable quantities year-round was cabbage, so the staple of many a meal at the Schmidts featured sauerkraut or cabbage soup. Along with cabbage, potatoes and beets became the staples of their diet, supplemented by whatever wild greens they could pick. Meat was a luxury. Nevertheless, Hertha appreciated her children's efforts and did her best to turn out interesting and tasty meals with whatever foodstuffs they managed to bring into the household.

During the three years that they lived there, Burg Hohenscheid proved a continuous wonderland. Naturally the family could not afford too many toys, but the boys found old bikes, stripped of chains and brakes. These made excellent "gliders" down the steep hills around the castle, as long as the rider was careful about dodging trees!

The younger boys (and Barbara, no doubt) found a natural playground just over the hill from the castle. The long downhill slope served as a dumping ground for the refugees' garbage. The Schmidts found another use for the slope, however; they would slide down on pieces of cardboard, creating their very own makeshift "roller coaster" ride.

The younger children spent hours exploring the dark forests around their medieval fortress home, scared of the goblins they were sure they would encounter if they strayed too far or stayed out too long. The old spring house was an especially frightful place, for it was reputed to be the home of an evil witch!

Meanwhile, poor farmer Birschel was always getting "dumped on" by the Schmidt boys—and on at least one occasion that proved to be literally true. Because there was no indoor plumbing, one of the most unpleasant but necessary tasks was emptying the chamber pots and buckets that substituted for indoor toilets. On one occasion when Einhard had the dubious distinction of being responsible for this task, he was feeling particularly lazy and did not wish to schlep the bucket all the way down two flights of steps and out to the side of the hill where the family normally disposed of the waste. Instead, he took it down the steps to the end of the elevated walkway leading to the farmer's outbuilding and dumped his bucket onto the top of the shed., assuming it would dry before it was noticed. Unfortunately, the shed roof was porous, and some of the refuse dripped through—right onto the farmer's tractor!

Despite occasional lapses like this, the older Schmidt children knew they had to help their mother manage the family's affairs. They helped to care for the younger ones, changed diapers, babysat, and made sure Mike, Joe, and Barb did not get into too much trouble inside the castle grounds. Sometimes on the weekends, older brother Rolf would gather up the youngest children and take them for walks in the woods outside Solingen—perhaps remembering that his father had done the same thing when he, Lori, and Wolfgang were much younger.

These sojourns must have provided a welcome respite for Hertha, as she could spend a few moments without the little ones under foot. There would be time for visiting with neighbors at the castle, or catching up on housework, or simply resting for a few moments while the apartment was quiet.

Joe remembers one Easter walk proved to be very special. As he and Barb walked along the path behind their elder brother, Rolf surreptitiously dropped candy along the way for them to find and pick up. It was a glorious time for them! Of course, Rolf was simply carrying on a tradition his father had started when he and Lori and Wolf were the same ages as Joe and Barb.

Not all the memories of life in their new home were good ones, however, especially for the two youngest Schmidts. Sometime, while the family was living at Burg Hohenscheid, a young man who worked on the Birschel farm attempted to molest five-year-old Barbara, exposing himself to her and encouraging her to "experiment" with him. Scared, she ran away before anything could happen.

Several years later, Joe was the victim of a similar incident when he was accosted by a young man whose family was friendly with the Schmidts. One day the man separated Joe and Barb, and when he was alone with Joe, began making lewd advances. They told no one in the family, though much later they did confide in one of Lori's friends, Sigi Weinberg.

Neither Barb nor Joe ever knew if their mother was aware of what had "almost" happened to them; Hertha never raised the matter with her children, and they refrained from speaking about it to her. Had she known, she would have no doubt been further distraught at her inability to protect her children in this new environment where she was at the mercy of government officials for the family's very existence. And besides, no one would have done much to help her. After all, the Schmidts were just refugees.

Even in those early years, the Schmidts' became aware of the discrimination they would suffer for the next decade in West Germany. While there were no spies lurking around to imprison them for uttering an ill-timed criticism, there were other, more subtle ways in which they were made to feel inferior, even by their landlord at the castle. Shortly after they arrived, the landlord had restored the plumbing in the basement so guests at the restaurant would have toilets and washing facilities available. The Schmidts were strictly forbidden to use these conveniences, and were forced to continue using a slop bucket and chamber pots in their apartment.

The landlord was equally unsympathetic about the Schmidts' requirements for fuel. For months the family gathered wood for their stove and stored it in the basement. But suddenly the landlord decided the wood was blocking his guests' access to the toilets downstairs, so he tossed it all out into the court-yard—in the process blocking off Herr Birschel's entrance into his utility shed adjacent to the castle tower. Now the Schmidts were in real trouble!

The landlord did not want their firewood in his base-ment, and Birschel did not want it in his way either. One of them finally called the police. Hertha managed to turn the tables on both the landlord and the farmer, however. Somehow she convinced the authorities to let her family keep the woodpile in the basement—and Herr Birschel ended up cutting their wood into smaller pieces for them. Hertha may have won the day, but it was clear from this incident the Schmidts were not wanted at the castle, and might not be welcome anywhere else, either.

Like so many other refugees, the Schmidt children were made to feel inferior by being labeled *Rucksackdeutsche*— "knap-sack Germans"—by the sons and daughters of people who had grown up in Solingen and surrounding villages. Like West Ger-mans all over the country, these families resented refugees, who seemed to be given preferential treatment by the authorities while the people who had suffered through the bombings in Solingen received no special attention. Whether this was true or not did not matter. Name-calling frequently led to scuffles, and the Schmidt boys quickly developed a reputation as "tough guys." Hertha was told on more than one occasion her sons would no doubt end up in jail before too long.

Only a few people showed the Schmidts any real shred of human decency. Among them was the mother of Klaus Wester, one of Bill's best friends. The Westers lived near the school in Hästen, and for years Frau Wester extended her generosity to all of the younger Schmidt children, inviting them into her house for sandwiches and cookies.

Decades after they were both grown, Klaus told Bill he was surprised to learn the Schmidts had suffered discrimination, since no one in his family ever said anything disparaging about the family—or about any of the refugees, for that matter. The Westers were the exception, however; both institutional and personal discrimination ran rampant throughout the country, and thousands of refugees like the Schmidts learned first-hand what it meant to be considered less than human.

In this hostile environment Hertha was busy all the time, trying to put enough food on the table, tend to her household chores, and get the family a permanent place to live. She knew they could not stay in the castle forever. As long as they did, they would be part of the Refugee Placement system, a stigma Hertha wanted to remove as soon as she could.

Additionally, the castle smelled of mold, smoke, and wet dirt. It was constantly damp—not a healthy place to raise children who had suffered under the harsh conditions they had experienced in the past five years. She may have been especially worried about Einhard, who continued to show signs of tuberculosis. Fortunately, he was able to go to another facility, this time in Bavaria, where he received special treatment.

But Hertha was determined not to take "just anything" in the way of permanent housing. For three years someone from the refugee agency tried diligently to help the family relocate, taking Hertha into Solingen to look at apartments. Time after time she was shown places she considered too small, too decrepit, or otherwise not suitable. Eventually, insistent and anxious government officials began to pressure her to accept one of their offers. But she remained steadfast, no doubt staring down one hapless official after another as she demanded a place where she could raise her children in relative comfort and safety.

At the same time she was caring for her children and looking for more permanent housing, Hertha continued to pursue information about her husband. Shortly after arriving in the West, Hertha renewed her correspondence with Jochen Lemme, an official associated with the West German Foreign Office

whom she had met in Berlin in 1949. Actually Lemme's organization, a front for the American government that was actively
trying to learn what it could about operations in the Soviet zone,
was engaged in a number of secretive activities inside East Germany. Lemme had moved to Bonn shortly after the Schmidts
had relocated to Solingen.

Hertha went to great lengths to curry favor with Lemme,
often preparing meals for him with special purchases such as
asparagus, a delicacy her children rarely enjoyed. In turn, Lemme
put Hertha in touch with an organization that had been formed
to assist victims of the Communists. The group met regularly in
locations in West Germany, and Lemme encouraged Hertha to attend one of their seminars. She did so, but found the experience
demoralizing; no one there seemed to care about her plight, and
no one was able to help her. Eventually she lost her contact at the
Foreign Office when Lemme was dismissed from his job.

In 1952, the family managed to put some closure on
one part of their painful experience. In response to pressure
from the Allied powers, the new East German government had
begun to notify families about the fate of thousands of men and
women taken prisoner by the Soviets or the German Communists during the first years after the end of the war. The news
came to the Schmidts in the form of a small urn, purported to
contain the ashes of August Wilhelm Schmidt.

There was no explanation regarding the cause of death.
But then, there was none needed; Hertha knew her husband
had died at the hands of the East Germans or their Russian
masters. Of course there was no way to know if the ashes in the
urn were really those of Willi Schmidt. Nevertheless, Hertha
arranged for a burial, and the ashes were placed in a cemetery
in Solingen. It may have been an act of faith on her part, but
Hertha told herself she now knew what had finally happened to
her husband. The family could move on with their lives.

"Knapsack Germans"
(1952-1957)

In 1952 government officials finally found an apartment that passed muster with Hertha. It was located on the second story of a building on Wilhelmshöhe, a quiet by-way just off Mangenbergerstrasse, one of Solingen's major streets on the west side of the city. A row of hawthorn trees with beautiful red flowers and long, spiked thorns stood along the wide sidewalk. The building had originally been erected to house workers at a local business; the tenants were mostly engineers and business owners.

Wilhelmshöhe 43-45, Solingen. Hertha Schmidt and her family lived in an apartment on the second floor from 1952 until 1959. (photographed 2006)

The owners of the apartment building begrudgingly allowed the Schmidts to move in. They were none too pleased to see so large a family (and one on welfare) occupying one of their flats, but they had no choice. The government had insisted one or two of the units be made available for refugee families. The owners succumbed to this pressure, and the Schmidts finally had a place Hertha thought might serve as home for more than a few months. One can only wonder how the downstairs neighbors felt about having so many children—especially noisy young boys—tramping around above them.

The living space consisted of two bedrooms, a bathroom with a separate toilet closet immediately adjacent to it, a large kitchen, a small pantry, and a living room. The family was allocated space in the attic and a storage room in the basement. They shared the laundry facilities in the basement with other residents of the building.

The space was actually too small for the family of nine, but apparently Hertha decided she would take this at least temporarily, until something more spacious could be found. As it turned out, the family would remain there for seven years, gradually gaining a bit more room when Rolf and then Wolf moved out to set up their own homes with their new wives.

Inside the apartment, sleeping arrangements were cramped, to say the least. The children occupied the two bedrooms. Barb, Joe, Wolf, Bill, and Mike shared the larger room; Rolf, Einhard, and Lori were in the smaller one. The living room, which doubled as Hertha's bedroom, contained a table, a couch, a Grundig radio, and a small oil heater Hertha turned on occasionally to take off the chill. Oil for the heater was kept in a five-gallon can in the basement.

All of the Schmidts reveled in having indoor plumbing (a great improvement over the castle!). The bath had a copper water heater, though they had to be careful not to use too many coals to heat the water; hot baths occurred only once a week.

Hertha used the tub for some of her washing as well, hanging the family's clothes out on the kitchen balcony to dry.

All of the beds had down comforters, but the rooms were cold, since only one had a stove tucked away in one corner, and Hertha could not afford enough coal to keep it lit through the night. The children shared not only rooms, but beds as well. The two youngest were paired up, and Barb was constantly complaining because she had to sleep on "wet" sheets. At one time or another, the Schmidt boys ended up wetting their beds while they slept—a result, no doubt, of the trauma they experienced during the last months of the war and the years in Hagenow and Vellahn.

Once she was settled in Solingen, Hertha spent even more time visiting the agencies charged with helping the widows of war veterans and assisting those receiving some form of welfare. She had two goals, neither of which she ever lost sight of: to restore her husband's reputation, and to care for her family. To accomplish the latter, she felt she needed to get off welfare. In fact, she believed she was entitled to a War Widow's Pension, since Willi's death had been caused indirectly by his wartime service. But until she was able to shed the stigma of being in the welfare system, she was determined to get from it everything she thought her family deserved, and whenever she saw someone else receive some benefit or privilege, she demanded the Schmidts receive equal treatment.

Unfortunately, even though the administrators did not appear to be corrupt as they had been in the East, they were not particularly efficient. Many of the men who had been the "stars" of the German bureaucracy before the war had been killed; their replacements simply were not as adept at their work. Compounding the problem was a constant shortage of staple goods such as coal, clothing, and foodstuffs, making it harder for the bureaucrats to meet people's basic needs. As a result, paperwork did not move as quickly, and people had to wait longer to receive what was rightfully theirs. Additionally, this new crop of bureaucrats seemed to labor under a stringent set of rules that made it difficult to process any action expeditiously. None of this sat well with Hertha Schmidt!

After her initial fights with the authorities, Hertha received monthly stipends for necessities such as food, coal, and clothing. The allocations were never sufficient to meet the family's needs. Hertha wrote numerous letters to various officials reminding them of their obligations to help relieve her family's plight. She would visit their offices to cajole anyone who would listen, "nickel-and-diming" them for a few more *Deutschmarks.* She reminded them in writing and in person that her family was not a nuisance, but a group of human beings who wanted to be out of the welfare system and into the mainstream of the new German society.

It is likely that before too long, every bureaucrat who had anything to do with refugees or pensions or any form of assistance knew Hertha Schmidt quite well. No doubt some of them would cringe, and the call would go out through the office—"Look out! Here she comes again!"

For her part, Hertha had little use for these government toadies—"unwashed hands in an unwashed suit," she would say of them. Nevertheless, the feisty, tenacious woman would latch onto one or another of these unfortunate drones like a terrier and threaten not to leave his office until she got what she needed.

Some of these bureaucrats actually became her friends, despite her constantly haranguing them about her family's circumstances. Some helped because they seemed to understand the Schmidt family really was owed something by the German government. Others did her bidding simply to get her off their backs. For her part, Hertha didn't care about their motives; she was only interested in getting results.

Hertha would prepare carefully for her meetings with government officials. Often she would write out her argument and spend time rehearsing her appeal. She would work out her plan of attack with the meticulous care of a general staff officer. Woe to the bureaucrat who dared to cross her, especially if he did not have his facts straight! Then she would return home, exhausted, but usually pleased with herself for having won some small victory. Her visits usually ended up in the family's being able to buy a little extra food—or even an occasional bottle of wine!

When she was not out seeking redress from the welfare office, Hertha was at home handling the duties any mother with eight children faced in a time before the widespread availability of electric appliances made housework easier. The apartment had to be cleaned—at least as well as the doctor's house in which she had worked twenty years earlier. Meals for nine had to be prepared. And of course, laundry had to be done every Monday. Since there was no washing machine, Hertha had to clean everyone's clothes, as well as the family's linens and bedding, by hand.

With nine people in the house, washing clothes and bedding proved to be a time-consuming task. Sometimes she could use the bathtub in the apartment, but routinely she would carry her laundry down to the communal area in the basement, boil water on a large stove, and dump in her washing and some soap that resembled petroleum jelly. After stirring the clothes to be certain the dirt had come loose, she would rub each piece against a scrubbing board. What she faced each Monday would have overwhelmed many other women. The younger boys continued to soil their bed sheets at night. Those engaged in apprenticeships brought home work clothes covered with grime and dust. School clothes were often just as dirty. And as her boys grew older, she made sure their best shirt would be freshly washed and pressed for the weekend.

No doubt there were times when the younger Schmidt children wished their mother did not do laundry by hand, because the instrument she used to stir her wash in the tub was a hardwood stick, some three feet long and more than an inch thick. In addition to being a useful tool for beating out the wash, it proved as effective as the carpet beater for instilling discipline in her children. She also employed with great effectiveness a wooden salad bowl that could easily go from the cupboard or the table onto the noggin of an unruly or obstinate teenager—including her almost-grown-up daughter Lori. Later she acquired a short horse whip that was particularly effective in getting the children's attention. Such methods of instilling discipline in children were practiced routinely in Germany (and elsewhere), and Hertha resorted to them only when she became increasingly frustrated with her children's behavior.

The boys always seemed to be unruly, talking back and insisting on having the last word. Hertha would not stand for such behavior. She might be shorter and smaller than several of her children, but she was still their mother. Willi's absence did not deter her in the least; she simply enlisted Rolf to help with the discipline. In the evenings she would sit at one end of the dining table, he at the other, and between them the younger Schmidts would arrange themselves on either side, knowing if they misbehaved, their mother or their older brother would have little compunction in using a well-placed "tap" to enforce appropriate standards of behavior and decorum on them.

In Solingen, there was no fear of starvation, but the daily diet did not vary very much. The evening meal became predictable, as Hertha usually repeated the menu on a weekly basis. Even when the Schmidts began to have enough food in the house, Hertha made her children consume everything they put on their plate. It was okay to say "no" to something, but whatever you took, you had to finish. And there was no dessert if you didn't eat the main meal.

Hertha was able to obtain staples for simple meals from the neighborhood grocer, who extended credit to her until her welfare check came in on the first of each month. As she had done for most of her life, she found ways to stretch whatever she could acquire. Because she could get them cheaply, Hertha would make great mountains of potatoes, boiled or fried with onions and seasonings. Her scalloped potatoes became a hit with virtually all of the children. Somehow she managed to afford an occasional strip of bacon for her potato soups. When she had some money, she would buy little ampules of seasonings for cakes. No one could beat her apple cake with fresh sliced apples!

When they were in season, she obtained fresh vegetables to supplement the ever-present potato dishes. Occasionally, she was able to procure fresh fish as well. When she fried them in batter all of the children were thrilled. But once in awhile, she would indulge in a typical Germany method to prepare them—plunging them whole into boiling water and letting them poach until the flesh could be flaked easily from the bones. When they were ready, she scooped them from the pot and set them on dinner plates, and when the children gathered at the table, they saw their dinner staring back at them. Some of the younger ones did not find this a very appetizing prospect!

It seemed Hertha was always preparing food for one of her children. Though they could never afford a steady diet of the rich cuisine for which Germany was famous—items like wursts and German pastries—Hertha loved to see her sons and daughters eat their fill. The scrawny young Schmidt boys all had great appetites, especially Wolfgang. Surprisingly, although he was known as "Shrimp" at the foundry where he worked, he may have been the most prodigious eater of the bunch.

To Barb it seemed as if Wolf could eat an entire loaf of bread at one sitting. Routinely, he would come home from work and eat a plate of sandwiches—five or six slices of bread with various toppings, such as tomatoes and onions when these were in season. Then three hours later he would have dinner—sometimes four or five helpings before Hertha would finally say "Enough!"

Once they were in Solingen, the school-age children settled into a regular routine. Unfortunately, just as had been the case in the East, the educational system in West Germany was not academically strong. The pool of qualified teachers had been sorely depleted by the war, and because of the shortage the best teachers had to teach a variety of subjects. Nevertheless, the Schmidt children from Einhard down to Barbara received a creditable education, while Wolf, Lori, and Rolf managed to make up for deficiencies suffered as a result of interruptions caused by the war and the family's displacements during 1945-1949.

What was truly surprising, and in retrospect disturbing, was the fact that no one in the Solingen schools talked about the war. It was almost as if the events of 1939-1945 happened somewhere else. Even teachers who had been in the service rarely mentioned what the Germans had done, or what had happened to them as a consequence. Of course, the Schmidt children, especially the older ones, knew first-hand about the war, and the Soviets had indoctrinated the population in their Zone about the atrocities committed by the Germans. But many of their classmates had heard and read only what the Nazi government had wanted them to know about the war in other places, and the new regime in the West seemed reticent to share with the rising generation information about the atrocities committed by Hitler's henchmen.

Not all of the Schmidts enjoyed attending school, but what made it a bit more enjoyable were the meals. Food was prepared by the school district in a central kitchen and shipped to the individual classroom buildings. The children would carry an empty container, such as a small milk pail, which would be filled with soup for their lunch. When there was extra soup remaining after all the children had been fed, school officials allowed the boys and girls to receive "seconds" to take home. No doubt Hertha appreciated this as well, since it meant one less meal for her to prepare from her meager resources.

Once a week some of the school children received candy bars, long blocks of chocolate divided into rectangular squares. The Schmidts knew they would have to share this candy with their brothers and sisters, so the lucky child who divided the candy, would nibble off the little edges that joined the larger rectangular pieces just to get a little more!

Unfortunately, the prejudice and discrimination that characterized the treatment of refugees from the East extended into the classrooms as well. Lori learned the hard way about this prejudice. She completed her final year of formal schooling, enjoying the opportunity to renew serious study of mathematics, geography and history, all taught by the same teacher. She did not mind that the teacher never called on her during the year. But at the end of the year Hertha was notified that Lori had failed her courses. Hertha was mystified; she knew Lori was a good student, even if the stresses of the past several years had dulled her edge for academic work. So she marched off to the school to confront the teacher, who had a simple explanation for Lori's failure.

"She never answered a question all year long," he said.

When Hertha relayed this information to her daughter, it was Lori's turn to be indignant. "He never called on me!" Lori retorted angrily.

So Hertha went back to the school, this time to harangue the principal, whom she hoped would get to the bottom of this matter. The two of them confronted the teacher with Lori's version of affairs. Nonplussed, the teacher simply responded, "I hate refugees."

That was enough to send Hertha through the roof, and the principal was not ready to take the kind of heat she threatened to bring down on him and his school. Lori was given passing marks, and allowed to proceed to her internship.

Even Barb suffered from the stigma of being an interloper in the West, and that may have contributed to the special notoriety she achieved at her school. As a consequence, Hertha spent quite a bit of time with school officials, bailing her youngest out of trouble. When Barb was about seven or eight years old, she was reprimanded for allegedly exposing her underwear to a group of boys on the playground and told to stay after school for punishment. Knowing that what had happened was an accident—a gust of wind had tossed up her dress—Barb instead ran home to tell her mother. At first Hertha was skeptical, but as she listened to her daughter's version of the story, she began to think the authorities had acted hastily in accusing Barbara. She marched back to the school, young Barb in tow.

"How dare you have such dirty thoughts about my daughter!" she lashed at them. She then proceeded to denounce the behavior of some of the school's former students and administrators. At this point the officials became quite conciliatory, and the incident was "forgotten."

The older siblings tried hard to ignore or deal constructively with this discrimination as they readied themselves for careers. This was important, since the family had no income other than what Hertha was receiving from the authorities. The limited support Rolf could provide from his apprenticeship earnings was barely enough to pay the family's food bill for a week. Later, both Wolf and Einhard would enter apprenticeships and contribute to the family's living expenses, easing the financial strain a bit. But when Rolf moved out of the house in 1954, Hertha lost most of his income, so Wolf's apprenticeship money simply replaced his elder brother's, as Einhard's did when Wolf moved out in 1958.

After serving his apprenticeship, Rolf went to work for the largest cutlery manufacturer in Solingen. By that time, West Germany was embarking on a spurt of industrial growth that would come to be known as the "Economic Miracle," and jobs for young men like Rolf were plentiful. But new prosperity also meant new opportunities for corruption, and while the West remained better than the East in holding down illicit activities, there is no doubt some people profited by other-than-legal means. Rolf remembered, for example, that before he left Germany for America he saw the son of a scrap dealer in Solingen driving a Porsche. There was no way for the father to have made the kind of money needed to purchase such a car through his everyday trade.

When Wolf finished secondary school, he became an apprentice in the pattern-making trade. Unfortunately, he did not like the work at all, so he became a molder in a foundry. As was typical of those serving apprenticeships, Wolf worked four-and-a-half days and attended school one day each week to continue his education, learning the technical and mathematical aspects of his trade, which included learning to read blueprints and understand basic machinery. The work was difficult, especially for an undersized youth, but he managed to haul the heavy containers of molten metals and work the machinery that heated metals before they were poured into molds.

After Wolf completed his apprenticeship he was retained at the foundry as a full-time employee. By this time, however, he had become bored with the routine of the job, especially when he was given the job of producing the same mold over and over. So he complained to his boss—and was immediately fired! He was a bit more careful at his next job.

In his first year as an apprentice, Wolf's Unterstützung, or stipend for support, was DM18 per week (about $4); this stipend increased to DM22 per week in the second year, and DM29 in the third. The foundry at which he was employed was only a few blocks from the Schmidts' apartment, so he could easily walk to work. Occasionally, on his way home, he would stop at a kiosk to purchase some fresh-roasted peanuts. Usually he ate all of them before he arrived home, but once in awhile he would keep some in his pockets to share with his brothers and sisters.

Despite these purchases, after Wolf completed his apprenticeship he managed to save up enough to buy a moped, a motorized bicycle that provided great transportation to work and allowed him to roam about in Solingen and the surrounding countryside.

Like Rolf and Lori before him, of course, Wolf ended up turning over the bulk of his pay to his mother. Hertha got DM 16 per week during that first year—and Wolf was glad to pocket DM2 for himself! His share did not increase much over the next two years, either.

Wolf remembers Hertha was constantly borrowing from the older children. Normally he was perfectly happy to turn over most of his wages to his mother, and to help her out with his pocket money when she needed it. But once, when he was planning to use his share of his earnings for a special weekend, he found himself having to think fast to avoid becoming flat broke. Just before the weekend he was standing on the street talking to friends when his mother leaned out of the window and asked to borrow two marks from him. Wolf realized he had only a five-mark piece in his pocket. He knew if he gave his mother that five-mark piece, she would not give him change! So he raced to the corner store to get change so he could give his mother what she needed and keep the rest for himself.

Einhard was the next to enter the work world, and through a stroke of good luck he was able to get an apprenticeship in a field where he already had some work experience. As soon as they arrived in Solingen, the Schmidt boys were always on the lookout for ways to earn additional cash. Einhard had landed a particularly attractive part-time job at a local cookie factory. He liked the work immensely—which not surprising, since his father had loved to bake when he was home on weekends—so when it came time for him to choose an apprenticeship, he went to work at Krombach Bakery to learn the skills of a confectionary baker.

The hours were long at the Krombach Bakery—undoubtedly the others in the family thought Einhard had the worst apprenticeship of anyone among the Schmidt siblings—but Einhard found several "perks." First, every Saturday he was allowed to bring home bags of broken cookies or damaged pastries that could not be sold. Moreover, he found frequent opportunities to separate the thin layer of crust that developed between individual loaves of bread as they baked side by side, providing himself a welcome snack. Naturally, when he started earning money from his apprenticeship, he shared his pay with his mother.

In the spring of 1955, Bill began his four-year apprenticeship as a machinist at Böntgen & Grah, a major manufacturing firm in Solingen. Like his brothers, Bill had to make his way to his workplace on foot or on the trolley. Then in 1958, he got lucky. Wolf got married and agreed to give his moped to Bill. The bike provided transportation to work on sunny days (he still took the trolley in bad weather), but it also gave him "status" among his friends—until the moped broke down!

To provide his share of the family's expenses, younger brother Mike went into the laundry business. In the afternoons after school, Mike traveled through the neighborhood on a bicycle, collecting laundry from the establishment's customers. But he almost lost his job when one evening he was out late making deliveries—so late that he violated the curfew law. He was stopped by a policeman who gave him a citation. His protests that he was actually walking the bicycle home fell on deaf ears.

The punishment for those who broke this law was assignment to defensive driving school. Little Mike had to attend a class with adults who had received citations for a variety of offenses including drunk driving, and he had to watch gory movies that highlighted the consequences of recklessness on the roads! Nevertheless, his entrepreneurial spirit and willingness to help earn money for the family was much appreciated by his mother, and earned him the respect of his elder brothers and sister.

During his final year in secondary school, Hertha took Mike to the local office of the Department of Labor, which maintained an employment bureau for those wishing to enter the workforce. As his brothers and sister had done before him, Mike was put through a battery of tests to see what he might be suited to do for a living. Of course, officials knew what trades were in demand at the moment and which would be needed in the future, so their recommendation (which carried the force of a directive) was often based as much on what the economy required as on the individual's aptitudes.

In Mike's case, officials decided he had the skills to be a fine tool and die maker. They found an employer where he could apprentice, and the next year Mike was off to learn his trade. Neither he nor his mother had much to say in the matter. The family was receiving public assistance, so it was important (in the government's eyes) that the children develop a useful skill so they would not end up on the welfare rolls.

Typical of the routine being followed in Germany at the time, Mike's four-year apprenticeship, began with classroom work that lasted a year before he got to work on the production line to gain hands-on experience. The highly regimented environment didn't sit well with him, and as a consequence he was constantly watching the clock. Once he stayed home suffering from a bad headache. About midday the plant manager showed up at the Schmidts' apartment and told Hertha if her son did not get to work, he would be fired. Mike had no choice but to drag himself over to the factory and suffer through the day.

When Mike began his apprenticeship, he passed on his laundry route to younger brother Joe. Actually, Mike spent considerable time training Joe to take over from him, tying a sled to the back of the bicycle during the winter months so he could drag Joe along the snow-covered streets to learn the route. Joe was ecstatic about inheriting the job from his brother, since he could now earn enough money to buy a few things for himself.

But the work had its hazards. Sometime after Joe got the job, he managed to get his bicycle wheel caught in the trolley tracks that ran along Solingen's main streets. When he jerked the wheel to pull out of the track, the load of freshly cleaned laundry went tumbling into the street! Needless to say, the laundry owners were not pleased.

Even before he was old enough to take on this kind of real work, Joe and his sister Barb did odd jobs to earn spending money of their own. For a time they sold flowers and fruit they picked up in the meadows and orchards outside of the city—or from neighbors' gardens. All the children knew how precious food was to everyone, and how nothing could be wasted, especially not special purchases. The younger ones took this measure to the extreme one day when their mother sent Barb and Joe to the grocery for some marmalade. On the way home, Joe managed to crack the jar so badly that shards of glass got into the fruit. When Hertha saw what had happened, she told Joe to toss the jar in the trash bin outside. Instead, he and Barb went downstairs and proceeded to eat the marmalade, trying their best to avoid the glass shards. Fortunately, they suffered no ill effects from their reckless behavior.

The youngest Schmidts attempted to bring some joy into their mother's life as well—although the results were not always successful. For Hertha's birthday one year, Joe and Barb got up very early to clean the kitchen. While their mother slept, they crept into the kitchen and located a can of cleaner—a product similar to Comet or Ajax—and proceeded to cover the floor with it. Naturally, when they applied water, the substance caked up, foamed, and made a terrible mess.

When Hertha came into the kitchen, she discovered the disaster and spent the rest of the day fixing her children's well-intentioned mistake. Perhaps she forgave them for this transgression since their hearts were in the right place and they had done no real damage. Such was not the case on Mother's Day, however, when they decided to surprise her with a bunch of fresh roses—

snipped from the garden of a neighbor at the house on the corner. Half an hour after they had made their presentation to gushing "thank-yous," they were both standing before their irate mother to get their "whuppin'" after the neighbor reported to Hertha how the flowers had ended up at the Schmidt apartment.

One trait Hertha instilled in her children was responsibility for others. They were expected to help their neighbors, especially elderly neighbors, without expectation of anything in return. Nevertheless, the little ones always seemed to benefit from their efforts. Frequently Barb and Joe would do chores for neighbors for which they would be given a treat. Getting something for free meant one did not have to spend the few pennies that came to the children from their various enterprises.

While their financial circumstances may have been difficult, during their time in Solingen, the Schmidts were a close-knit and generally happy family. They worked hard and played hard and though there were inevitable squabbles, they enjoyed spending time together. In their apartment, Hertha had a radio that the family loved to listen to in the evenings. Sometimes on Thursdays, Hertha let her younger ones stay up later than usual to listen to two special shows. The first was the "Chris Howland Show," an immensely popular program featuring American Top Forty tunes. It was hosted by a British disc jockey who had developed a following among German listeners and remained in the country after the war. This show was followed immediately by "The Shadow," and the children were glued to their seats listening to the suspense drama as it unfolded.

Hertha could not afford a television, of course, but from time to time the downstairs neighbors allowed the Schmidts to view programs on their set. The children could also count on seeing some television at the homes of friends whose families were fortunate enough to own a TV.

Though the younger Schmidts were busy during the academic year with schoolwork and outside jobs, they often found

An evening of cards in the Schmidts' apartment in Solingen. (l to r): Heinz Bölling, Hertha, Einhard, 1957.

time for relaxation during the summer. A favorite destination was the public swimming pool in Ohligser Heide, a Solingen suburb. On hot days they would walk the long distance from Wilhelmshöhe out to the pool, stopping along the way to ask for a glass of water from people who happened to be out on the street in front of their homes.

Sometime after the Schmidts moved to Solingen, Hertha became friends with Heinz Bölling, a gentleman slightly older than she who seemed to have an interest in her—despite her having eight children! He would come over to the apartment regularly, often spending hours in the evening playing cards or other games with Hertha and the children. He developed a bond with everyone in the Schmidt clan, and even took Joe to a football game in Düsseldorf.

Once in awhile, Heinz would take Hertha out for dinner and a movie. None of the children knew whether Hertha and Heinz shared more than conversation and occasional outings—though some suspected there was more than card-playing to the relationship—but the older ones appreciated then, and the younger ones realized later, that having Herr Bölling around was a very good thing for their mother.

Hertha also spent time with Lilli Lemke, whom she had met when both families were living at Burg Hohenscheid. They would visit each other and periodically go to the cinema to catch the late show. Sometimes the movie let out too late for Hertha to catch a bus back across town, so she would have to walk. Normally that was not a problem, since the city was relatively safe, even for a woman out alone near midnight. But one evening as she was returning home she found herself in real trouble.

Traveling to and from the Lemkes' apartment, Hertha had to pass by a business that kept guard dogs inside the fence surrounding the establishment. As she was approaching the fence line that evening, she noticed that the gate had been left open. Too late to retreat! The dogs ran out of the enclosure, barking fiercely, fangs bared! Hertha backed up against the fence and began calling frantically for help. What went through her mind she never revealed, but it must have seemed like an eternity before the owner, who lived beside his business, awoke and came out to rescue her.

The holidays continued to be special occasions in the Schmidt household. Even in the darkest times in Hagenow and Vellahn, Hertha had tried to do something special at Christmastime. Before the war, Willi had always decorated a tree on Christmas eve, keeping it from the children's view before it was ready. No doubt Rolf, Lori, Wolf, Einhard, and perhaps even Bill had memories of those holiday seasons when they were dazzled by the trimmings and candles, and when there were presents to be shared with everyone.

Hertha revived this tradition in Solingen by having her older children help decorate a tree to dazzle Mike, Joe, and Barb.

The littlest ones would wait with great anticipation for the signal to enter the room, where before them they would see the tree lit up with candles and sparklers. They would sing songs and exchange simple presents.

During the years when they lived in Burg Hohenscheid, several of the Schmidt children were sent on Christmas day to the homes of families who had agreed to share what they had with the children of refugees. In later years, when they had settled in town, their grandparents began sending them a duck or a goose and some fresh butter to dress up the Christmas table. Hertha tried each holiday season to obtain oranges to send to her parents in East Germany, since it was particularly difficult to acquire citrus fruits there.

Though there was not enough money to buy gifts for everyone, the children were sure to receive a special plate of fruit with chocolate, nuts, and cookies. Hertha also continued the tradition of decorating the tree with *Traubenzucker*, a special candy ornament with, as its name suggests, a high content of grape sugar. The round or star-shaped morsels would melt in one's mouth. Hertha pretended they were decorations, but when the younger children discovered they were edible—and delicious!—they began stealing them one at a time, starting from the back of the tree. They would take only one a day so the candies would last and their mother would not realize (so they thought) that the "decorations" were missing. Only later did they learn she had known all along what they were doing—and that she had bought these candies so her children would have something special for the holidays.

Occasionally one of the younger children received a real present, frequently because one of the older children would buy something for them. Many presents did not seem to last long, though, as items such as toy cars and even soccer balls ended up in the trash after rough treatment caused them to break or pop. Unfortunately, some presents were sources of embarrassment.

After he had gone to the United States, Rolf sent Joe a pair of argyle socks—all the rage in America—and Joe proudly wore them to school, only to discover that they evoked not admiration but ridicule from his classmates. He never wore them again.

Since store-bought gifts were a rarity, home-made presents were received with as much joy as most children expressed for expensive toys. The Schmidts may not have had money, but their mother saw to it that they had love—sometimes tough love, to be sure, but the kind of love that binds a mother to her children no matter how much they may quarrel.

The Christmas season provided only a brief interlude in the otherwise grueling routine for Hertha Schmidt. The pressure to provide for her family, combined with the loss of her husband, was sometimes too much for her to bear. She managed to get through the days, probably because she was too busy tending to household chores or dealing with government authorities to take time to think about her own predicament. Of course, she had her older children to help, and no doubt she truly valued their efforts. But sometimes, late in the evenings, the children who had not yet dozed off to sleep could hear faint sobbing coming from the living room where their mother lay. Perhaps she shed tears over her children's behavior; they were always in trouble, and she was always having to discipline them or get them out of scrapes with school officials and others. Certainly she was bewailing the loss of her husband. She loved Willi Schmidt, and she knew she would never see him again. No doubt, she also cried for the loss her older children had suffered—the loss of their youth and innocence, as they had been forced to grow up so quickly.

She may too have wept for her younger children, who had known nothing but deprivation and hardship. Hertha lamented the fate all of her children had suffered, being uprooted constantly, shifted from home to home and school to school, forced to grow up without a father. She cried, too, for what her family had experienced under the Communists: the constant degradations they endured while Willi was in prison, and the daily struggle to obtain the basic necessities for living. But she may well have been in tears because, even though they had escaped to the West, the family was still living from hand to mouth. She wanted something better for all of them.

Living in the West now gave the Schmidts a chance to see their paternal grandparents more frequently. That was, of course, a mixed blessing. Spending time with Oma Paula and Opa Schmidt proved to be one of the most unpleasant experiences any of the children could remember from their years in Solingen. The elder Schmidts were still living in the small village of Horumersiel on the North Sea, where Rolf had visited them some years earlier. They condescended to make periodic visits to see their grandchildren, sweeping down on Hertha and her family in Solingen and taking over the family's routine.

Willi Schmidt's parents, Paula and Wilhelm Schmidt, at their Diamond Wedding Anniversary, 1964.

Oma Paula always insisted on being the center of attention. She insisted on planting wet kisses with her large, puckered lips on the cheeks and foreheads of her grandchildren, who shuddered each time she touched them. She demanded the place of honor at the dinner table, and insisted on being served the best food. Far from being a loving grandmother, she treated Hertha and her family as if they were bond servants, far beneath her socially and good only for ministering to her every whim.

Had Oma Paula's imperious behavior been the worst thing the family had to endure, that would have been plenty. But Opa Schmidt was worse, although the younger children did not suspect anything amiss because he always treated them especially well. Barb was quite happy to see the Schmidts arrive, because Opa made her feel special, taking her for ice cream or on excursions. Joe has similar memories of his grandfather going out of his way to make him feel good. What neither of them knew at the time was that their grandfather was a philanderer and a molester who preyed on young women and teens.

Hertha would dread visits from Willi's parents because she knew her father-in-law would try to put his hands all over her—and do even more if she were not vigilant. On one visit, when Lori was a teenager, her grandfather asked if she had a boyfriend. When she said no, he said he would be happy to show her what it was like to have a real boyfriend. Somehow Hertha found out about his proposition—whether Lori told her, or she overheard the conversation, or simply guessed at what had transpired—and she threw him out! In fact, she tossed his suitcase out the door.

The air of superiority and selfishness that characterized their paternal grandparents' behavior extended to their aunts as well. One of Willi's sisters lived in Wuppertal just ten kilometers away, so the Schmidts got to see her occasionally. Because she had a daughter who was close in age to Lori, she invited

Marie Sadler Dittmann, Hertha Schmidt's mother, on her visit to the family in Solingen, circa 1957.

Hertha's teenage daughter to spend time with her family. Lori gladly went—but soon regretted her decision.

The first day passed well enough, and Lori was looking forward to dinner; she could smell something quite aromatic being prepared in the kitchen. When she went down for her meal, however, she was served a bowl of cream of wheat. Displaying some of her mother's feisty spirit, Lori asked why she was not given some of the food she knew was being prepared that evening. Her aunt replied testily, "That's for the adults!" Apparently, though, Lori and her mother were thought "good enough" to be invited to her aunt's annual birthday—so long as they brought a present.

While Oma and Opa Schmidt visited periodically, Omi Dittmann managed only one trip to the West, and Opa Dittmann never crossed out of East Germany. Marie was able to obtain a visa because the East German government was glad to allow those who had reached a certain age to travel on the other side of the border. The government's rationale was that, if these people failed to return, the West Germans would have to care for them in their old age, and the East Germans could confiscate their property for the State. So Marie came to visit, stayed quite a while, noted the progress Hertha and her grandchildren were making in adjusting to life in the West, and returned to Flecken Zechlin convinced her daughter had made the right decision to flee from the Communists.

In 1957, Bill and Mike were allowed to visit the Dittmanns in East Germany. What they discovered in the East was a world too tragic to be believed. The Communist Party controlled everything, and government officials ruled the lives of the populace in even the smallest matters. As a consequence, people were despondent, afraid to say anything negative about their situation lest someone inform on them.

Everyone knew of people who had been taken away in the middle of the night. Even Omi Dittmann was different. In Solingen she had exhibited a feisty spirit, carrying her own suitcase and out-walking everyone in the family. Now, just a short time later, she was quiescent and resigned. The Schmidt boys recognized immediately what a decade of Communist rule had done to the places where their family had lived. The stores they visited to shop for their grandparents were invariably empty. Even though ration coupons were abundant, there was nowhere to use them.

Inevitably, Hertha Schmidt had to face the fact that her children would one day begin adult lives on their own. The first departure must have been the most painful, though. By 1954, now that he had begun to solidify his career, Rolf felt it was now possible to marry. He turned twenty-one that year, and although he was starting to lose some of his wavy blonde hair, he cut a handsome figure. He had always been industrious, and his brothers and sisters marveled at his capacity for hard work and his drive to improve himself through education.

For some time, Rolf had been dating a girl he had met at school in Hagenow. Renate Ursula Spingies was originally from East Prussia, but like so many Germans living in that region during the war, she had come west with her family ahead of the advancing Russian army. Her mother had died of cancer when

Renate was ten. Her father raised her, but he was imprisoned and forced to work in a uranium mine for some time. Although he was eventually released, he became ill and never recovered his health. He died in 1952.

On one level at least, Hertha accepted the idea that all of her children would one day marry. Probably she was even thrilled at the thought of having grandchildren. In the abstract, she was delighted with the prospect of having a bevy of new young women around the house, married to the sons she had worked so hard to raise. But when abstract thought turned to reality, it was a different matter. For instance, she had known Renate Spingies since 1952, when the young woman slipped out of East Germany by negotiating a solitary border crossing much as Rolf had done years earlier to visit his grandparents. She planned to stay with the Schmidts at Burg Hohenscheid for a few days, but Rolf was intent on keeping her close by.

Afraid that Renate would be apprehended and punished upon her return to the East, Rolf lobbied her to stay in Solingen and look for work. Hertha joined her son in attempting to persuade Renate to remain in the West, knowing that her son was more than casually interested in his former schoolmate. Renate was accepted into the family circle, even helping to bathe the younger children on occasion! Yet when the time came for Rolf and Renate to tie the knot, Hertha still had mixed feelings about seeing her oldest move away. Later, she would have similar misgivings when her other sons introduced her to the girls they planned to marry. In time, however, she came to accept them as part of her family, making them welcome as daughters and friends.

On July 29, 1954, Rolf and Renate were married. As part of their "honeymoon" they obtained visas to visit the Dittmanns in East Germany. Upon returning to the West they found an apartment in Solingen—a one-room flat that they divided with blankets to make separate areas for eating, sleeping, and working.

While working full-time during the day, Rolf went to school at night. Interested in engineering, he completed a postsecondary diploma program that would have served him well had he stayed in Germany. Unfortunately, he learned several years later, it was not recognized as equivalent to a college degree by American educators.

The young couple's marital bliss was heightened less than a year later when, on June 17, 1955, Renate gave birth to Petra Hertha Helene Schmidt. The youngster quickly became something of a family celebrity. Regularly one or more of Rolf's brothers and sisters would make the long walk across town to visit, and they would take the baby out for a stroll. Even Joe spent some of his precious earnings to buy her chocolate mints, her favorite candy. Petra's birth marked a significant milestone for all of the Schmidt family. For years, all her children had called her "Mutti." Now Hertha Schmidt was a grandmother. There was someone to call her "Omi."

*   *   *   *   *

For years Hertha badgered the German government about receiving a War Widow's pension. Just because her husband had not died in combat, she insisted, did not mean she should be denied what she felt was justifiably hers. But, she could not prove her case because she had no documentation. It had all been confiscated when Willi was arrested. For years her plea fell on deaf ears. Then one winter day in the late 1950s (no one remembers the precise year), she was notified that her requests had been reviewed again, and this time officials had decided she was right after all. She was told to report to the Post Office to receive her back payments.

This was not the first time Hertha had received a substantial payment. Once before she had been given enough to buy her older boys nice suits—all the same kind, of course, but classy and eye-catching. But this time, this grosse Nachzahlung—the great back payment—would finally offer some real financial security!

It was the Christmas season, and the Schmidt children were ecstatic as well. This would be a Christmas to remember— perhaps there would even be real presents! Barb had her eye on a new doll to replace the worn-out one she'd been carrying around for years. Wolf knew what Barb wanted, but he was afraid if his mother waited until she received her money, the doll might be gone from the store shelves. So he advanced Hertha money from his earnings so she could get Barb's doll.

Hertha directed the older children to dress in their best clothes and gather up the shopping nets they used to bring home goods from the market. She figured they would need these to carry home the items they would purchase once they had that money in hand. Why, she must be owed thousands of marks! Thousands! Imagine what they could do with all that money. Now she would be able to do something for everyone in the family.

At the Post Office the family crowded around the desk as the official began calculating what was owed to Hertha. It was a large amount—larger than most of them could ever have imagined! But their jubilation turned to disbelief as the man began explaining how the government pensions and welfare payments "offset" each other. Since Hertha had been receiving welfare payments for years when she should have been getting the pension, she would have to pay back all the "welfare money" she had received out of the proceeds of the pension money owed to her.

As the bureaucrat dutifully calculated the sums, the family watched in dismay. When he arrived at the final total, everyone's jaw dropped in disbelief. Hertha Schmidt would walk away with less than 20 marks! There was hardly enough to pay back Wolfgang for the money he'd given his mother to buy Barbara's new doll.

Coming to America
(1957-1959)

❧

*I*t is not clear exactly when the idea of emigration became the focus of Hertha's efforts. It is almost certain she began thinking about leaving Germany long before many of her children did, although she may have entertained serious thoughts about this matter only after Rolf and Renate started applying for visas to other countries. The idea may not have seemed radical to her; after all, when she was a young woman, her mother had encouraged her to move away from the farm in Flecken Zechlin to pursue her dreams.

By 1957, conditions in Solingen were much improved over what she had experienced in the East. But Hertha was convinced that, as long as the family remained in Germany, they would continue to be stymied in their efforts to improve their lives financially and socially. The stigma of being *Flüchtlinge*—refugees—still hung over them. Welfare payments and pensions may have kept her from poverty, but she still could not provide adequately for those who remained at home with her. Something would have to be done.

Rolf was the first of the Schmidts to actively pursue opportunities to emigrate. After arriving in Solingen, he had begun corresponding with the American Red Cross official whose apartment he had visited in Berlin. Although Rolf was always a bit put off by the thought that the man was gay—and skeptical about the man's claims that he was an undercover agent—he thought at the time that writing to him would be a good way to practice his English. The man had returned to the United States and was now running a dry cleaning business. He offered to be Rolf's sponsor if Rolf wanted to immigrate to America. Rolf considered the offer, but by the time he became serious about leaving Germany, he was married. When he informed his potential sponsor that he would be bringing his wife with him, the man suddenly became less enthusiastic about helping him. Rolf decided that, if America were to be their choice, they would need another sponsor.

At first Hertha was not eager to see Rolf leave Germany. She was afraid he might not succeed overseas. Indeed, others in Germany also thought Rolf was making the wrong move. His employers at Henckels were angry. He had just begun a training program there to become a foreman, with the possibility to advance to further management positions. They felt he had simply used them to gain valuable skills, and now he was abandoning them just when he was becoming of real value to them. They informed him he should never have accepted the promotion—and immediately sent him back to the work bench!

Some of Rolf and Renate's friends felt the same way. They thought the young couple should stay in Germany to help the country recover. After all, these people reasoned, every family whose breadwinner earned a good living and whose children would grow up to become good German workers and citizens was helping to restore the country's economy and its reputation. In their minds, leaving Germany was an act of selfishness.

Ignoring these criticisms, in 1956 Rolf and Renate began making serious plans to emigrate. They both felt they could adjust well in an English-speaking country, since they had studied English as their second language in school. Rolf applied for visas at both the American and Australian consulates. The Australians answered first, and Rolf had his visa and airline tickets in hand when he read an article outlining the poor conditions for immigrants in Australia and New Zealand. He sent back the tickets.

The Americans were much slower to respond, as they conducted a lengthy investigation and required additional documentation and a physical. Rolf was patient, however, and eventually his visa for America arrived. The Consulate found sponsors for Rolf and Renate through the World Council of Churches, a group that made it their special mission to help refugees resettle in the United States. That was the last piece of good news Rolf and his family needed. After months of bureaucratic wrangling, he was finally granted a visa.

To win over his mother, Rolf shared with her the brochures and documents provided to him by the American Consulate, and eventually Hertha came to realize that America was not "gangsterland," as she and many other Germans had been led to believe. In March 1957, Rolf, Renate, and Petra said goodbye to Hertha and the other Schmidt family members. They were on their way to Hamburg to catch a plane for America.

In the 1950s, American sponsors were required to guarantee that the new immigrant would be provided a place to live and receive assistance in locating work. Presumably, however, people realized immigrants from Solingen who had completed apprenticeships in one of the region's outstanding manufacturing plants would have no trouble getting work in America, no matter where they settled. He and Renate flew to Idlewild (now John F. Kennedy) airport outside New York City. Once they passed through customs, they were met by representatives of the Mount Hope Episcopal Church, located in Manheim, Pennsylvania. This group, it turns out, was to be their local sponsors. Rolf, Renate, and Petra were driven from Idlewild to the town of Manheim, some two hours west of Philadelphia, Pennsylvania, and given their own small apartment.

How Rolf and Renate ended up in Manheim, Pennsylvania, was a matter of pure serendipity. The Mount Hope Episcopal Church in Manheim was scheduled to sponsor an Italian family arriving at the same time as Rolf and Renate. But when church officials learned the size of the family, they indicated they could not accommodate such a large group. At the last minute, the Schmidts were sent to Manheim instead.

Manheim proved to be a most hospitable place for immigrants like the Schmidts. The region had been settled centuries earlier by the Pennsylvania German immigrants who had fled intolerable conditions in Europe for the new world. Many of them were Mennonites, followers of the sixteenth-century religious reformer Menno Simons who had come to America to farm the rich lands of south-central Pennsylvania. As early as the eighteenth century, industry began to grow in and around Manheim, and it became a population center in agricultural Lancaster county.

By the twentieth century, people of many other nationalities had settled in the area, but the Mennonites continued to dominate local government, including the planning commission. As a result, the region remained predominantly rural. Few of the amenities of the big city were allowed in the area.

When Rolf's family arrived in 1957, the only "fast food" restaurant in town was the Twin Kiss Diner on Main Street; more than twenty years later, it remained the only place to get a quick meal or an ice cream cone. Manufacturing continued to be strong in Manheim, though, so that when the Schmidts took up residence there, the town could boast of several large factories producing metal works, asbestos, and other products necessary for industries in the region and nationwide. For a young German trained as a tool maker, it was a perfect location.

Their sponsors provided Rolf and Renate limited financial support until Rolf was established in his first job. After that, the Schmidts were on their own—exactly as Rolf wished to be. Once they were settled, Rolf and Renate were able to assist other family members who wanted to come to America. They could not be sponsors, but they could provide a place for brothers and sisters to stay until they found permanent lodgings. Rolf could help them find jobs, too, so they would not be on their own when trying to become independent in their new homeland.

Less than two years later, Wolf and his new bride, Sigi Weinberg, would follow Rolf and Renate to the United States. Sigi had become friends with Lori and was a member of the folksdancing group to which Wolfgang and Lori belonged. She had grown up in Güstrow, not far from Mirow. She had lost her father during the war, and like the Schmidts, she and her family had fled to the West after the Communist takeover of her region. She had even been in the same refugee camps, though not at the same time.

In Solingen, Sigi lived with her mother and sisters only fifteen minutes from the Schmidts, on the other side of one of the city's parks. Often when Sigi came to visit the Schmidts, she and Wolfgang would stroll through the park back to her home. As a result of their membership in the folkdancing group, the two of them went along with Lori and Mike on a number of trips around the country, dancing at various festivals in *Dirndls* and *Lederhosen*. By 1957, it appeared that the two had developed more than just a friendship.

Both Wolf and Sigi had decided they did not want to remain in Germany; however, they had no plans to marry immediately. Instead, they thought they would both emigrate to America, get jobs, and then wed at a later date. When they went to apply for visas at the American Consulate, however, they learned that if they were not married when they traveled to the United States, they could not be guaranteed resettlement in the same location. So they decided to accelerate their marriage plans. They became officially engaged in December 1957.

By the time Wolf asked Sigi to marry him, he had become enamored with "The American Dream." His own experiences—and no doubt some prodding from his mother—had convinced him that his future lay across the ocean. What Wolf felt is what his mother believed as well. His rationale provides a kind of "case study" of what drove all of the Schmidts, except perhaps Joe and Barbara, to look forward to boarding a plane for the United States.

In Wolf's view, there were three good reasons to resettle in America. First, he felt he had no real roots in West Germany. Living in Solingen was like living in a foreign country, far different from his home in Mirow. The people in the region spoke a different dialect, had different customs—and had little use for refugees. In Germany, people expected to die where they were born. They were, Wolf thought, too tied to a single place, and he could not return to the place in Germany he thought of as "home." In Solingen he would always be an outsider.

Second, he thought Germany was too close to the Iron Curtain. Surveying the tense political climate of the 1950s, he felt there was no guarantee the Communists would stay on their side of the border. He remembered life in East Germany, and he did not want to raise a family in a country controlled by Communists. He wanted to get away before things worsened.

Third, and perhaps most importantly, he hated the class system in Germany. He could see there was no intermingling between commoners and the upper classes who thought themselves too good for the likes of the Schmidt family. One incident stood out with particular vividness to illustrate the kind of discrimination the Schmidts could expect for the rest of their lives if they did not leave the country. One evening, Wolf and Sigi went with Hertha and her friend Herr Bölling to dinner at a nice restaurant. It turned out that the restaurant had an area upstairs reserved for the higher classes; the Schmidts, of course, were directed to a table on the ground floor.

That might not have bothered Wolf had his dinner party been left alone to enjoy the evening. But while they were eating and drinking their beer, the waiter brought a bottle of wine. Wolf protested that they'd not ordered any wine. The waiter gestured up toward the balcony seating and said it was from the "*Herr General Direktor.*" Looking up, Wolf saw the general manager of the foundry where Wolf worked. The *Direktor* gave them a condescending glance to await their acknowledgment and thanks—after all, it was expected that people of Wolf's class would be appreciative of any small gesture their "betters" made toward them. Even if the *Direktor* may have intended well in sending down a bottle of wine, there was *no* chance that he would come down to share a glass with the Schmidt party! Wolf knew this was as close as he would ever get to socializing with his "superiors." The experience rankled him.

Wolf and Sigi tied the knot on March 21, 1958. Their early wedded bliss almost ended before it began when the couple decided to visit Wolf's grandparents in Horumersiel for what was to be a week-long honeymoon. Wolf was aware of his grandmother's imperious behavior, but he had no idea what his grandfather was really like. As soon as they arrived, Oma Paula began dictating to Sigi what she could eat and ordered the young couple around like servants. But Oma Paula's highhandedness paled in comparison to Opa Schmidt's behavior. The newlyweds had not been there a day when he propositioned his grandson's wife. Sigi, frightened and in tears, ran to tell Wolf. Indignant and angry, Wolf told his young bride to pack, and they left on the second day of their visit.

Several months later, with a loan from the World Council of Churches, Wolf and Sigi paid for a flight and headed off for the United States. On December 17, 1958, they landed in New York. Rolf met them and took them to Manheim, where he and Renate put them up while they looked for a place to live. They settled into a brick row house at 420 Main Street, east of the city center.

While Rolf was away at work, Renate helped find some

second-hand furniture and household items from the Water Street Rescue Mission in Lancaster. Wolf had no trouble getting hired, but his early days at the Lancaster Malleables Foundry were especially taxing. Each molder was expected to pour his own metal. In the stifling Pennsylvania summer, the heat became almost unbearable, especially for the (then) diminutive Wolfgang Schmidt, who weighed only 123 pounds and who was accustomed to the more temperate summer climate in Germany. But he persevered, and slowly he and his wife became accustomed to the "American way" of getting things done. After several months'

At home in the apartment on Wilhelmshöhe, late 1950s. Left to right: Hertha, Einhard, Lori, Bill, Bill's girlfriend Brigitte Heyer.

Seeing off Lori, Einhard, and Bill to the United States in April 1959. Left to right: Mike, Brigitte Heyer, Hertha, Barbara, and Joe.

commuting to Lancaster, he was able to secure a job at the Manheim Brass Foundry just a short distance from his home on Main Street.

Back in Germany, however, Hertha Schmidt was far from content. Two of her children were gone, and if it were not so earlier, it was now crystal clear to her that the future for all the Schmidts lay across the ocean. She did not consider this move lightly. Wolf remembers her being distressed at Rolf's leaving, and doubly so when Wolf followed him. But she was growing increasingly frustrated by the German bureaucracy, and she could see that her sons and daughters would fare much better in a land where the children of farmers could grow up to be successful business owners and political leaders. There is no doubt that, by 1958, she had determined to relocate to the United States. So she set out to help all of her children prepare to emigrate.

In the spring of 1959, Lori, Einhard, and Bill left Germany for America. They each borrowed money from the Revolving Fund of the World Council of Churches, signing a promissory note to repay the loan as quickly as possible. They were sponsored by the St. James Episcopal Church in Lancaster, Pennsylvania. Their plane left Frankfurt on April 8, 1959. When they landed in New York, big brother Rolf was on hand to pick them up in his yellow 1952 Mercury. Rolf took them straight to Manheim, where he and Wolf proved helpful in getting them settled into the apartment that had been rented and partially furnished by their sponsors.

The apartment was in a large white frame house just a few doors down from Wolf and Sigi's place. Their arrival in the region created something of a stir. On April 11 the Lancaster *New Era* newspaper ran a feature story about the Schmidts, complete with a photo of the new arrivals sharing a happy moment with Rolf and his family. The article contained the story of the family's escape from East Germany, and provided some candid observations about life under the Communists. The reporter quoted Renate's observation that the people of East Germany were being told that, "America is a desert where capitalism sucks the blood of everyone." In these Cold War years, the American community welcomed people like the Schmidts, who had escaped the clutches of the East Germans and their Soviet masters.

Omi's insistence that all her children learn a useful trade paid immediate dividends for the Schmidts once they settled in America. Rolf had found work shortly after arriving in 1957, and Wolf had done the same when he emigrated the following year. Similarly, within days of their arrival, Bill also had a job at the Fuller Company in Manheim; Lori found work at Bearings Company in Lancaster; and Einhard landed a position at Pepperidge Farm in Downingtown, an hour's drive east of Manheim. He remained there for six months, renting a room in the home of a Mrs. Reed, an elderly widow, during the week and returned to Manheim on weekends.

While Rolf and Wolf were working to support their families, Bill and Einhard were thinking of starting theirs. Both had sweethearts back in Germany. Bill was negotiating to have his fiancée, Brigitte Heyer, join him in America. Einhard was not sure the family of his intended, Erika Winterhagen, could afford to send their daughter to the U.S., and he could not see how he could save enough money to pay her way across the ocean. But then he hit upon a scheme that would solve his problems nicely. He enlisted in the United States Army, with a guarantee of choosing his first duty station. Naturally, he chose Germany. In October 1959, he left Pepperidge Farm for Fort Benning, Georgia, to begin his basic training.

In Solingen, Hertha was preparing to bring the remainder of the family to America to join her elder children. When she knew she would soon be leaving, she had Barbara accelerate her schoolwork, enrolling early in the eighth grade so she could reach her new home with a certificate of completion from the German secondary school system. Hertha herself enrolled in English language classes, although as she discovered after arriving in the United States, she had not learned anything of practical value.

Mike, who was now the oldest child at home, would have to listen to her practicing what she'd picked up. He recalled years later that she was immensely proud that she had learned to say, "A new broom sweeps clean!" And she knew what it meant, too. But as they all found out just a few months later, knowing how a broom works didn't help much when trying to order something in a restaurant.

Hertha began final preparations for the trip to America in the fall of 1959. The family was to be accompanied by Bill's fiancée, Brigitte Heyer. The daughter of parents who had lived in the West during the war, Brigitte was "a step up" in the German class system from the Schmidts. Brigitte's parents thought the refugee family from the other side of the border little better than the foreign guest workers who were flooding into Germany to help with the country's reconstruction. Ultimately, they decided to let their daughter join Bill in America. Hertha was only too glad to have the young woman accompany the Schmidts on the flight to New York. A wedding would be a great way to start their new life in the States!

The Schmidts were scheduled to fly out of Munich. Prior to leaving Solingen, they were feted by neighbors at a farewell party, and the family received going-away presents from friends. Among the most special gifts were hunting knives for Mike and Joe. Unfortunately, the knives were missing from their luggage when they unpacked after arriving in the United States—pilfered, no doubt, by an airline employee or perhaps even a Customs agent who admired them and assumed these immigrants would not know how to file a complaint even if they discovered the theft.

On December 16, 1959, the day before their scheduled departure, Hertha brought her traveling party by train to Munich. They were billeted overnight in a processing center reserved for departing emigrants, inside a compound near several commercial attractions. Joe and Barbara decided they wanted to spend their last night in Germany at the movies. Reluctantly, Hertha agreed to let them leave the compound to go to a theater just outside the gate. Barb and Joe slipped out without difficulty. But they decided they did not like the feature film playing at the nearby cinema, so they wandered about until they found one with a movie that caught their interest. Unfortunately, the film ended late, and by the time they returned to the compound, the gates were locked shut.

One can only imagine what Hertha must have been going through when her children did not return on what was to be their last evening in the country. Certainly the scene that took place the next morning when the errant teens were reunited with their mother would not have been pretty to witness.

The next day the five members of the Schmidt party boarded a plane bound for America. No commercial aircraft was able to fly non-stop from Munich to New York, so the Schmidts found themselves taking one of the typical routes from Germany to America, touching down in Holland and again in England before setting off across the Atlantic.

Once they reached the North American shore, there was another stop in Newfoundland, where they were encouraged to deplane to wait out the layover in the terminal. No one mentioned, however, that a blizzard was raging outside, and when they stepped outside in sweaters and light clothing, they were almost blown over. They struggled to put on overcoats that were whipping behind them in the gale-force winds. The "rest" they got in the terminal was most welcome! Even more welcome was the call to re-board for the last leg of their journey. That afternoon, they touched down at Idlewild airport.

When the family completed their customs inspection, they exited into the terminal, only to be disappointed again. Rolf was late in coming to pick them up. The woman in charge of the group of immigrants was indignant. She was not going to keep them company forever! Hertha was told her group would have to wait for their transportation alone. Not knowing how long it would be before Rolf arrived, they decided to get something to drink, and found a nearby coffee shop in the terminal. Unfortunately, no one in the family spoke English, so placing an order turned into a real adventure. Mike was designated to try to get something for them. He went up to the counter and quickly discovered the waitress spoke no German. There was only one item he could recognize—Coca-Cola—so he began signaling with one hand and holding up five fingers on the other. Only by employing such "sign language," did he manage to get his order placed.

As they sat sipping their drinks and gazing out the windows of the terminal, the family saw a steady stream of limousines pull up to the door to pick up passengers. "So this is America!" Mike thought. "When will our limousine arrive?" About two hours later, Rolf finally showed up—with only a car, not a stretch limo—and the family were off to their new home.

Meanwhile, back in Manheim, Sigi Schmidt was completing final preparations for the family's arrival. For ten days she had been sewing curtains for the freshly painted room in her house where Barbara and Brigitte would sleep, and helping spruce up the apartment down the street where Omi and Mike would stay with Bill, Lori, and Einhard, who was home on leave from the Army. Joe was to sleep on the couch at Wolfgang's next door until more suitable arrangements could be made for the entire family. Sigi took time out from her last-minute housecleaning on that day to drop a note to her mother in Germany, relaying the joy she and Wolf felt about the family's arrival. "It's all so exciting!" she wrote. How ironic those words would seem in just a few short days.

It was with a great deal of anticipation and excitement, too, that Hertha Schmidt and the other new arrivals headed out across New York City and into the Pennsylvania countryside. Nearly five hours later they arrived in Manheim. That evening there was a tearful but joyous reunion. Hertha was introduced to her first grandson, Rolf-Achim "Bootie" Schmidt, who had been born in November 1958, and to her second granddaughter, eight-month-old Marianne Schmidt, Wolf and Sigi's firstborn. They spoke excitedly about going house-hunting after Christmas so the newcomers would not have to stay in Bill and Lori's apartment, which was suddenly very cramped. They decided that, for a couple of days, though, they would all just enjoy the thought of being reunited in America, the land where dreams could come true.

Their euphoria was to be short-lived.

Tragedy struck the Schmidt family on December 20,

Wolfgang and Sigi Schmidt's home at 420 Main Street, Manheim, Pennsylvania. Site of the fire that claimed the life of Brigitte Heyer, led to Barbara Schmidt's serious injuries, and devastated the Schmidt family, the last of whom had arrived in the United States only three days earlier. (photographed 2008)

1959. The entire clan went that evening to a Christmas celebration at the home of the Conrads, one of the families who had sponsored Omi and her youngest children. The group coming from Germany had loaded up on Christmas presents, since they were arriving close to the holiday. These were placed in Wolf and Sigi's living room so the family could open them on Christmas Eve. Joe took one present with him to the Conrads, a box of the special chocolate mints Petra had liked so much. But when he presented them to her, he learned (much to his dismay) that her tastes had changed and she no longer wanted them! However, this small disappointment did little to dampen the joy everyone in the family felt that evening.

The Schmidts returned home late, and while Omi and Mike walked down to Lori's apartment, those staying with Wolf-gang stumbled sleepily into his house and prepared for bed. Barb and Brigitte headed upstairs to their second-floor bedroom. Joe slipped into his pajamas and dropped off on the couch in the living room. Wolf and Sigi also went upstairs. Tired themselves, they decided that their infant daughter, already asleep, could spend the night in her snow suit, so they laid her in her crib, which was in their own bedroom.

Initially, all seemed well; the house was warm, despite the bitter cold of the Pennsylvania winter night. Sometime in the early hours of the next morning, near 2:00 a.m., Joe awoke feeling uncomfortably hot. Groggily he stumbled around before discovering that the curtains in the living room were on fire! He tried to dash up the stairs to alert Wolf and Sigi, but flames and smoke drove him back. In something of a panic, he ran out of the house, then tried to get back in to warn the others. But he was locked out. Clad only in his pajamas, he began trying to kick loose some stones to throw at the window to wake Wolf and Sigi. When that did not work he went to Lori and Bill's apartment to get help. Einhard was the first to come out. Quickly the rest of the family dashed over to Wolfgang's to see what they could do to help avert disaster.

Upstairs, Wolf and Sigi had finally awakened to the sound of shattering glass. Wolf tried to open his door into the hallway but he, too, was stymied by the flames and smoke. The bedroom walls were beginning to give way, and suddenly the one next to the crib collapsed on their sleeping child. Wolf snatched Marianne from her crib and told Sigi to take the baby onto the balcony at the rear of the house. As she headed toward the door, Sigi stumbled and apparently passed out momentarily. Wolf was able to get her and Marianne out of the room.

As Sigi stood on the balcony overlooking the yard behind the house, she could see Bill standing below them—no doubt frantic not only for his brother's family, but especially for his fiancée. Wolf tossed the baby down to him; fortunately, Bill caught her and carried her off to safety. Wolf and Sigi climbed down from the balcony on the drain spout, escaping essentially unhurt. They were the lucky ones.

In the other bedroom Barb and Brigitte had been sleeping soundly. A noise from outside woke them. Someone was shouting "Fire!" Barb made sure Brigitte was awake. By now they could smell the smoke which was billowing out in the hallway, seeping in under the closed door of their bedroom. Brigitte seemed paralyzed. She crawled back under her covers, moaning that someone would come to save her. Barb had no such illusions; she knew the girls would have to act—fast!—if they were to escape. She raced to the window and yanked on the frame to throw it open.

The windows would not budge.

Barb turned back to Brigitte, trying to pull her toward the window. Brigitte would not cooperate, but kept hanging on to Barb, dragging her back toward the bed and the door, closer to the fire. By now Barb could hardly breathe. She broke away and dashed toward the window, picking up a pillow to protect herself as she punched a hole in the glass. The panes shattered, ripping her arm in the process. She then kicked out the window and scurried out onto the roof just outside the room in which she and Brigitte were sleeping.

As Barb emerged onto the roof, Einhard climbed up from the street and tried to enter the girls' room through the broken window. He was driven down by the intense heat and the flames, his hands and arms burned badly.

Barb heard someone yelling at her to jump. The fire had burst out several windows in the house, and flames were shooting out into the night sky. She could see tongues of fire jetting through the roof. Quickly she retreated to one edge of the roof, then raced toward the other side, leaping toward the roof on the adjacent house. But she did not make it. Instead, she fell on the concrete sidewalk.

The fire department arrived and mounted a concerted effort to rescue Brigitte, who never emerged from the window Barb had broken out. When they finally reached her, however, they discovered she was beyond help. She had died of smoke inhalation.

Two doctors arrived on the scene almost immediately. Barb had received the most severe injuries, so she was taken in an ambulance to the hospital, where doctors discovered she had broken her back, several ribs, and her ankle. She would be in a body cast for months. One of the doctors took Sigi and Marianne to the hospital in his car while the other stayed to tend to injuries suffered by others in the family. Wolf and Sigi's little girl had suffered severe burns on one foot, but her winter jumpsuit had saved her from further injury. Wolf had cuts on his arms and hand, and burns on his fingers and ears. All of Sigi's fingers were blistered, as were her earlobes. Every one of them had singed eyebrows and hair. In attempting to help with the rescue, Einhard cut his forehead and burned his fingers and ear lobes.

Later, an investigation revealed the fire had been caused by faulty wiring. There was little the family could have done to prevent the conflagration. But no one could have anticipated the tragedy that rent a hole in the family's blanket of optimism which had covered them so snugly just a day before.

Almost immediately after the fire, Wolfgang sent a telegram to Frau Weinberg back in Solingen to let her know what had happened and to assure her that everyone except Brigitte was safe. He then made a tape recording for her, giving a detailed account of the catastrophe. Sigi sent it via express mail.

Bill was disconsolate. He lay for hours on his bunk in

the upstairs apartment, staring out a window at a shaft in the middle of the building. What could anyone say to him? Worse, what was he to tell Brigitte's parents?

The Schmidts knew that telephoning was both expensive and unreliable, but they had decided to place a call to the Heyers rather than send a telegram. What they could not decide was, who was to call (Bill volunteered, of course) and, more importantly, what should they say—and not say.

While they were deliberating about how to break the news, they heard from the Heyers who had read about their daughter's death in their local newspaper.

What the Schmidts had not realized was the worldwide reach of the news media. The wire service in Germany picked up the story of the fire, and since it happened to a family that had only recently left the area, papers in the Solingen area carried an account. Unfortunately, either the wire services or the German newspapers got the details terribly botched up. The headlines announced that "THREE GIRLS BURNED TO DEATH." The "awful news from America" was that "three young girls, two of whom stood joyful and happy at the Ohligs train station only a week ago, were killed in a fire in a wooden farm house." German papers cited the Associated Press as the source for reporting the fatalities.

"Three girls could not be rescued," the paper reported. "Brigitte Heyer, 18, Barbara Schmidt, 14, and the 8-month old daughter of Wolfgang and Sigrid Schmidt." The papers reported erroneously that Wolf and Sigi were living in a farmhouse (they would move to a farm a short time later), and that Bill was living with them (he was still in the apartment several doors down from their townhouse).

The cause of the fire was identified as an exploding oil furnace, rather than faulty wiring. According to the paper, Sigi's mother had been notified by the Consulate and had been asked by American officials to deliver the news personally to the Heyers. But no matter how many details were wrong, one was horribly right: Brigitte Heyer was dead, and the family had learned about it second-hand.

To make matters even worse, Brigitte's family wanted Hertha to ship their daughter's body home for burial. Hertha did not have the money to pay for what would have certainly been an expensive transport. The Heyers, angry over what they considered insensitive treatment by the entire Schmidt clan, did not offer to pay. So Brigitte Heyer was buried in the Mount Hope Episcopal Church Cemetery outside Manheim, in a plot donated by the Church. For years afterward, even after he had married, Bill's sense of duty—instilled in him by his mother, no doubt—compelled him to visit the cemetery regularly and tend Brigitte's grave.

Barbara spent a week in the hospital before coming home with a cast covering her torso and another over her leg. All of the other family members were healing well within a week, except Wolf and Sigi's daughter. She had suffered third-degree burns on one foot, and was hospitalized for a long time so that skin grafts could be placed on the injury; fortunately, none were required.

If the tragedy of Brigitte's death were not enough of a blow to him, Bill was now left to deal with her belongings. She had brought with her quite a bit of clothing and housewares. To make matters even more painful, her "hope chest" with special items for her wedding arrived several days after the fire. Bill knew he would have to send all these items back to Germany, as the Heyers had indicated they wanted their daughter's possessions returned. But he was handicapped by his unfamiliarity with the American systems for mailing or shipping items, and by his inability to speak English.

For several weeks Rolf did his best to investigate options for getting these goods back across the ocean, but the delay seemed excessive to the Heyers, who accused the Schmidts of trying to profit from Brigitte's death. It was just as she expected, Frau Heyer wrote to them; after all, weren't the Schmidts refugees?

Of course, Wolf and Sigi had lost everything, including the Christmas presents they had bought to send to relatives in Germany and those the Schmidts had brought with them to America. Nevertheless, they gathered as a family on Christmas eve to offer thanks for their lives, and for the blessing of being together, despite the tragedy.

Bill was insistent that they try to have a normal Christmas; he even went out and bought a tree. Petra—old enough to understand something of Christmas but too little to realize the extent of the tragedy her family had just suffered—became the center of the family's attention. She got to see Santa Claus, thanks to her Uncle Mike, who dressed up for the celebration.

Almost as soon as they learned of the fire, Sigi's family began sending much-needed replacement items to the family, for which they were all most grateful. What was also exceptionally gratifying to the Schmidts was the generosity of their Manheim neighbors. Beginning the day after the fire, people began coming to them with food, clothing, furniture, appliances, towels, blankets, and even money—more than $800 in all. Stores in town contacted them to let them know there were boxes awaiting pickup, marked simply "For the Schmidt Family." So much food was collected that the family had to rent extra freezer space to store everything given to them.

Some of their neighbors simply stopped and left gifts without waiting to be thanked. Others stayed a few moments to pray with the family. Even though the newest arrivals did not understand everything that was being said, the entire clan

Living the American Dream

(1960-1985)

felt comforted to know that so many people cared so much.

The tragedy that marked Hertha Schmidt's first days in the United States might have crushed someone of weaker spirit, but this woman was determined to make a go of life in America. Instead of giving in to despair, she rallied her family and urged them to focus toward the future. In the years to come, her own life in this new land would be filled with new adventures, and she would be

Hertha Schmidt, circa 1960.

known to the next generation as "Omi"—the grandmother and matriarch of a family that would, over the next three decades, live out the American dream in a way that would make her most proud.

In the days following the disastrous fire at Wolf's home, the first item on the family's long agenda was to establish some sense of normalcy for everyone. Wolf and Sigi moved in with the crowd staying at Lori and Bill's apartment until they found a place of their own. Their daughter came home from the hospital in early January 1960, and the Red Cross provided baby clothes, blankets, diapers, and a voucher good for purchasing additional items Sigi might need for her. The owner of a sewing machine store in Ephrata donated a machine to the family. By mid-January, Wolf had gone back to work. A few weeks later he and Sigi settled into a new apartment.

Barbara was still in a body cast, but the doctors were certain she would heal completely. Bill was understandably still feeling low, but he had thrown himself into his work. Now that he had a job in Ephrata, he needed better transportation, so he bought a 1953 Pontiac from the Conrads, the family's American sponsor. Although Bill was slow to recover, he was fortunate to have his mother and siblings with him to ease the pain he was most certainly feeling.

In addition to helping one son deal with the death of his fiancée, another cope with the loss of his household belongings, and a daughter handle the recovery and rehabilitation required after her serious accident, Omi had to find a place large enough to accommodate her family comfortably. Even though Einhard would not be staying with them, the apartment in which Bill and Lori had been living was simply not large enough for everyone. They needed a new place—quickly! Fortunately, a two-story home on North Main Street was available. The place had a kitchen, dining room, living room, and laundry on the first floor, three bedrooms and a bath upstairs. But the Schmidts were able to stay there only temporarily, and Omi had to continue looking for suitable housing. As luck would have it, a local farmer owned a home in town on Hazel Street, a quaint one-story bungalow with an attic that could be used for extra living space. The owner agreed to rent it to Omi at a very reasonable rate.

Though the place was small, the Schmidts managed to shoehorn themselves into these quarters, creating a bedroom in the attic for some of the older children. Outside there was room for a garden where Omi could plant flowers to brighten up the place. Unfortunately the location turned out to be bad for Bill and Mike, who were working the night shift; it was near the high school, and the noise from the school band practicing out on the field disturbed their sleep constantly. What made this even more excruciating was every day the band played the same song! It was probably the school's fight song, but the weary brothers were not in the least bit interested in the music; all they wanted was a little extra shut-eye!

A top priority for everyone in the family was to learn English. By the time Omi and the last of her family arrived late in 1959, Rolf and Wolf had already become adept in their new language, and the siblings who had arrived in April 1959 were rapidly mastering the vagaries of English on the job. Joe and Barb were exposed to English at school—although there was no one to help translate from German. Barb remembers sitting at the back of the room, "like a bump on a log," not comprehending anything being said in any of her classes. She spent many weeks gazing at the pictures in old books her teachers gave her.

Living in a region of Pennsylvania that had been settled centuries earlier by German immigrants actually proved frustrating for a family that wanted to assimilate quickly. All around them descendants of the Amish, Mennonites, and other German sects who had come to America in the eighteenth century spoke to Omi and her children in "Pennsylvania Dutch," a patois of corrupted German that made perfect sense to the locals but was confusing to people who spoke modern German. After two weeks in America, Omi announced to the family, "Look! This Pennsylvania Dutch that people are trying to use on me is all boogered up! Let's try to speak English at home!"

One of the ways the new immigrants sought to learn English was by watching television. Someone had advised them they could pick up the nuances of the language if they listened attentively and followed the actions on the screen. The Schmidts had never owned a television. Not only were sets expensive, one had to pay for the service. Even though it would have been easy to subscribe—like so many services in Germany, all one had to do was fill out a form at the Post Office—the state-run German television had been too costly for a family on welfare. They had seen German TV, of course, at the homes of friends, but they were not prepared for one of the most important differences between their old country's "boob tube" and the American version: commercials. Imagine what the family must have thought as they were sitting in front of a television watching a western like Wagon Train, trying their best to associate speech with action, when, all of a sudden, the scene changes. A woman in a long gown is waltzed away by a man in a tuxedo; they pause, smile at each other, and light up a cigarette! It took awhile for the Schmidts to realize these advertisements were not part of the program, but were inserted by sponsors who were paying the bills so television could be free for anyone who owned a set.

The Schmidts had not been in their home on Hazel Street more than a year when the owner told Omi he would need his house. She was ready to move anyway; she knew the family could use more space. So she and five of her children—Lori, Bill, Mike, Joe, and Barb—moved to a duplex at 15 South Fulton Street, just five blocks from the town square in Manheim. Not only was this two-story structure more spacious; in the rear, behind the small yard, was a garage where Bill could keep his 1958 Mercury—the car he bought to replace the 1953 Pontiac, which was totaled in a wreck. The Fulton Street duplex would be the Schmidts' home for several years.

Beginning in 1960, more of Omi's children began to leave the nest. Once he enlisted in the Army, Einhard never returned to live at home. In 1960, while serving in Germany, he married his childhood sweetheart, Erika Winterhagen in 1960.

Relaxing at Rolf's farm house outside Manheim, Pennsylvania, Easter 1960. Foreground: Marianne and Petra; first row: Wolfgang, Mike, Joe, Omi; second row: Barbara, family friend Jürgen Walbrecht; background: Renate and Bootie.

Lori married in February 1961, to Richard Stoltzfus, a co-worker at the Bearings company. Bill managed to rebound from his devastating loss, and in 1961 he began dating Peggy Ann Southern, a young divorcee who had moved to Pennsylvania with her first husband from her home in southwestern Virginia. She was working at a store where Bill's sister-in-law Renate ran the diner, and Bill would see Peggy when he stopped for gas. They married in 1962.

Before Bill and Lori left home, they were the principal providers for the Schmidt household, using their wages to support Omi, Mike, Joe, and Barbara. It must have been especially hard on Lori, since she worked at a union shop where, because she lacked seniority, she was laid off from time to time. Bill had steadier employment at the non-union Ephrata Tool, but earned only $1.60 per hour—hardly enough to be considered a real bread-winner. Yet when it came time for him to file his first income-tax return, he had a pleasant shock: He was able to declare five dependents on his tax form, and as a result receive money back from the government! In Germany workers had money taken from their paychecks for taxes, but there was never a return.

While her older brothers and sister seemed to be adjust-

ing quite well to life in America, Barb— still a teenager—did not fare as well. She had been rebellious while in Germany, staying out late in the evenings and lying to her mother regarding her whereabouts. Things actually got worse when the family settled in Manheim.

Omi Schmidt with Wolf and Sigi's daughter, Andrea, in 1960.

Barb flaunted her mother's rules, dating someone three years older and eventually becoming pregnant. Angry words were exchanged, and eventually she moved out of the house. She dropped out of high school and married in 1962 at the age of 16.

There were other ways family members were starting to become increasingly independent. In 1960, Omi got a taste of what the phrase "America's mobile society" meant. That year Rolf got his first real engineering job in the design section of Electro Mechanical Research Company, which had a contract to make components for the Gemini and Apollo rocket projects, the United States' first real ventures into manned space flight. But accepting the position meant he had to move his family to Sarasota, Florida. For nearly three years, Omi got to see her eldest son and his family only infrequently.

Omi may have taken some consolation in knowing that Bootie and Petra were both having a great time learning gymnastics and acrobatics from a retired member of the Ringling Brothers Barnum & Bailey circus, which had its winter quarters in Sarasota. Their escapades were even written up in the local newspaper. But she was overjoyed in 1963, when Rolf turned down the company's offer to relocate for a new job in Birmingham, Alabama, and moved the family back North.

When Rolf's family returned to Pennsylvania, they stayed briefly with Omi while Rolf looked for suitable lodgings. Eventually he rented a place in Mohnton, a suburb of Reading, Pennsylvania, forty miles northeast of Manheim, where the family lived briefly. Then he purchased a home at 515 West Madison Street. The modest dwelling built in 1926 was on property that had a barn where the previous owner had tried to keep horses. Most importantly, it contained a sizable cinderblock garage—a structure that would figure largely in the family's future endeavors. The house and grounds would prove large enough for the Schmidt family to hold occasional reunions beginning in the 1970s.

*Enjoying the summer sun at Lake Cordoba, York, Pa.,
sometime in mid 1960s.*

As her children moved away, Omi became even more
convinced that she needed to become financially and personally independent. This was America, after all, the land of opportunity. Certainly there was no reason she could not earn her
own living! The fact that she had not worked outside the home
since her marriage in 1933 did not deter her. So she sought
out a position in a business for which she felt qualified—the
garment industry. Intrepidly, she headed into downtown Ephrata to Ephrata Apparel, a division of Terre Hill Manufacturing,
which operated out of a one-story brick factory at the east end of
Main Street. The company manufactured underwear and other
specialty garments for ladies. At the time, manufacturing was

still in its heyday in Pennsylvania, and the people at Terre Hill were happy to take her on. She became a garment inspector, checking the work of seamstresses who were often young enough to be her daughters.

For months she joined Bill, Peggy, and the others on their drive from Manheim to her place of work in Ephrata. But eventually she decided to move to Ephrata to be nearer to her job. She vacated her place in Manheim and located an apartment on State Street across the street from the Donecker's complex in Ephrata. She was immensely proud of her little place, even though it was furnished with hand-me-downs. Now she felt truly on her own—almost.

She had learned quickly that to be on one's own in America, one needed an automobile. She was tired of relying on her children and their spouses to cart her around everywhere she wanted to go. So she bought an old car—a dilapidated Chevrolet Corvair—and coerced her family to teach her how to drive.

Omi relaxing in 1967 with Barbara's daughter Tonya, Bill's son Carlton, and Barbara's son Jimmy.

Wolfgang tried briefly, but gave up, having quickly run out of patience. It did not take him long to have his mother crying at the wheel. Her daughters-in-law soon found themselves saddled with this unenviable task. For hours they would patiently coach Omi in the basics of good driving as she maneuvered around a parking lot or on some side road.

When she thought she was ready, she had her daughter-in-law Peggy accompany her to the Motor Vehicle Administration to get her license. She managed the written test without any problem, but the driving portion of the examination was another matter. The evaluator sat quietly as this little woman went through the mandatory stops and starts and turns and traffic maneuvers, ever so cautious lest she do something wrong. When she was finished, the evaluator reluctantly decided he would pass her. But he encouraged her not to drive alone for awhile—and he instructed Peggy to make certain someone ride with her mother-in-law until Omi became more familiar with her car and the American roadway system.

But Omi would have none of that! From the very first day she had her license in hand, she was off on her own to explore the neighborhood, do her own shopping, and show her children she was not going to be a burden to them any longer! She never became an expert driver, probably because she had learned to drive so late in life and did not adjust well to the demands of the road. She managed to master the basics, but there were times when mishaps seemed unavoidable. Her luck did not improve much when she traded in her Corvair for a Rambler. Because she was exceptionally short, she had trouble seeing from behind the wheel. In the 1960s and 1970s, American cars were not built for short people, so she had to use a pad of some sort on the seat of the car, and then had to have blocks placed on the pedals so she could use the accelerator and brake. None of this made it easy for someone approaching sixty to handle an automobile in city traffic! What made things worse was that the Rambler had power steering and power brakes—both of which were inoperative when the car stalled, which it did with some regularity.

Omi lived on State Street in Ephrata for about a year, but then her landlord decided to take over the building for his own use, and she was forced to move again. She moved in with Mike and his wife Thelma for a time, but eventually decided she wanted to be truly on her own. So she located and rented a small apartment in a run-down tenement on Reamstown Road, five miles north of Ephrata. When that apartment proved to be unacceptable, she found another, similar accommodation in Denver, Pennsylvania, just west of Reamstown. The tiny place on the first floor was always neat, but sparsely furnished. Yet like other places Omi had kept, there was a basket of toys for the grandchildren to play with. Here her black and white television received only one channel. That may have bothered visiting grandchildren, but Omi didn't seem to mind. "I get all the shows I watch on that channel," she explained to one of them. Every day she traveled back and forth to her workplace in Ephrata, piloting her unreliable automobile up and down the country road at speeds that would make a turtle want to pass her.

Finally in 1971, Omi allowed her children to persuade her to upgrade her lifestyle. She obtained a comfortable first-floor apartment in Ephrata's Cloister Gardens Apartments on Dawn Avenue just off Highway 272 west of the town center. Bill and Peggy had lived in Cloister Gardens for some time after they sold their house so Bill could generate cash to invest in his own business. Her sons and grandson Bootie helped her move to the new place. For the first time in her life, she bought decent furniture, including bedroom and dining room suites. Outside her door she had her very own flower garden, which she meticulously tended. The side of her building was always ablaze in color. Inside, she could watch her favorite shows on television: news shows and soccer matches. She was an avid fan of soccer, perhaps because it reminded her of happier times in Germany.

The Cloister Gardens apartment complex, Ephrata, Pennsylvania. Omi lived in the first- floor apartment (shown here with chairs and table outside) from 1971 until her death in 1985.

Everything she did at the new apartment was carried out under a permanent haze created by the smoke from the cigarettes she puffed on constantly. She had taken up the habit years earlier, and she was not about to quit now.

By the time Omi moved to Cloister Gardens, Bill and Peggy had moved into a home on North Academy Drive just around the corner from the apartment complex. Living so close to their grandmother's new place was especially appealing to Bill's children, who could slip out the gate in their back yard and race through the parking lot to their grandmother's apartment door. Carlton and Tia looked forward to dropping in on Omi who relished their brief visits. She would have treats for them every day, much to their mother's dismay!

The apartment was nice enough for her to entertain, too. Family and friends visited regularly, including Bill's mother-in-law, Grace Southern, who lived with Bill and Peggy for some time during the 1970s. Bill himself stopped by every other Wednesday after he got his hair cut. Omi would take out a bottle of wine from behind a curtain, and they would sit and reminisce about bygone times, or discuss current political events, something in which Omi took great interest. She could get into heated debates on such matters, and visitors to the apartment in the Cloister Gardens soon learned that the little lady who lived there was no retiring grandmother content to knit quietly and watch soap operas! She may not have had extensive formal education, but she kept abreast of political matters and would not be intimidated by anyone who came to share food and conversation with her.

Visitors to Omi's apartment were certainly a varied lot. When Wolf was working as manager of a foundry near in the area, Omi would make lunch for him and other plant officials. Wolf would bring the Chair of the Board, the owner, and the accountant to the apartment once a month. His mother would prepare a big pot of soup—beef noodle, vegetable, or whatever struck her fancy. Whatever she fixed was sure to be good. Twice during the 1970s, Omi was able to host Lilli Lemke, her friend from Solingen who came to the United States for extended stays.

Omi loved to get out of the apartment, too, hopping in her car to go shopping whenever she needed something. She was quick to accept invitations to lunch or dinner, or to join family and friends for day outings—especially shopping trips with her daughters-in-law. For several years she would drive up to Rolf's on Saturday, where Bootie would wash her car. She even accompanied her grown children on vacations when any of them asked her along, relishing long trips with Dick and Lori, who took her with them to gatherings of various antique automobile clubs. Once she accompanied them as far as Maine, enjoying the scen-

All smiles in America: Omi with daughter-in-law Sigi (Weinberg) Schmidt in 1976.

ery in a part of the country she had only heard of before the trip.

Holidays remained special times for Omi in her adopted homeland, even though she was not able to follow all of the German traditions. In most years, after enjoying Christmas Eve with Bill and his family, who were always close by, she would spend Christmas day visiting her other children, eager to see the beaming smiles of grandchildren who were ecstatic to discover what Santa had brought them.

Whenever they gathered, the family was eager to hear stories of Omi's driving, the source of quite a few humorous (and sometimes frightening) stories. Sigi remembers being in the car with Omi, who at the time had only a learner's permit, in the Nightwear Company parking lot, trying to help her learn to park where she worked. Slowly, ever so slowly, Omi advanced toward a parking space at the rear of the lot. As they edged closer, Sigi noticed that the lot sat on a small bluff; beyond the shrubbery lining the lot was a sharp drop-off. Suddenly, Omi began to accelerate. Sigi raised her feet up and placed them on the dashboard, certain they would end up through that shrubbery and down the bluff! Fortunately, Omi managed to stop just in time to avoid catastrophe.

Once, while driving on Main Street into downtown Ephrata, Omi stopped at a light when another car pulled beside her on the right. When the light turned green, that car darted in front of her to make a left-hand turn. Startled, Omi tried to slam on her brakes, but was unable to avoid smashing into the other vehicle. She sat for a moment, dazed perhaps, wondering what to do next. Then she spied a phone booth on the corner where she had come to a stop. She knew she had to report the accident, so she climbed out of the car, made a beeline for the phone, and dialed the number for an emergency.

A voice came over the line. "Ephrata police!"

Omi told the young woman who had answered her call what had happened. The woman listened carefully, then began to laugh a bit.

"Oh," she finally said, "is that the crash I heard outside!"

Omi glanced around at her immediate surroundings. The telephone was just outside police headquarters.

When Omi was living in Denver, the family pitched in to buy her a new car—an American Motors Company Pacer, a little compact whose "bubble top" provided better visibility than she'd experienced in the Corvair or the Rambler. Unfortunately, this didn't make her a better driver. One day after she had moved to the Cloister Gardens complex, she left her apartment and headed toward the bank some three blocks away. The bank building was located on a busy corner of Route 272 and Martin Avenue across from a very popular—and very crowded—McDonald's restaurant. Attached at the side of the bank was a drive-through window. The roof over the drive-thru was supported by poles extending upward from a short flagstone wall. Cars would drive between the flagstone wall and the side of the building, where the teller window was located.

To avoid having to travel on the busy Route 272, Omi came from home on side streets and pulled through the parking lot that led past the McDonald's to the exit that allowed her to cross directly into the bank parking lot. Naturally she looked carefully before attempting to cross Martin Avenue. But as she began to accelerate, she saw another car coming as if out of nowhere. She went to hit her brake, but instead stepped on the accelerator—and drove across the street, through the lot, sideswiping a car as she sped along, finally zooming right into the drive-thru shelter and up the flagstone half-wall, where the car came to rest, balancing precariously on the stones.

Ironically, Mike was driving by at almost the moment his mother drove into the bank parking lot, and he saw a car perched upon the wall. But he did not "put two and two together" until he got to work. As he parked, Bill came running out of the factory toward his car. Mike thought this unusual, so he asked what had happened to make Bill leave work long before his shift was up.

"Didn't you see Mom?" Bill yelled at him.

"Where?" Mike asked innocently.

"At the bank!" Bill shouted back. Omi had walked from the bank to Bill's house, where she told Peggy what happened; Peggy's call to Bill had prompted him to leave for home just as Mike was driving into work.

The best was yet to come, however. Two months later, Omi was traveling on the Route 30 by-pass north of Lancaster, where she had gone to shop. As usual, she was making sure she was traveling at (or below) the posted speed limit of 40 MPH. Observantly Omi checked her rearview mirror, where she noticed a state trooper following her. For several miles he stayed immediately behind the Pacer as Omi inched toward her exit. Finally she turned off the bypass, and the trooper signaled for her to stop. She pulled over, nervous and afraid. She could not recall what she had done wrong. She had hit no one, passed no one on the right—certainly she had not exceeded the speed limit! The trooper got out of his car and strode toward her. Timidly she rolled down her window and leaned out.

"Officer, is there something wrong?" she managed to squeak.

"No," he boomed out, "not at all! In fact, you have done everything just fine! We need more drivers like you! I wanted to stop you to give you this certificate for safe driving!"

When she told the story to her children later that week, she admitted sheepishly, "I wonder what he would have done if he had known what I did two months ago!" Predictably, the story left the family in stitches.

Perhaps because she had suffered severe deprivation for so much of her life, in later years, Omi was always sure she had enough of everything in her house. Her refrigerator was constantly stocked, bulging with more food than any one person might eat before it spoiled. In her hallway stood a pyramid of umbrellas. The drawers of her dresser were filled with costume

"Going home again . . ." Omi on a train traveling from Frankfurt to Solingen, Germany, 1978.

jewelry and scarves in an array of colors to match the dozens of outfits she had bought with her own money. She discovered that one could get nice clothing for a very modest price at the Goodwill store. Buying second-hand was just fine with her. In America, she would never want for anything.

Now that she could afford to look stylish, she insisted on always being well-groomed and well-dressed. On one occasion, her penchant for noticing others who also dressed impeccably was cause for a great laugh. She was out shopping with her daughters-in-law in a local department store when she noticed someone walking her way. "Look at that nicely-dressed lady coming toward us!" As it turned out, Omi was looking at her own reflection in a mirror! When she realized her mistake, she found the incident worth repeating to her family—and she joined in when they all had a hearty laugh at her expense!

On the other hand, Omi was never comfortable talking about the period between 1945 and 1949. She wanted to forget that part of her past. Her hatred for the Communist government in East Germany was so great that she became angry at the thought of anyone in her family traveling there, even for business. In 1978, however, Wolfgang and Sigi convinced her to go back to Germany for a visit. Omi accompanied Wolf, Sigi, and three of their children. Despite her initial reservations, she enjoyed a visit in Solingen with her old friend Lilli Lemke.

She also went north to visit her sister Anni, who was living in the town of Winsen outside Hamburg. It was probably a good thing, however, that she did not accompany Sigi and Sigi's two youngest children to East Germany. Before they crossed the border, Sigi had to provide a detailed itinerary to East German authorities, and every day they were in the country she had to report to the local police station to confirm her whereabouts. That kind of control by the authorities might have brought back too many bad memories for Omi.

However, Omi did not let her aversion for "the Old

A happy reunion: Omi and her sister Anni in 1978.

Country" prevent her from staying in touch with her mother. They corresponded regularly, and Omi learned first-hand how hard life had become for Willi and Marie under the Communists. Despite the government's efforts to control the media, the people of East Germany were not totally cut off from news of world events. After John F. Kennedy was assassinated in November 1963, Marie Dittmann wrote to her daughter in America to express her deep sadness; in Marie's view, the world had lost a great hero. The Dittmanns never made it to America.

Willi Dittmann died in 1958. Marie moved to a retirement home in Rheinsberg, twelve kilometers from Flecken Zechlin. She hardly considered this a retirement, however. She took her sewing machine with her, and made clothes for herself and other residents. She even made curtains for the entire facility.

Marie continued to write regularly to her daughter Hertha and granddaughter Margarete in the United States until she died in 1967. Though her life never improved materially, Marie Dittmann seemed pleased to know that her daughter and grandchildren were doing well in America. At least that was some reward for the sacrifices she had made for them during her lifetime.

Omi's sisters all remained in Germany. Anni, who had served with the *Wehrmacht* as a communications specialist, had married a German soldier during the war. When hostilities ended, the two had managed to stay in the West, settling in Winsen. Hedwig stayed near her parents in Flecken Zechlin, dying of cancer in 1950. Elli had moved to Berlin after the war, settling in the Soviet sector. Marriage to a man some years her senior led to the birth of one son, Peter, who was raised an ardent Communist. Elli remained in Berlin after her husband died and her son moved away, spending her last years in a small apartment in a section of the city that had been bombed out during World War II and never repaired.

Willi's sisters had remained in the West, of course. Änne, a homemaker all her life, resided in southern Germany. Käthe worked as a hospital nurse, and Hertha became a visiting nurse, as did her daughter. Like their parents, the Schmidt sisters believed their brother had married beneath his class. When newlyweds Wolf and Sigi stopped by to see one of them in 1958, they were treated with overt condescension. Apparently, they never forgave their brother for what they considered a tragic mistake.

By the time she retired from the Nightwear Company, Omi had become a venerated icon within her own family. Her children all realized what she had done to secure their futures. Her grandchildren adored the kindly little lady who was so fond of all of them. None of them would believe she had ever raised her voice in anger; they would have been incredulous if someone had told them their grandmother had been the disciplinarian in the Schmidt household, and that those little arms at one time packed quite a wallop! But her habit of directing her children remained with her as she grew older. When she said that she wanted to see them at a reunion, they showed up.

At these reunions, the grandchildren got to mingle with dozens of cousins as their grandmother oversaw the gathering. It was not out of the question for Omi to hike up her skirts—metaphorically, at least—and join the players in a game of badminton, although she was known to swing and miss that little birdie time after time. Fortunately, rather than be embarrassed, Omi would simply laugh uproariously at her ineptitude, happy all the while in knowing her family was enjoying the benefits that living in America had brought to all of them.

Often when family members would visit Omi's apartment, the grandchildren would gather in the kitchen where Omi would join them to share stories about their parents, aunts, and uncles. In her quiet voice she would tell the youngsters about her life in Germany. Before long, many of the adults would wander into the room, captivated by her accounts. One or another of the children would invariably clamor to hear more.

"Tell us about eating turnips all winter long!"

"Tell us about Uncle Joe complaining about having to eat cabbage all the time!"

Slowly but surely, the family saga was passed on to the next generation.

The little matriarch also possessed an uncanny ability to laugh at herself. In 1982, when Evalina McCuiston, who would become Mike's second wife, first met Omi, she was struck by how happy her future mother-in-law was—all the time! Evalina was even able to tease Omi about "an old Southern custom" of having the mother of the groom sing at the wedding. Omi was concerned at first, but when she learned her leg was being pulled, so to speak, she took the joke quite well.

For years one of Omi's favorite pastimes was to ride with one or another of her children and their families out into the Pennsylvania countryside on weekends. These jaunts were most pleasant in the fall, as the leaves changed colors, making the hillsides blaze in yellow, red, and gold. Often as she stared out the window, she would muse wistfully how she wished Willi Schmidt could have come to America to see this spectacular scenery.

Until the day she died, Omi spoke with reverence and love about Willi, preserving his memory as a devoted husband and provider. Whatever quarrels may have occurred, whatever infidelities on Willi's part may have marred their seventeen years together, all of this seemed to be forgotten—or perhaps repressed. Of course, she had been annoyed, even angry, that he had never been able to keep silent about the injustices he saw going on all around him in the Communist-controlled zone of Germany after the war. He simply would not "dance with the devil," and the combination of honesty and outspokenness had been his doom.

One can only wonder what might have been. If Willi had lived, would he have been a driving force in helping his community rebound from the devastation of World War II? Would he have eventually acquiesced to Communist rule, and kept the family together in East Germany? Would he have led the family out of the East, as his wife did?

* * * * *

For more than sixty years, Omi Schmidt was strong physically as well as mentally. Eight pregnancies did little to sap her energy. As a young woman, she seemed to relish the demanding life of a German *Hausfrau*. The hardships she experienced in post-war Germany never dampened her fighting spirit, and never seemed to get her down. But in the early 1970s, her body began to turn against her. In 1971, certainly the darkest year of her life, she was diagnosed with cervical cancer.

The initial prognosis was not promising. At the time, patients diagnosed with this disease were typically given no more than six months to live. She was admitted to the hospital on January 3, 1971, and those who visited her were told she would probably never come home. The only hope doctors could offer would come at great personal cost. If Omi were to have any chance that she might recover or that the cancer would go into remission, she would have to submit to a painful form of radiation therapy known as "cobalt treatment." Cobalt pellets were inserted into the body near the site of the cancer; gamma rays emitted from the cobalt attacked and killed the cancerous cells. Unfortunately, the cobalt could also kill good cells, and doctors had to be careful in administering dosages so the patient was actually helped, and not harmed, by the treatment.

After what she had been through earlier in life, however, Omi was not going to give up easily. She allowed her doctors to complete a series of cobalt treatments, enduring excruciating pain while trying to be her normal, cheerful self. The treatments lasted for months, and finally the doctors announced the result she and the family had hoped to hear. By June, the cancer seemed to be gone. The family was naturally ecstatic. Omi had beaten the odds! Little did they know then that the cure would prove to be as bad as the illness.

Once she had beaten cervical cancer, Omi went home and gradually resumed her normal activities. There was one immediate drawback, however. Even while she was still at Lancaster General Hospital, one of the more immediate negative after-effects of the cobalt treatments emerged. Omi developed life-threatening uremic poisoning. The cobalt treatments had caused tissues surrounding the urethra to swell, preventing the passage of urine into the bladder and causing her whole body to become bloated. To relieve this pressure, a surgeon had cut slits into her sides near the waist to insert drainage tubes into her kidneys. These were connected to collection bags that had to be secured to Omi's body. For months after returning to her apartment, Omi made jokes about the pouches strapped to her thighs, but it was a relief to her and the entire family when first one tube, then the other, was removed after doctors

determined her kidneys and bladder were functioning properly
again.

It is possible that the years between the time she "beat
the odds" in her bout with cervical cancer and 1980 may have
been the happiest time of Omi's life. She had her health restored. She went back to work briefly but then retired, confident she could live comfortably on her small Social Security
payment and the pension she received from the German government.

Unfortunately, sometime in 1980, Omi began feeling
some discomfort in her stomach area. A visit to the doctor led to
a battery of tests that revealed the long-term effects of the cobalt
treatment. Some of her lower intestines had been burned by the
substance that had eradicated her cervical cancer years earlier.
Now she would have to deal with a new form of illness brought
on by the cure for the earlier one. The only solution this time,
however, was surgery to remove the damaged portion of her intestines. So Omi "went under the knife."

The surgery was successful—as far as it went—but post-op-
erative testing revealed the possibility of cancerous tissue resid-
ing in her stomach. Physicians ran another battery of tests. This
time the results were clear: cancer was present, and a second surgery required. Once again, Omi entered the hospital. When the
surgeons opened her up, they realized the damage was extensive;
they were forced to remove nearly 90% of Omi's stomach just
to be certain they'd cleared out what they could see. Then they
prescribed a series of chemotherapy treatments to eradicate all
remaining cancerous cells.

Omi bore up remarkably well during this new crisis. Although she remained in her apartment at the Cloister Gardens,
she allowed her family to help her much more than they had
during the previous fifteen years. She submitted to chemotherapy, hoping it would destroy the cells eating away at her body. But
this time things were different. The chemo treatments caused

her to lose her appetite. Her weight began dropping rapidly, and she was forced to subsist on liquids.

In the midst of this new suffering, Omi must have quietly taken stock of what she valued most about life, and decided she would joyfully live her remaining years. She did not want to spend months suffering from treatments that may not really cure the illness that was slowly taking her life. She decided it was more important to spend what time she had left reveling in her children's successes, watching her grandchildren grow to adulthood and start families themselves, enjoying time with friends and acquaintances, and traveling with Lori and Dick. She stopped the chemotherapy treatments.

A seemingly remarkable thing happened. Almost immediately, her appetite returned. She seemed to regain her strength as well. But that was a false hope.

Although she ate well, her body was unable to digest anything and extract nutrients needed to keep her healthy. While she did not suffer inordinately, she began to waste away slowly. Her blood pressure and her blood cell count varied wildly. For-

tunately for her, Ephrata Community Hospital had only recently installed a program to provide special assistance for elderly patients. Omi was given a device which she could press to alert the hospital when she needed immediate help. Additionally, a special alert device was installed on her telephone to let someone at the hospital know if the phone

Clowning around: Omi puts on her "Schwälbchen" face (the "little swallow beak"), in 1970.

was not used for more than twenty-four hours. At that point someone would call to check on her.

During her final years, Omi was in and out of Ephrata Community Hospital, but each time she recovered. Both she and her family knew, however, that the end was drawing near. In the late fall of 1985, she entered the hospital for the last time. Rolf and Renate were the last of the family to see her alive. They visited on the evening of November 2, leaving near midnight. A nurse on duty encouraged them to let Omi rest. They promised to come back the next day, but before they could return they received a call from the hospital informing them that Omi had passed away in the early hours of the morning, November 3, 1985.

The official death certificate ascribes the cause of Omi's death to acute heart failure brought on by malnutrition and a long-standing condition known as short bowel syndrome. Renal failure was listed as a contributing cause. What the certificate

Omi relaxing outdoors with her daughters-in-law Renate and Betty, circa 1980.

does *not* say is that Hertha Anna Marie Jürgens Schmidt went out the way she lived: on her own terms, after a bout against odds that no one could beat, fighting until she was satisfied she could give no more of herself to the struggle.

Two days after Omi died, the family gathered at the Stradling Funeral Home in Ephrata at 2:00 p.m. for a memorial service. Presiding at the service was the Reverend Doctor Merlin Conrad, a family friend, but the highlights of the afternoon were remarks delivered by two of Omi's children, Wolfgang and Rolf.

Wolfgang spoke first. With an air of reverent confidence, he looked out at the family and friends assembled in the parlor and offered his heartfelt reminiscences.

"We're here to reflect one more time on our mother," Wolf began. We come here, he said, to honor the memory of a woman known by many different names. "To some she was 'Hertha'—although she preferred 'Hart-a,' the German pronunciation of her name. Many called her '*Mutti*,' or '*kleine Mutti*'— 'Mother' or 'Little Mother.' But to most she was known simply as 'Omi'—'Grandmother.'"

"Who was this woman that we call 'Omi'?" Wolf asked. He provided a brief history of her life, emphasizing the courage and determination she showed when her husband was taken away from her, first by the war, then later by the Communist authorities in the Soviet Zone.

"When I think back, she reminds me of a wolverine fighting for her young, scratching, fighting, not caring for her own life or wellbeing. All she wanted was for her family to survive." Most of the children did not fully comprehend the impact of their father's being taken away, but Omi realized "this was the end of the family as we knew it; there would be no father and mother to raise the children."

She also knew, Wolf said, that she could not stay in East Germany. "So this little woman took four of her children and without permission traveled into West Berlin, to safety. Then again, like a mother animal, she returned into East Germany and got the other four!"

Nothing seemed to get her down: not the refugee camps where the family lived for years, nor the news of Willi's death in a concentration camp. "What was her response? She just reared up and said, 'This is not going to kill the family! Now it's finally all on my shoulders, and I'm going to raise these kids, and I'm going to do it right!'"

With great passion Wolf told of his mother's efforts to provide for her children, taking on the bureaucracy in West Germany, looking the other way when one or another of her offspring broke the law so the family would have food on the table or fuel for the fires that would keep them warm in winter. "She would *never* have permitted any of us to go into a store to steal a candy bar," Wolf emphasized, "or go into the woods to cut a tree to sell it, or steal a bike so we could have fun. But she taught us to survive, by whatever means necessary.

"As we grew older, she insisted that every one of us finish school, and every one of us learn a trade," Wolf remembered. "It would have been easier to send us into the labor market to earn money to support the family," but Omi took the longer view. And then, as the children grew older, "this little woman sent us away from home, to this far-away land, that she knew as the promised land."

Wolf spoke with obvious pride about his mother's decision to live independently. "She went out and learned how to drive a car, and at an age when most people are thinking about retirement, she got out and found a job. This woman, who only knew how to raise a family, went into the labor market and worked next to teenagers to make a living for herself."

"How proud she was when she bought her first piece of furniture!" Wolf exclaimed. "All her life she had hand-me-downs, never anything her own." She appreciated what she was able to do in her adopted country, and proud of her children,

Birthday celebration in 1981.

whom she implored constantly to work to realize the American dream.

"She was a grand old little lady," Wolf said. "We, her family, and I'm sure you, her friends, have never known a person, nor shall we ever know a person like her again. I think nobody ever stood as tall as she did."

Rolf, too, spoke reverently of his mother. "I recall the last time I said goodbye to Omi," he began. "At first, I cried because I felt guilty for not taking greater care of her," as she weakened from her disease. "I know so many in her condition have long opted to go into the care of others. She never let herself do that."

"Then I felt pride," he continued, "in her determination which was strong until the very last minute, not to be a burden to her children, to her neighbors, to the state." Reflecting

*Taking a break beside the pool at Bill's house in the
year she died, 1985.*

on the principles she had tried to pass on to her children and
grandchildren, Rolf said, "Finally, I cried for joy," because his
mother had accomplished the goals she set for herself and her
family. She had died at peace with herself, knowing her family
would carry on in the spirit she had instilled in them.

"So I am happy today," he concluded. "She gave us all a
mother can give. I saw in that frail person a giant."

Pastor Conrad saw in Omi's life an important lesson
for those who remained behind. Having known her for a time,
and also observed how respected she was by her friends, and
how revered she was by her family, Conrad reflected on a story he learned from his own father, who had passed away some
time before. The elder Conrad, also an immigrant, once wrote

about seeing a bushel of wrinkled, shriveled potatoes that initially seemed worthless. But he saw that if he planted them, they would come to life again. The pastor's father had written that, "Some day soon people will look at me in a box, and I'll be old and wrinkled, and for those who know no better, they will say, 'He is dead'—but don't you believe it!" Such was the lesson Conrad encouraged people to draw from Omi's death. She, too, would continue to live on, as what was essential of her nature had indeed been planted in her family, through whom she would continue to live.

After the memorial service, Omi's body was sent to the Ferris Company in West Chester for cremation. The ashes were returned to the family. Rather than place her remains in a cemetery or mausoleum, however, the family decided to let her rest in one of the spots she had enjoyed so much in her last years with them. A beautiful weeping cherry tree was purchased and planted in Bill's yard, and Omi's ashes were placed near the base.

Wolfgang's daughter Marianne, who was working at a foundry at the time, had a plaque made containing an inscription that Omi had always admired: "Let there be peace on earth, and let it begin with me."

Finally, beneath these words from the Prayer of St. Francis of Assisi, this little woman who had labored tirelessly all her life for her family could now rest forever.

Omi's Legacy

❧

$\mathcal{B}$ill Schmidt, who served as Omi's executor, did not have much work to do to settle his mother's estate. She had left little real property. There were no elaborate trusts to manage. There was not even a home to sell. The little woman from East Germany whose obituary took up only a few lines in the local papers left this world as simply as she had entered it seventy-five

Omi Schmidt standing in the center amidst her children, 1980. Kneeling, left to right: Bill and Mike. Standing left to right: Rolf, Lori, Joe, Barbara, and Wolf. Living in Germany, Einhard was not available for this photograph.

years earlier.

But Omi Schmidt left a legacy far greater than earthly goods. She left a part of herself in each of her eight children.

The events of 1933-1959 transformed Omi Schmidt from a feisty young girl into a remarkably strong woman with a sense of perspective that made the last twenty-five years of her life a perpetual joy. Difficulties and setbacks during her years in America could not compare to the ones she had undergone in Germany. And the toughness she developed dealing with the privations of war, the terrors of communism, and the frustrations of German bureaucracy rubbed off on her children.

Throughout her life Omi had been exceptionally proud of her sons and daughters. Certainly they had not all been angels growing up! And she was wise enough to see that not all of them had been able to overcome adversity in their adult lives, either. But she realized they had all survived a horrific ordeal with their sense of self-worth intact. That may have been her greatest gift to all of them.

But there were other bequests as well. Certainly there was something in her genes that made Omi strong in the face of adversity. She looked for ways to make the best of even the most oppressive circumstances. That kind of opportunism seems to have been inherited by her sons and daughters. Many of the siblings—especially those who had lived through the war and were old enough to remember the privations of those post-war years—developed a strong sense of purpose and self-preservation. Remembering the dark years when the family lived under the thumb of the Communists, and the time they lived as refugees and welfare recipients in West Germany, they were determined to succeed in America. They were not going to let small defeats get them down.

How *did* Omi's children fare in America?

After returning from Florida in 1963, Rolf landed a job at Textile Machine Works, later the Rockwell Corporation in the Reading, Pennsylvania, suburb of Wyomissing. What he really wanted, though, was to start his own business. In the late 1960s, he mentioned his dreams to Bill, who had been thinking along the same lines. They decided to join forces and after working nights and weekends to build machinery and develop a manufacturing process, they began fabricating products for sale and lining up customers. In 1969, they received their first large job to prepare wire blanks for a suture company in New York. Shortly thereafter, they formally launched Sharpoint, a firm targeted at producing surgical needles for this specialized industry. They put quite a bit of their own money into the venture—money they obtained largely by refinancing their homes. Both Renate and Peggy went to work to help pay family expenses.

Omi was not at all thrilled that her sons were being so "adventuresome" with their hard-earned money. She did not really understand the American system of entrepreneurship, and she had never been close enough to any of the upper classes in Germany to get a real sense of how businesses are owned and managed. She may have taken some solace in knowing that the brothers were operating out of Rolf's garage in Mohnton, and that, as the business expanded, they hired other family members to help them. It would take her years to acknowledge they had made a good decision, and at that point her pride would swell even more to know that "her boys" had made it after all.

Sharpoint was a gamble, of course, but one that would pay off in years to come. Rolf and Bill became major employers in their area, moving in 1972 from Rolf's garage to a building at 111 Chestnut Street in Mohnton. As the years passed, Sharpoint provided the brothers a business platform from which they could launch a number of other ventures. In 1986, the brothers sold most of the assets of Sharpoint, obtaining capital to explore other business opportunities. Their collaborative ventures with other businesses in locations around the world made them financially successful. Throughout all the ups and downs of their entrepreneurial activities, however, they remained close to their families, including their siblings. They took special pride in helping to care for Omi in her later years.

In 1962, Lori and Dick blessed Omi with another grandson, John Henry Stoltzfus. A year later Lori gave birth to twin boys; unfortunately, both died within days of delivery. Two years later, however, her son Michael was born. Lori worked for most of her adult life, remaining for years at the Bearings Company where Dick was also employed. She was one of the first employees at her brothers' new business, remaining at Sharpoint for several years on the production line and in quality control.

Later in life, Lori took a job as a manager in the seafood department of a local grocery market before retiring just a few years ahead of her husband. Avid antique car buffs, the Stoltzfuses spent considerable time attending shows around the region. When they traveled, they made sure Omi was invited to join them, giving her a chance to see the country she had admired from afar as a girl growing up in Germany.

One of Lori and Dick's favorite destinations had always been Florida, where Dick's mother had spent the winter since 1978. So after retiring, Lori and Dick bought a home in Sarasota, and began escaping the cold Pennsylvania winters every year.

The fire that devastated their home in late 1959 did not crush Wolf and Sigi's spirit. They produced three more grandchildren for Omi: Andrea in 1960, Wolfgang, Jr. in 1961, and Karen in 1963. They remained in the area near Manheim for several years while Wolf worked at various foundries in Lancaster, Manheim, and Reamstown, before taking a job as plant manager at Alcast Metals in Montgomeryville, Pennsylvania.

While still working in Lancaster, he enrolled in college via correspondence and completed a course in psychology to improve his skills as a manager—something he would never have done had he remained in Germany. Wolf was reminded of that later when he was working as President of Alcast Metals. Wolf attended a trade show in Philadelphia where he discovered that among the foreign attendees was Harald Rautenbach. Wolf had tutored Harald, the son of the foundry owner where Wolf had done his apprenticeship. But when Wolf went to renew the acquaintances, Rautenbach claimed he did not remember Wolf at all. Barely acknowledging Wolf's presence, the man walked away almost immediately. It seemed to be too bitter a pill to swallow, discovering that a former refugee from the lowest classes of society could now be an executive. But thanks to his mother's encouragement, it had happened to Wolfgang Schmidt—in America.

Einhard decided to make a career of the Army. After completing basic training and advanced training as a tank gunner, he headed off to his first assignment in Germany, where the Army in its wisdom made him a cook. He and Erika were married in 1960, but the expense of overseas travel precluded members of the family now living in America to attend; the Schmidts were represented, however, by relatives from his father's family who were on hand for the occasion.

An accident that eventually brought on epileptic seizures caused him to change career fields within the Army; he ended up in data processing. His assignments took him around the globe, including tours of duty in Korea and Vietnam. He and Erika provided Omi three more grandchildren: Akis Helene in 1961, Ralph Einhard in 1963, and Kirk Wilhelm in 1966. Although Erika and the children lived in Manheim, Pennsylvania when Einhard was serving in the Far East, this branch of the Schmidt family settled in Germany, where they felt quite at home. After retiring from the Army, Einhard worked in a variety of professional positions until 1998, when he became Managing Director of Syntacoll, a drug delivery device company owned by his brothers Rolf and Bill.

In six months at the Fuller Company in Manheim, Bill had learned a valuable lesson about the union environment in

American manufacturing. He saw that men who did little could rely on seniority to retain their position while younger workers struggling to be more productive were chastised for exceeding performance rates set by the union contract.

The move to Ephrata Tool, an open shop, in late 1959 proved most beneficial; Bill continued working there for over a decade. He and Peggy moved to Ephrata from Manheim in August 1964. Their son Carlton was born in 1963, and daughter Tia in 1968; and a second son, Adam, arrived much later, in 1982. His business ventures with Rolf made him financially independent, but no matter how hard he worked, he gave priority during his off hours to his family. Until his mother died in 1985, Bill and his family lived close by and gave her what help she needed—or what she was willing to accept. When Bill and Peggy's daughter Tia died of cancer in 1999, her remains were laid to rest beside her Omi, who had loved her dearly.

Mike had a rougher start in America than his older brothers did. He discovered when he arrived in the United States that, because he had not finished his apprenticeship in Germany, the State of Pennsylvania would not recognize any of the work he had done. He would have to repeat *all* of his training. Dutifully he enrolled in a program, and when he finished he joined his brothers on the workforce at Ephrata Tool. Like Bill, he enlisted in the National Guard, doing a stint on active duty in 1965.

In 1966, Mike married Thelma Smith and moved to Lancaster. He remained at Ephrata Tool until he was asked by a friend to take over a small machine shop in North Carolina established to supply parts for AMP, a manufacturer of electrical equipment used in automobiles and appliances. The company had opened a major facility in North Carolina but found it difficult to get the specialized tools and diecast parts needed for their own manufacturing.

Initially, Mike went down to help put the operation on

sound footing. He ended up buying into the business, and relocated to North Carolina permanently. Though the company
would eventually be sold to Burle Industries, Mike stayed on
and continued to work in the tool and die business, both as an
owner and later as an employee of Phillips Electronics, which
had bought out the business he was running. He and Thelma
had no children.

When Thelma became seriously ill, Mike provided for
her care until she died in 1982. In the following year he married
Evalina McCuiston Barker, who had a thirteen-year-old daughter Cynthia. Evalina was working in real estate, but retired in
1999 after suffering a major heart attack and stroke. Once again
Mike found himself caring for an ailing wife. Although he never
had children of his own, when Cynthia married and became
a mother, Mike became—like Willi Dittmann—the proud step-
grandparent to her four children. Mike finally retired so he and
Evalina could spend time with their grandchildren, helping with
the handicapped, and doing volunteer work such as fund raising
for the Fire Department that saved Evalina's life.

The adjustment to living in America was much harder
for Omi's youngest children. A typical teenager, Joe found the
loss of familiar surroundings distressing. In the fall of 1960 he
entered ninth grade at Manheim Central High, but soon transferred to Stevens Tech in Lancaster, a school that offered a high
school diploma program and opportunities to learn a variety of
skilled trades. Joe lived in Lancaster during the week, coming
home to Manheim on weekends. He managed on his $5 weekly
allowance, buying an occasional pack of cigarettes or ice cream
cone. Having no car, he spent most of his time on the campus,
looking forward to weekends, no doubt.

After completing Stevens Tech, Joe entered the work-
force as a carpenter. He, too, joined the Pennsylvania National
Guard, then settled down in the Manheim area. He married
Bonnie Ewing in 1967, and their son Mark was born three years

A part of Omi's legacy, 1980. Bottom row, l to r: grandson John Stoltzfus, daughter Annlore Stoltzfus, grandson Michael Stoltzfus, grandson Carlton Schmidt, Carlton's friend (seated on grass), son Michael, daughter-in-law Renate (Spingies) Schmidt, Hertha "Omi" Schmidt, great-grandnephew Sebastian Laun, great-grandniece Christiana Laun, Ulrich Laun, grandniece Ulrike Laun, granddaughter Andrea (Schmidt) Walton holding great-granddaughter Shana Walton, Dean Walton, daughter Barbara (Schmidt) Frankford, granddaughter Tonya Smith. Top row (l to r): son Joe, daughter-in-law Betty (Knier) Schmidt, niece Margarete Preiss, Heinz Preiss, son-in-law Dick Stoltzfus, son Bill, daughter-in-law Peggy Schmidt, granddaughter Tia Schmidt, son Rolf, Mary Schmidt (Bootie's wife), granddaughter Petra Schmidt, grandson Bootie Schmidt, David Adelson (Petra's husband), grandson Wolfgang Schmidt II, son Wolfgang, daughter-in-law Sigi (Weinberg) Schmidt, Jim Becker beside granddaughter Marianne (Schmidt) Becker, granddaughter Karen Schmidt, Karen's friend, grandson Jimmy Smith.

later. The marriage lasted only six years. In 1973 Joe married again, to Carol King; their son Joe Jr. was born that same year. Divorced again in 1979, Joe remarried in 1980, to June "Betty" Michael (Knier). Meanwhile, he continued to ply his trade as a carpenter, working for several businesses before settling down at Sharpoint, the company owned by brothers Rolf and Bill, and later at Surgical Specialties.

Fellow employees at Sharpoint remember him as amiable, low-key, humorous—and exceptionally skilled at his craft. As the years passed, the hell-raising young man began to mellow and develop a strong sense of personal responsibility—traits that would make it possible for him to give himself over to caring for Betty as her health began to fail.

Barbara and James Smith, the man she married in 1962, had two children, James in 1963 and Tonya in 1965. After five years, the couple divorced, and in 1968, Barb married William Frankford. With Frankford, Barbara had two daughters, Cynthia in 1968, and Billie Jo in 1970. Barb worked in the garment industry, for a time at the same establishment where her mother and Bill's wife were employed. She also held down jobs as a bartender and a domestic.

For several years, Barb lived in Georgia and Texas, but eventually returned to Pennsylvania, settling first in Lancaster then in Manheim. Although she was not always living near other members of her family, she kept in touch with her mother who always kept a soft spot in her heart for her baby.

When Barb needed help, Omi was there—even if her unconditional love and support annoyed others in the family. From Barb's perspective, Omi seemed to demand more of her daughters than she did of her sons, especially when it came to domestic chores. Barb recalls Omi insisting that the girls help with the ironing. And of course, *everything* had to be pressed, including bed sheets and even her boys' underwear! Perhaps, Barb speculated much later in life, that's why she always found herself

Omi's children: Rolf, Lori, Wolfgang, Einhard, Bill, Mike, Joe, and Barb. (photographed 2002)

looking to buy drip-dry clothes. But she also found herself looking out for those in need—something she no doubt learned from her mother, who was always making sure that those she loved were cared for.

*   *   *   *   *

As they grew older, the Schmidt children came to appreciate the extent to which their mother had sacrificed for them. No matter how difficult things got for any of them, they knew their struggles paled by comparison to the trials their mother had faced in raising them during three turbulent decades. Looking to her as an example, they could always find inner strength to face even the most difficult personal and work-related challenges. They did not always succeed, but they always fought hard. And when they failed, they shrugged off defeat and started over again. After all, that's what their mother had done, and they all learned from her example.

From the day she arrived in the United States until the day she died, Omi never expressed regret at leaving Germany. She hated the Communists; she despised the class system. And she was sure that neither was going to be "overthrown" any time soon, so she knew that coming to America had been the right thing to do. Unfortunately, she did not live long enough to see the Berlin Wall come crashing down in 1989, and to witness the transformation of the region around Flecken Zechlin and Mirow after the Communists were ousted from power. Shed of the yoke of totalitarianism, the citizens there have once again become the outgoing, generous people that made them among Germany's most likable before the war. With the exception of a few scars on the land caused by the Soviets and the East German government's ill-fated attempts to industrialize the region, the area remains one of relatively unspoiled natural beauty.

There is considerably less small farming than there was

when the Dittmanns made a living off the land, but tourism is returning to the region. The lakes and hills still beckon to city-dwellers wishing to escape the crush of urban living. Perhaps it is once again a place that Omi Schmidt could love.

It is also unfortunate that Omi did not live long enough to share in another important success, one that saw her children band together in a way that would have pleased her immensely. In 1996 Rolf and Bill provided an opportunity for their brothers and sisters to invest in a company they called Omi Partners. In turn, through Omi Partners the Schmidts all became shareholders in Closure Medical Corporation, the company Rolf and Bill had formed some years earlier after selling Sharpoint. Over the next decade Closure Medical did quite well, and in 2005 when the shares held by Omi Partners were sold, the payoff was substantial for all of them.

Harking back to his mother's receipt of her husband's back pension, Rolf called this latest payout the *grosse Nachzahlung*—the big "back payment," the settlement the Schmidts merited after lifetimes of hardship and hard work. This time, though, there were no collections from the welfare office to offset the payments; the money was theirs, free and clear. Finally, *all* the Schmidt children could say with some certitude that they had "made it" in America.

This was the legacy Omi Schmidt, a lady of immense courage, had wished for all her children.

A Note on Sources

The story told in *Omi, Mother Courage* is based on recordings, interviews, and family documents, as well as information from Internet sites and published materials that tell the story of Germany in the twentieth century. I am grateful to the living members of the extended Schmidt family (and their spouses) for their willingness to spend a great amount of time reminiscing about their life with Hertha Schmidt—their mother, mother-in-law, grandmother, aunt—and for being frank in their revelations about other people and about themselves. Both my wife and I owe a special debt of thanks to Rolf and Renate Schmidt, who hosted us for a week in Germany, where Rolf took us to places where the Schmidts had lived before coming to America. I am also particularly indebted to Bill Schmidt, who has been my counselor, advisor, mentor, and (from my point of view, at any rate) steady friend in bringing this project to fruition.

In preparing this book I was given access to three tapes Hertha Schmidt made in 1982, at the request of her family, to set down for posterity some details about her life in Germany from the time she was born until the days she and her eight children made their daring escape to the West. I was also given a copy of the tape made at her memorial service in 1985, at which her sons Wolfgang and Rolf paid tribute to their mother. During the months between the fall of 2005 and the spring of 2007

I interviewed all eight of Hertha Schmidt's children, several of her daughters-in-law, one of her nieces, and a number of her grandchildren. These "oral histories" allowed me to construct the portrait presented in the pages of this book.

In Germany we were aided most graciously, if indirectly, by the caretakers of the *Dokumentationzentrum des Landes für Opfer Deutscher Diktaturen*, the Museum for the Documentation of Victims of German Dictatorships, located in the annex of the old Ministry of Justice Building in Schwerin. There we visited the cells where Willi Schmidt was held awaiting his first trial, and possibly his second, secret one as well. We also received a bit of incredibly important information from a man we met by chance in Alt Lutterow: Joachim Mahnke, the grandson of Ewald Mahnke, who bought the Jürgens farm from Marie Sadler in 1918 or 1919. Not only did he identify the house in which Hertha Jürgens was born; he also provided us a bit of lore about the village and its surroundings that I hope has helped to bring a part of this story to life.

No one's life story can be told adequately without reference to the world in which that person lived. To say that times were turbulent in Germany during Omi's childhood and the years of her marriage to Willi Schmidt would be a serious understatement. Perhaps no country in Europe suffered such political and social upheaval as Germany. One could argue persuasively that German leaders brought on much of that suffering, but as Bertolt Brecht's title character in *Mother Courage and Her Children* observed, both defeat and victory are a costly business for those "little people" caught up in the maelstrom.

To help place Omi's story in historical context, I consulted the following books and articles:

For cultural, social, and political background: Monika Adomeit, *Flecken Zechlin* (2001); Gordon A. Craig, *Germany 1866-1945* (1978) and *The Germans* (1982); Matthew Hughes and Chris Mann, *Inside Hitler's Germany* (2000); Walter Laqueur, *Wei-*

mar: *A Cultural History 1918-1933* (1974); Tim Mason, "Women in Germany, 1925-1940: Family Welfare and Work, Part I." *History Workshop* (Spring 1976), and "Women in Germany, 1925-1940: Family Welfare and Work, Part II." *History Workshop* (Autumn 1976); Alexandra Richie, *Faust's Metropolis: A History of Berlin* (1998); R.H. Samuel and R. Hinton Thomas. *Education and Society in Modern Germany* (1949); Charles Whiting et al., *The Home Front: Germany* (1982). Eric Weitz's *Weimar Germany* (2007) appeared after I completed this book, but it appears to be the best study yet of Germany in the years between 1918 and the rise to power of the Nazis under Hitler.

For military operations before and during World War II: James S. Corum, *The Luftwaffe: Creating the Operational Air War 1918-1940* (1997); Martin Gilbert, *The Day the War Ended: May 8, 1945: Victory in Europe* (1995); Max Hastings, *Armageddon: The Battle for Germany 1944-1945* (2004); David Irving, *The Rise and Fall of the Luftwaffe: The Life of Field Marshal Erhard Milch* (1973); Fritz Morzik, *German Air Force Airlift Operations* (1968); Richard Suchenwirth, *The Development of the German Air Force 1918-1939* (1970).

For information on the Soviet occupation and life in East Germany after 1945: Gary Bruce, *Resistance with the People: Repression and Resistance in Eastern Germany 1945-1953* (2003); William F. Buckley, *The Fall of the Berlin Wall* (2004); John H. Koehler, *Stasi: The Untold Story of the East German Secret Police* (1999). Norman M. Naimark, *The Russians in Germany: A History of the Soviet Zone of Occupation, 1945-1949* (1995), and his review of Jörg Morré, *Hinter den Kulissen des Nationalkommittes: Das Institut 99 in Moskau und die Deutschlandpolitik der UdSSR, 1943-1946* in the *Journal of Modern History* (2004); Charles F. Pennacchio, "The East German Communists and the Origins of the Berlin Blockade Crisis," *East European Quarterly* (Fall 1995); Gareth Pritchard, *The Making of the GDR 1945-1953: From Antifascism to Stalinism* (2000); and Gregory Sanford, *From*

Hitler to Ulbricht: The Communist Reconstruction of East Germany 1945-1946 (1983).

For information on West Germany after 1945: Jane Carey, "Political Organization of the Refugees and Expellees in West Germany," *Political Science Quarterly* (June 1951); Charles Harris and Gabriele Wülker, "The Refugee Problem in Germany," *Economic Geography* (January 1953); Morris Janowitz, "Social Stratification and Mobility in West Germany," *American Journal of Sociology* (July 1958); and Robert Selig, "1945-1948: America's Long Road to the Federal Republic of Germany" *German Life* (June/July 1998).

In addition, I found two memoirs particularly enlightening: Sigfried Knappe, *Soldat: Reflections of a German Soldier 1936-1949 (1993)*, and Wolfgang Samuel, *German Boy (2002)*.

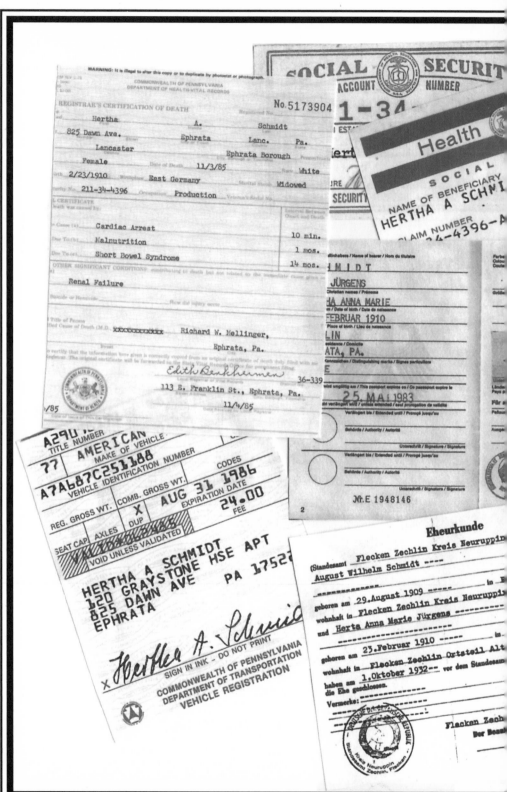